D1458440

The Fraternity of the Estranged

The Fraternity of the Estranged

The Fight for Homosexual Rights in England
1891–1908

Brian Anderson

Cover Artwork credit to Henry Scott Tuke (1858-1929), *The Critics*, with
acknowledgment to the Leamington Spa Art Gallery & Museum for permission to
reproduce it.

Matador
9 Priory Business Park,
Wistow Road, Kibworth Beauchamp,
Leicestershire. LE8 0RX
Tel: 0116 279 2299
Email: books@troubador.co.uk
Web: www.troubador.co.uk/matador
Twitter: @matadorbooks

ISBN 978 1788037 815

British Library Cataloguing in Publication Data.
A catalogue record for this book is available from the British Library.

Printed and bound by CPI Group (UK) Ltd, Croydon, CR0 4YY
Typeset in 11pt Aldine 401 BT by Troubador Publishing Ltd, Leicester, UK

Matador is an imprint of Troubador Publishing Ltd

For HC

Author's Note

Although this book resonates with contemporary academic research, in the fiftieth year since the decriminalisation in England and Wales of sexual relations between men in private, it is intended to speak principally to the LGBT community and, in a time more accepting of sexual diversity, to a wider readership. For many, Carpenter and Symonds remain dead to the world: their brave stand against persecution and intolerance not widely known. This narrative recounts the writing of important books, but it also offers a glimpse of what it was like to be homosexual in late-Victorian England.

Contents

Introduction

July 2017 marked the fiftieth anniversary of the decriminalisation in England and Wales of sex between two men in private. The law that had made such relations a crime had been passed in 1885, and remained in place for 82 years. But this restriction on same-sex love did not go unchallenged: between 1891 and 1908 three books appeared in England on homosexuality and the rights of homosexual persons. They were written by two homosexual men, Edward Carpenter and John Addington Symonds, and a third, Havelock Ellis. Setting out in life as young university dons, Carpenter and Symonds seemed the least likely of individuals to court notoriety as defenders of homosexuality, whilst the shy and retiring Ellis was a most improbable student of sex.

At the time, the study of what was then called '*sexual inversion*' was the almost exclusive preserve of writers on the European continent. Books on homosexuality that circulated freely there were hardly known in England, where, apart from its occasional discussion in medical journals, anything published on the subject was liable to be prosecuted for obscenity. Men who loved men were pushed to the margins, in a society where masculinity was strenuously upheld. In such a hostile environment, the appearance of these publications was highly significant. They were the first English contributions to the scientific understanding of homosexuality, and at the same time opened the long fight for the legal recognition of same-sex love that was finally won in 1967.

The special circumstances under which these books came to be written has not before been comprehensively documented. Here, through a combination of history, biography and textual analysis, the full story of the individuals who opposed this legislation and argued for homosexual equality is told. And, as the hazardous progress of these books towards publication is recounted, what was written is critically examined.

Chance pervades this narrative at every level. If certain events had not combined with the twists and turns of coincidence and circumstance, it is highly unlikely that any of these ground-breaking books would even have been conceived, let alone published. There would be nothing to tell if Carpenter had not discovered the homoerotic poetry of Walt Whitman at a time when he was deeply troubled by his homosexuality. Equally, if, after a crisis of belief, he had been able to resign as an Anglican curate but remain at his Cambridge college. When this was denied him, he became a peripatetic lecturer in the industrial towns of northern England, which radicalised him and brought him into contact with Ellis.

Similarly, if Symonds had not been forced to leave his Oxford college after a homosexual scandal, and had not also read Whitman at a time of crisis over his homosexuality. And if he had not abandoned the study of law for literary criticism, he would not have been approached by Ellis to contribute to a series of books that he was editing. In turn, this led to their collaboration in the writing of what turned out to be a fateful book on homosexuality.

Further, this story could not be told if the adolescent Ellis had not been taken to Australia by his sea captain father. Alone in the outback, where books were his only consolation, by chance he came across James Hinton's *Life in Nature*,[1] and discovered that, at about his own age, he had studied medicine. His future being unclear to him, in a flash he decided that he too would become a doctor. Perplexed by his sexual awakening, precociously he resolved to make the study of sex his vocation. But, once back in England, the cost of a medical education thwarted his ambition, until "the gift of Heaven, without any effort of mine, fell miraculously upon me". The Hintons, who had befriended him, loaned him £200, without which the life that he had mapped out for himself would have been "forever closed and my whole life-course altered".[2]

Finally, there is a fourth individual in this story, without whose intervention the history of homosexual law reform in England may have taken an entirely different path. In 1885, Henry Labouchère, the Member of Parliament for Northampton, succeeded in having a five line clause inserted into a piece of legislation that had nothing to do with sex between two men. It was its inclusion in the 1885 Criminal Law Amendment Act that made any intimate behaviour between men, whether in public or in private, potentially a criminal act. It would ensnare countless individuals before it was revised in 1967.

The iconoclastic poet Walt Whitman was the dominant presence in the lives of Carpenter and Symonds. He is woven into this story. In fear of the rigid taboo against the physical expression of their homosexuality, early in life both adopted a romanticised form of male-loving: an aesthetic idealization of their erotic instincts. Whitman's fervent espousal of male *comradeship* sanctioned the expression of their sexual natures but, more importantly, the empowerment to write about homosexuality flowed directly from him. Of discovering

---

1   James Hinton (1822-1875), English surgeon and writer on scientific subjects.
2   Havelock Ellis, *My Life* (Heinemann, 1940), p. 144.

Whitman, Carpenter recalled: "I find it difficult to imagine what my life would have been without it".[3] And Symonds would write, barely a month before Whitman's death, "You do not know, & I can never tell anyone, what Whitman has been to me".[4] Whitman was also a significant figure for Ellis, who placed him among the new breed of realist writers of his day. He was given a whole chapter in his first book, *The New Spirit*, in which he sought to capture the ethos of his times, expressed in the writing of leading literary personalities. Whitman was also the subject of Symonds's first exchange with Ellis on homosexuality, and it was through the chance discovery of Carpenter's Whitmanesque long prose poem *Towards Democracy*[5] that Ellis first came to know him.

It was when Symonds's friendship with Ellis grew, that he asked him if he would take a book by him on homosexuality, for a series of scientific texts then under his editorship. He had written and privately circulated two monographs on homosexuality, which were outcomes of personal and contemporary events in his life. Both were defences of homosexuality, but in origination and purpose were essentially different. The first, which is referred to throughout as the *Greek Problem,*[6] was the product of a Platonising phase in his life, which lasted from adolescence until his late twenties. It was an examination of the practice of *paederasties*, of boy-love, found in the refined civilisations of the ancient Greek city states. The second, referred to as the *Modern Problem,*[7] was

3   Edward Carpenter, writing in *The Labour Prophet*, (May,1894).
4   Symonds to Horace Traubel, 27 February 1892, *The Letters of John Addington Symonds*, ed. Schueller and Peters, (Wayne State University Press, 1967-69), vol. 111, p. 667.
5   Edward Carpenter, *Towards Democracy*, (Bradway, 1883).
6   John Addington Symonds, *A Problem in Greek Ethics*, (privately printed, 1883).
7   John Addington Symonds, *A Problem in Modern Ethics*, (privately printed, 1891).

a direct outcome of the passing of the 1885 Criminal Law Amendment Act. Under the Offences against the Person Act of 1861, the crime of buggery, if no longer a capital offence, remained in place, but at the instigation of Labouchère, the 1885 Act introduced the *misdemeanour* of 'gross indecency' between male persons. Symonds wrote the *Modern Problem* to contest this legislation, by advancing a case for the decriminalisation of homosexual acts between consenting adults that took place in private. It was a political manifesto: the first to fully address the plight of homosexuals in England.

When the cautious Ellis prevaricated over taking a book on homosexuality for his series, considering it too risky, Symonds, out of the blue, suggested that they might write a book together on the subject. His approach was timely, as unbeknown to him, Ellis was preparing to make the study of human sexuality his life's work. But of much more significance, he was equally unaware that, at this very time, Ellis was facing a personal crisis, after discovering that the woman who he had married only six months earlier was lesbian. This was the decisive factor in Ellis's decision to collaborate with Symonds on the writing of *Sexual Inversion,* the book for which he is now best known. If Ellis had not agreed to collaborate, this book would never have been written. Acutely aware of Victorian attitudes towards homosexuality, Ellis knew that, rather than collaborating on a book on the subject, he should have passed it over as an unpleasant topic on which it was not wise to enlarge. Later, he would acknowledge that writing the book was a mistake, and claimed that it had never been his intention to launch his career as a sexual theorist with such a publication. He described the time spent on it as "this toilsome excursion".[8]

But it was Ellis's decision to collaborate that propelled Symonds, and then Carpenter, into the field of sexual politics.

---

8   Havelock Ellis, *Studies in the Psychology of Sex*, vol. 1, *Sexual Inversion*, (Wilson and Macmillan, 1897), p. 158.

Carpenter, then known only for his writing on economic and political subjects, had come to know Symonds through their mutual admiration for Whitman. Once drawn into the project, like Symonds, he wrote an account of his homosexual history and, importantly, each provided essential material for the book, in the form of autobiographical notes written by homosexual friends and acquaintances. The excessively shy Ellis, had he intended to write a book of his own on the subject, would have struggled to acquire such material.

Early in 1893, before much progress could be made on the book, or before he could even meet Ellis, the tubercular Symonds died in Rome. Given his nervousness about the wisdom of writing such a book, expressed time and again in an intense exchange of letters with Symonds, (the substance of chapter three), Ellis could have abandoned the book, reserving the subject of homosexuality, as he had intended, for inclusion in a more comprehensive work. But, intent on establishing himself as a serious writer on human sexuality, and to earn money, he worked on his own material and that provided by Symonds. In 1896, he had *Sexual Inversion* published, firstly in German, and the following year in English, with Symonds named in both books as the co-author.[9] When the English edition was already in circulation, following an intervention on behalf of Symonds's family all remaining copies were bought up and destroyed. Ellis then removed Symonds's contributions and all references to him and republished the book, only to have it prosecuted in England as an 'obscene libel' and banned.

Except for his analyses of the small number of case histories provided for him, Ellis's book was entirely derivative: a compilation of the findings of continental investigators, with his own observations added. Although now a certificated

---

9   Havelock Ellis and John Addington Symonds, *Sexual Inversion* (Wilson and Macmillan, 1897).

physician, except for a few months after he qualified, and occasionally when acting as a locum, he never practiced. It is not an exaggeration to say that almost everything he knew about homosexuality came from what others had recorded, and which he had a talent for weaving into a convincing synthesis. As one of his biographers wrote, he learned more about sex from books and less about it from personal experience, "than almost any man of his age".[10] He shunned social intercourse and relished solitude; undertook no empirical research on homosexuality, and is not known to have interrogated a single homosexual person, except perhaps his wife. This was in marked contrast to the continental physicians on whom he drew so heavily for the book. Their publications grew out of direct contact with individuals in prisons, asylums, and their own consulting rooms.

But, influenced strongly by his long-written exchanges with Symonds before his death, and afterwards with Carpenter, in *Sexual Inversion* Ellis concluded that homosexuality was not a pathological condition but a *congenital abnormality*. If he added little else of significance to what was then known about homosexuality, this alone marked him out as a progressive voice, and for England, made his book ground-breaking. Although banned, for the first time individuals able to acquire a copy could begin to understand their same-sex desires.

This is where Ellis's role in support of the homosexual can be said to have ended. Although he had a life-long commitment to scientific impartiality, he was unable to reconcile himself to his wife's lesbianism, which destroyed his marriage almost before it had begun, and could not bring himself to condone homosexual lovemaking. He ignored the evidence from his own case histories, in which respondents overwhelmingly confirmed its bodily and mental benefits. Instead, he consigned

---

10 Arthur Calder-Marshall, *Havelock Ellis*, a biography, (Rupert Hart-Davis, 1959), p. 68.

homosexuals to lives of unnatural chastity. His reluctance to discuss the subject was such, that when an individual who had read *Sexual Inversion* wrote to him, he invariably referred him to Carpenter. He also disapproved of homosexuals fathering children: a reflection of his long-held views on the influence of heredity, and his enthusiastic support for the new science of eugenics. It would be excessive to brand Ellis as homophobic, but however humane his treatment of the subject, the concluding chapter of *Sexual Inversion* reinforced Victorian social attitudes towards the homosexual.

After Symonds's passing, it was left to Carpenter to continue the long struggle in England for the legal right of consenting adult homosexuals to enjoy sexual intercourse in private. Such a right to privacy had not existed in any European country before it was granted by the French penal code of 1891 and incorporated in the 1805 Code Napoléon, but denied to homosexuals in England and Wales until 1967.[11] Within months of Symonds's death, encouraged by his close friend, the female emancipationist Olive Schreiner, Carpenter began to write a series of women-related pamphlets on sexual issues. At the same time, he penned a pamphlet on homosexuality, in which he embarked upon the difficult, and dangerous, task of constructing a homosexual identity that detached the innate homosexual bias from carnality. Skilfully written, and for private circulation, the pamphlet escaped the censor's pen. In 1896, he combined and expanded his pamphlets, judiciously leaving out the one on homosexuality, and published a pioneering book, *Love's Coming of Age*.[12] Many of its conclusions, if applauded by progressives, elicited a

---

11   The 1967 Sexual Offences Act decriminalised, in England and Wales only, sexual acts in private between two men aged over twenty-one. Similar legislation was passed for Scotland in 1980, and for Northern Ireland in 1982.

12   Edward Carpenter, *Love's Coming of Age*, (The Manchester Labour Press Society, 1896).

collective drawing in of breath, as one by one he demolished Victorian sexual codes. In a slightly more tolerant climate, the 1906 edition of the book included a chapter on the *nature* of the homosexual person, depicted as belonging to an 'intermediate sex'.

Two years later, he published *The Intermediate Sex*,[13] a book devoted entirely to the subject of homosexuality. It was the first widely-read, unambiguous defence of same-sex love to appear in general circulation England. Although his depiction of the homosexual person was controversial, as we discuss in chapter ten, in challenging attitudes towards homosexuality he was years ahead of his time, calling not only for the reform of the 1885 anti-homosexual legislation but for the social acceptance of the homosexual. Remarkably, he also called for institutional recognition of same-sex relationships. But some of his claims were likely to have impeded, rather than advanced, the position of homosexuals of his day.

Carpenter was the necessary corrective to Ellis, his always slightly distant friend. Both wanted to bring the discussion of human sexuality into the open, but Ellis's aim, despite his youthful enthusiasm for radical social reform, was a narrow one: to advance knowledge through the writing of what were, essentially, medical texts addressed to physicians and lawyers. In contrast, Carpenter began from the personal: from the need to defend his natural attraction to the male. He wanted to raise public awareness and acceptance of homosexuality, to argue for the value of the homosexual to society, and to offer comfort to those who made up his 'fraternity of the estranged'.

Together with Symonds, Carpenter contested the criminalisation of homosexual acts between consenting adults in private, but his radicalism went beyond claims

---

13   Edward Carpenter, *The Intermediate Sex*, (George Allen & Unwin, 1908).

for same-sex attachments. He wanted to change Victorian attitudes towards human sexuality. Ever conscious of the emotionally-constrained lives of his six sisters, it was to the then controversial question of the 'new woman' that he first turned. Believing that sexual fulfilment was a primary human need, he was one of the first men of his time to acknowledge women's erotic natures, and to argue for the breaking of the link between sex and procreation. For many of his detractors, he posed a greater danger as an instigator of sexual anarchy, than as a defender of same-sex love.

Drawing on self-knowledge and their life-experiences to challenge the entrenched view that homosexuality was a pathological condition, Carpenter and Symonds fashioned a counter-discourse, in which the homosexual impulse was presented as a natural variant of human sexuality. The morbidity claim, which had its origin in the study of inmates of prisons and mental institutions, was already being contested by the inclusion in the literature of a growing number of positive homosexual self-definitions. Such autobiographical narratives challenged established thinking and provided a foundation on which Symonds and Carpenter built their case. "What I am, is what I had to be," Symonds protested.[14] For both, the enfranchisement of their own sexual natures was essential for their psychological well-being and sense of personal worth.

Carpenter made his literary debut with a slim volume of unremarkable (and unremarked) poetry. Following the publication of his prose poem *Towards Democracy*, he found his authentic voice with a succession of tracts on political and economic issues of the day. Many of these pieces were combined in popular publications which, like subsequent books, articles and speeches over a period of forty years,

---

14 Phyllis Grosskurth, ed. *The Memoirs of John Addington Symonds*, (Random House, 1984), p. 53.

made him one of the most recognised of the early English socialists. But it is his books on human sexuality, especially homosexuality, that give him real contemporary relevance.

For his health, writing mainly in Davos Platz in the high Swiss Alps away from great libraries was challenging, but Symonds's output was impressive. His *magnum opus*, the seven-volume *Renaissance in Italy*, was supported by substantial works on Michelangelo, Dante, Shelley, Sydney and Jonson; translations of the autobiographies of Benvenuto Cellini and Carlo Gozzi; poetry and essays, and much incidental writing for the leading English literary journals of the day. He occasionally dismissed this endeavour as sterile, detached from real life. Conscious that he might be taken at any time, it was his two monographs on homosexuality and his memoirs, in which he recounted his tortured life, that he saw as his 'best works' and most wished to see preserved.

Serendipity

Aged barely sixteen, Henry Havelock Ellis was taken by his sea captain father on a voyage around the world, to prepare him for a settled life at home. On reaching Sydney, it was decided that he should remain for a time in Australia and a post was found for him as an assistant master at a private school. When it was clear that he could not carry his pupils far, he was dismissed. A year as a private tutor followed, after which he took up another post but left after nine months, "distinctly a failure".[1] To remedy his shortcomings, he trained as an elementary school teacher, and was then sent off to divide his time between two remote schools at Sparkes Creek and nearby Junction Creek. By now approaching his eighteenth year, it was here that he entered the world, without a single friend in the whole southern hemisphere into which he had been so unceremoniously dropped.

Living in an isolated one-room schoolhouse in Sparkes Creek, out of sight of women, his desire for knowledge "was more massive than my desire for love".[2] The physical efflorescence of puberty had begun early, and he had already taken to noting its occurrences in his pocket diary:

All the obscure mysteries of sex stirred dimly and massively within me; I felt myself groping helplessly among the

---

1   Havelock Ellis, *My Life*, (Heinemann,1940), p. 111.
2   Ibid. p. 111.

difficulties of life. The first faint germ was formed within me of a wish to penetrate those mysteries and enlighten these difficulties, so that to those who came after me they might be easier than they had been to me.[3]

He felt an impulse to intellectualise his personal situation, transforming it into an impersonal form, and "universalising it".[4] As he would later write, sex was the last frontier, standing before the coming generations as "the chief problem for solution".[5]

If he would later claim that the 'problem' of religion had practically been resolved, at Sparkes Creek he struggled to find his own settlement. He had, sometime before, "slid almost imperceptibly off the foundation of Christian belief",[6] but the idea of the universe as a mechanical whirr of lifeless wheels was alien to his whole nature. The contrast between the consoling beauty of the religion that he had lost, and the scientific conception of the world weighed upon him, persisting until he chanced to come across a review of the writing of James Hinton.[7] He sent to England for his *Life in Nature*,[8] and the arguments he found there convinced him that they were different aspects of a single unity. In a post-Darwinian age, Hinton's mystical marriage of science and religion was deeply satisfying to Ellis, born in the year of publication of *The Origin of Species*. Reading Hinton was a turning point: "Its work was done, once and for ever, in a moment".[9]

---

3   Ibid. p. 124.
4   Ibid. p. 99.
5   Havelock Ellis, *Sexual Inversion*, (Watford, The University Press,1897), p. x.
6   Havelock Ellis, *My Life*, p. 90.
7   James Hinton (1822-1875) English surgeon and writer on scientific subjects.
8   James Hinton, *Life in Nature*, papers on 'physiological riddles', (London 1862).
9   Havelock Ellis, *My Life*, p. 132.

The idea of becoming some sort of clergyman had earlier stirred him, and at Sparkes Creek the thought of a legal career had also "floated passingly" across his mind. Then one day, lying on his bed reading an account of Hinton's life, he discovered that, at about his own age, he had entered medical school: "Suddenly I leapt to my feet as though I had been shot. I will become a doctor a voice within me seemed to say".[10] He had never before thought of such a life, but in an instant, his future role in the world seemed to be "once and for all decided".[11]

On his return to England, the cost of a medical education brought him down to earth. Fortuitously, as happened a number of times throughout his life, at the right moment, the "gift of Heaven" fell upon him. He had not lost interest in Hinton and wrote to his biographer inquiring about unpublished manuscripts. An invitation to meet his widow followed and he was soon on friendly terms with the Hintons, who interested themselves in his future. He sealed the friendship by helping to edit a volume of extracts from Hinton's unpublished manuscripts.[12] Grateful, and aware of his wish to be a doctor, he was offered a loan of £200 towards the costs. He hesitated before accepting, characteristically insisting on insuring his life for the amount of the loan. But recalling this single act of generosity, he reflected that without it the path that he had mapped out for himself might have been blocked, and his "whole life-course altered".[13] When the loan was supplemented by a family legacy he enrolled as a medical student at St Thomas's Hospital in London.

His memory was excellent for things that interested him

10   Ibid. p. 135.
11   Ibid. p. 135.
12   M Hinton, ed. *The Law Breaker and the Coming of the Law,* introduction by H.H. Ellis, (Kegan Paul, 1884).
13   Havelock Ellis, *My Life,* p. 144.

but unreliable for anything else. Hours spent in attempts to memorise the details of anatomy and other subjects for examinations, which he sometimes passed and sometimes failed, involved a great amount of drudgery. But he was driven on by his conviction that a medical qualification was necessary for his future work, although the day-to-day world of a practising physician would have been one of real discomfort. Excessively shy, he would always find it difficult to look a person straight in the eye, and throughout his life anything in his behaviour likely to attract public attention he found highly embarrassing. The truth was, that he did not want a doctor's life: he wanted a doctor's education, convinced that becoming an accredited practitioner was indispensable to fulfilling his ambition to write about human sexuality. He would be entering a field that was the domain of physicians and a medical qualification would signify his scientific competence. It was "the necessary portal" to his career.[14]

His studies were undistinguished, and he qualified only with a licence to practice from the Society of Apothecaries, although in midwifery he secured a certificate of honour. He said that he chose this specialism because it fell within the sphere of sex, whilst gratifying an interest in women, "at once scientific and emotional".[15] His direction of travel was now set. In his own time, he had begun an investigation into the sexual differences between men and women. Although this was primarily for his own enlightenment, there was a specific purpose in mind: it would clear the ground for his intended study of the primary questions of sexual psychology, by dealing with all differences between men and women that, in a narrow sense, were not sexual.

He took seven years to qualify because he was juggling his medical studies with other interests that, sometimes on

14   Ibid. p. 137.
15   Havelock Ellis, *My Life*, p.194.

the surface, at other times more fundamentally, would shape his work on human sexuality. Firstly, he wanted to establish himself as a writer, and secondly, he had a young man's enthusiasm for progressive causes. The years of voracious reading at Sparkes Creek had provided a storehouse of knowledge, honed his critical faculties and begun to develop his writing style. Excessively industrious, and not backward in seeking openings for his pen, he was soon writing book reviews and articles for journals on various subjects. His very first attempt at literary criticism was a much worked-over essay on Thomas Hardy's novels. He claimed: "It was in writing it that I learned to write."[16] His confidence was boosted when Hardy thanked him for what he described as, a "remarkable" paper. Some years later, he would defend Hardy's *Jude the Obscure*, when its explicit sexuality turned many against it. Then an article on Hinton, in the prestigious journal *Mind*, brought an invitation to review books, whilst his interest in religion led to a similar offer from the *Westminster Review*. Invitations to edit popular series of books would follow, and in 1888 he would float the idea of an ambitious series of books promoting the new sciences then coming to the fore. Under his editorship, the prestigious Contemporary Science Series would be launched.

For a person who would make the *spirit* of the age the subject of his first book, it was impossible not to share the excitement generated by the radical political and social ideas then circulating in London. His interest quickened when he had a few small pieces published in *Today*, a monthly magazine that served as an outlet for the pens of progressives of all hues. He took to stopping off at the office of its editor, John Foulger, and when he floated the idea of establishing a discussion forum, to be called the Progressive League, he became its

---

16   Ibid. p. 151.

secretary and assumed the role of organiser and amanuensis: functions best suited to an individual who claimed to have never spoken a word in public. The friendships forged after entering this small world of metropolitan societies that thrived in London in the 1880s remained the most important throughout his life.

*

In 1881, twenty-six-year-old Olive Schreiner, born of a German father and English mother and raised in the then Cape Province, sailed for England. The daughter of missionaries, from early adolescence she had rejected her parents' deep religious convictions and the predestination for herself as a woman that their strict Calvinist beliefs foreshadowed. Her escape was with her pen and story-telling soon revealed a precocious talent. The death of her father and subsequent dissolution of the family brought independence, and for ten years she earned her living as a governess, moving from farm to farm across the vast Karoo, experiencing at first-hand the lives of women in a tradition-bound, male-dominated society. When she left for England, with a half-formed ambition to train as a doctor, she was carrying with her the manuscript of a novel, which no publisher in her own country had been prepared to take. Its subject, the 'women question', was to become the driving passion of her life.

Initially, she had little success in finding a publisher for the novel but her fortune changed when she sent the manuscript under a *nom-de-plume* to Chapman and Hall, with the title *The Story of an African Farm*.[17] The company's reader happened to be George Meredith, who liked it. There was consternation

---

17   Ralph Irons, (pseud. Olive Schreiner), *The Story of an African Farm* (Chapman & Hall,1883).

when a small girlish figure appeared in the publisher's office and announced herself as Ralph Irons.

Full of magical pictures of life and nature on the African Karoo, the idyllic title masked its real subject: the helplessness and humiliation of its heroine Lyndall, who rejects her pre-ordained life and prays for the day when "to be born a woman will not be to be born branded". Although not widely reviewed, its significance was recognised in progressive circles and she was feted. The novel announced her future life as a protagonist in the battle, not just for the political and economic rights being claimed by suffragettes, but for a complete re-evaluation of womanhood.

Ellis read a review of the novel, wrote to Schreiner and, after exchanging letters, invited her to a meeting of the Progressive League. She knew it would not be easy to find acceptance as an equal in the male-dominated intellectual circles to which she now gained entry, and her friendship with Ellis, which for a time bordered on courtship, eased the way. It was soon clear that she did not have the funds to cover the long period of study needed to become a doctor and she switched to training as a nurse, only to abandon this because of crippling asthma. After the reception of her novel, a future as a writer seemed possible. Boldly, she told Ellis: "I have made up my mind that scribbling will be my work in life."[18]

Early in 1885, Ellis was at a meeting of the Fellowship of the New Life,[19] another reformist group that he had become involved with, when a youth from Sheffield sitting next to him placed a small book in his hands. After thumbing through a few pages, he returned it with the curt remark, "Whitman and water." The book was the first part of Edward Carpenter's

---

18   Olive Schreiner to Havelock Ellis, 2 May 1884, HRC.
19   The Fellowship of the New Life (1883). It sought social transformation through "the cultivation of perfect character in each and all". It spawned the Fabian Society.

idiosyncratic long prose poem, *Towards Democracy*,[20] a powerful critique of the very foundations of late-Victorian society and the ravages of industrial production and commercialism. It was also a psychological history: an account of personal catharsis; of the release of long-repressed feelings about both his homosexuality and the 'civilisation' exemplified by the family into which he had been born.

*

Edward Carpenter entered the world on 29th August 1844, at Brighton, then a fashionable resort on the English south coast, the third of four boys and a brother to six sisters. His father, after abandoning both a naval and a legal career, being as ill-suited to the foredeck as he was to the courtroom, settled into the role of a respectable *rentier*. Henceforth, his life would be overshadowed by the ever-present prospect of the family being reduced to penury because of some failure in his investments. As stocks rose and fell, the young Edward learned at first-hand what it meant to belong to a class for which financial return was everything: a class enjoying an existence of ostentatious contentment, as he would later write, with its face "turned away from the wriggling poverty which made it rich".[21] It was a childhood of privilege and ease, but not of happiness:

> I hated the life, was miserable in it – the heartless conventionalities, silly proprieties… To be pursued by the dread of appearances – what people would say about one's

---

20 Edward Carpenter, *Towards Democracy*. First published anonymously, (John Haywood,1883). References are to the complete edition, in four parts, (George Allen & Unwin, 1921).

21 Edward Carpenter, *Towards Democracy*, (George Allen & Unwin, 1921), p. 124.

clothes or one's speech – to be always in fear of committing unconscious trespasses of invisible rules… [22]

He thought his parents were the best people in the world, but looking back could not recall a single occasion when, if troubled or perplexed, he was able to go to anyone for consolation. Childhood and adolescence became a time of emotional concealment; a covered underground life. His two older brothers were no longer at home, and in a house overrun with girls he was left to fathom the mysteries of his sexual awakening alone. Long before he experienced any erotic feelings, he felt a friendly attraction to other boys, which developed into a passionate sense of love. At about the age of fourteen, his erotic feelings became identified with a good-looking young curate and it entered his mind that he, too, might become a clergyman.

When he arrived at Trinity Hall, Cambridge, in 1864, lean and athletic, he was soon found on the river, where rowing became entwined with romance. Moving daily among gilded and silvered youths, his eyes absorbed, his imagination invented, but his voice was mute. "I consumed my own smoke" was how he would describe his unspoken infatuations.[23]

He had a flair for mathematics and was encouraged to take his degree in the subject, but he had not given up his intention to be ordained and the prospect of a college clerical fellowship was held out to him, if he got a good enough degree. Although his eldest brother urged caution, believing that the sheltered 'Eddy' needed to experience more of the world before being allowed to take such a step, he could not be deterred. Brought up in the Broad Churchism of his father, antagonistic to any narrow interpretation of Christian belief, he was confident

---

22 Edward Carpenter, *My Days and Dreams*, (Charles Scribner's Sons, 1916), p. 14.
23 *My Days and Dreams*, p. 63.

that he would find the Anglican Church perfectly habitable, telling him:

> I have always thought that the life of a Don is rather a stagnant sort of life and I do not think I could make up my mind to settle down altogether as such. At the same time, I do not think that I ought to refuse such a good opening, because even if I do remain here altogether, it will be very likely to lead to something else, and a few years spent here would not have been wasted.[24]

In 1868, he took a good degree, was elected to a clerical fellowship and admitted to the Church of England as a curate. Relaxing that summer, his future seemingly secured, a fellow don came into his rooms, handed him a small blue-covered book and asked him what he thought of it. He turned a few pages, puzzled by its unusual format, particularly by the absence of rhyme in many of the pieces. The book was a selection from the 1867 edition of Walt Whitman's collected verse.[25]

Intrigued, for half an hour he was totally absorbed: spellbound by the overpowering individuality that leapt from every page. Here, cast in literature, was a life lived, a complete man, with all his pride and passion; encompassing the whole gamut of human life from end to end, all harmonies and discords, nothing concealed.

There was something else that clutched at his heart. He was thrilled by the poems that celebrated male *comradeship*. This, now so near and personal, he had never before found expressed in such a way. Whitman had crafted a new language for the expression of attachments between males: new

---

24   Edward Carpenter to Charles Carpenter, 28 March 1867, SA MS 339.
25   W.M. Rossetti, ed. *Walt Whitman: Selected Poems*, (Chatto & Windus, 1867).

words equalling the language of romantic love between man and woman. The selection, by William Michael Rossetti, did not include any of the overtly homoerotic poems from the *Calamus* cluster found in the 1860 edition of *Leaves of Grass*, but a small number of poems were clearly addressed to men: poems that spoke in natural, undisguised language of every-day fleeting encounters with men who caught and responded to Whitman's roving eye.

Instantly, he felt connected, but the unexpressed longings of the heart that Whitman had sanctioned could not be easily stilled. The suppression of his sexual feelings, condemned by the church whose teachings he was now required to pronounce, led to frequent bouts of ill health. His brother's warning appeared justified as, once ordained and immersed in ritualised worship, he felt the reality, and the *unreality*, of the priesthood. Any sentiment of romance that he had harboured for the ecclesiastical life began to drain away.

Over the following three years, in a college stuffed with lawyers, academic life became toilsome. Frustrated by the everlasting discussion of ideas that seemed to be unrelated to actual life, by cheap philosophizing and ornamental cleverness, he came to regard his donnish existence as "a fraud and a weariness". Yet this was as nothing to what really haunted him: the Christian abhorrence of his deviant sexuality. It was not until he came to write *Towards Democracy* that he was able to give voice to his then terror:

Was it really your own anxious face you used to keep catching in the glass...? did you once desire to shine among your peers – or did you shrink from the knowledge of your own defects in the midst of them...? Are you tormented with inordinate clutching lusts of which you dare not speak? Are you nearly mad with the sting of them, and nearly mad with the terror lest they should betray you…? All that is changed now.[26]

By the beginning of the 1872 academic year, his life as a don had become intolerable. He took leave of absence for two terms and embarked on a long sojourn in Italy, from where he informed the Master of the college that he intended to resign his clerical fellowship. When he returned to Cambridge in June 1873, he was determined to go through with it. In November, whilst in Cannes with a convalescing sister, he received the reviews of his first literary venture, a small volume of poetry.[27] A writer in the *Athenaeum* described the collection as "Keats writ indeed in water". As he often did when life seemed to be against him, he turned to Whitman for consolation, burying himself in his *Songs of the World*. The opening verse of *A Song of the Open Road* provides the clue to what was to be the most important decision of his life: "Afoot and light-hearted I take to the open road/Healthy, free, the world before me/The long brown path before me leading wherever I choose".[28] On the journey back to Cambridge the question of what he might do afterwards was constantly revolving in his mind. Then, "it suddenly flashed upon me, with a vibration through my whole body, that I would and must somehow go and make my life with the mass of the people and the manual workers".[29] Whitman had worked his spell, as he had with others, "saved them from their own little selves – from their own little virtues and vices – and united them in the solidarity of humanity".[30]

26 Edward Carpenter, *Towards Democracy*, pp. 35-39.
27 Edward Carpenter, *Narcissus and other Poems* (Henry S King and Co., 1873).
28 Walt Whitman, *Song of the Open Road*, (Limited Edition Club, New York, 1990).
29 Edward Carpenter, *My Days and Dreams*, p.77.
30 Edward Carpenter, *Days with Walt Whitman*, (George Allen, 1906), p. 58.

It was made clear that if he resigned his clerical fellowship it would not be possible for him to remain at Trinity Hall. Although urged by many not to take such a drastic step, he engaged a solicitor to set in train the process of ecclesiastical law that would enable him to renounce his orders. He was fortunate, as before 1870 and the passing of the Clerical Disabilities Relief Act, he would have been bound irrevocably to his calling and required to remain a clergyman for the rest of his life. In June the following year he surrendered all the rights and privileges belonging to the office of priest.

On the eve of his departure from Cambridge, he was drawn to write a long, intensely personal letter to the individual who had set him free:

> Because you have, as it were, given me a ground for the love of men I thank you continually in my heart... you have made men to be not ashamed of the noblest instinct of their nature. Women are beautiful; but to some, there is that which passes the love of women. I was in orders; but I have given that up – utterly. It was no good. Nor does the University do: there is nothing vital in it. Now I am going away to lecture to working men and women in the North. They at least desire to lay hold of something with a real grasp. And I can give something of mathematics and science. It may be of no use, but I shall see.[31]

Again, chance intervened in his life, as an opportunity had arisen that offered a step towards his desire to throw in his lot with "the mass-people and the manual workers", but not cast himself entirely adrift. The university's extension movement to open up education, especially to women, had been inaugurated that year: objectives that chimed with his vague

31 Horace Traubel, *With Walt Whitman in Camden*, (Boston, 1906), pp. 159-161.

socialistic outlook and the siren call of Whitmanic democracy.

He had to kick his heels in Brighton for several months but the following year he arrived in Leeds. The next seven years would be spent as a peripatetic lecturer, criss-crossing the north of England. It was a life of repetitious drudgery, of travelling from one smoke-hidden town to another, plagued by persistent bouts of exhaustion and nervous tension. In time, he once again felt trapped by circumstances that he seemed powerless to change. In April, 1877, he fulfilled a long-slumbering wish and went to America to meet Whitman. On his return, he told his closest friend, "[H]e came up to my expectations. He is magnificent".[32] Forced to resume his humdrum life, he swore a great oath that somehow he would break free and find his health again.

The following year, life took a turn for the better. Attracted by the heartiness of its folk, he settled in Sheffield, where he began to build up alliances: "Railway men, porters, clerks, signalmen, ironworkers, coach-builders, Sheffield cutlers, and others came within my ken… I felt I had come into, or at least in sight of, the world to which I belonged, and to my natural *habitat*".[33] One association led to regular escapes into the countryside from smoke-shrouded Sheffield, where he experienced manual labour for the first time, and was soon seized by the idea of an invigorating outdoor life. The open air, the hardiness of sun and wind, would build up his strength and combat his recurring bouts of ill health. He formed a plan "of coming to live if possible with these good people" and eventually took lodgings in Totley with a scythe maker, Albert Fearnehough, and his family. For the first time, he lived cheek by jowl with a working-class man: a relationship tinged with sexual overtones. "In many ways he was delightful to me, as the one powerful uneducated and natural person I had as yet,

---

32 Carpenter to Charles Oates, 22 August 1877, SA MS 351/2.
33 Edward Carpenter, *My Days and Dreams*, p. 104.

in all my life met with".[34] Later, they moved to a larger cottage at Bradway, and it was there that *Towards Democracy,* the work that was soon to define him, was conceived.

In 1881, his mother died and the mass of feelings, intuitions, and views of life which lay within his mind, and which had been set down randomly in scraps of prose and poetry, demanded expression. The urge to write was so strong that he could no longer resist the desire to cut loose. He threw up his lecturing work and felt "supremely happy".[35] With his father's passing in 1882 he came into quite a large fortune, and might have settled into an armchair literary life, but a fancy for manual work had seized him. He bought three small fields, amounting to seven acres, in the hamlet of Millthorpe, snuggled between Chesterfield and Sheffield, had a house built and, with the help of the Fearnehoughs, set himself up as a market gardener.

Soon after, *Towards Democracy* was published, a small, thin volume meant for the pocket. As a work, it was irregular in form, uneven in quality, and incomplete as either a system of philosophy or a socialist manifesto. The structure of the book certainly did not help: themes are intertwined, many sections seem to stand alone, connections between sections are often puzzling and sudden disconnections startling. But for Carpenter its intellectual coherence was of secondary importance. It had been written, as he said, in a mood of illumination and inspiration under the pressure of feeling. Whatever its defects, the uniqueness of its conception convinced him never to make alterations to the original text. He would always consider this first part of *Towards Democracy,* which really stands apart from its succeeding three parts, to be the "start-point and kernel" of all his later work, the centre from which all his other books "radiated".[36]

---

34 Edward Carpenter, *My Days and Dreams*, p. 103.
35 Ibid. p. 107.
36 Ibid. p. 190.

No serious estimate of the work appeared in any leading publication. Like a number of his books, it did not enter the literary fold through the accepted gate, but by stealth, "like a thief or a robber".[37] Many years later, he humorously summarised its prospects:

> That it should go its own way quietly, neither applauded by the crowd, nor barked at by the dogs, but knocking softly here and there at a door and finding friendly hospitality is surely its most gracious and satisfying destiny.[38]

Towards Democracy marked his entry into the world of radical politics. He soon came into contact with socialists and anarchists, with feminists and suffragettes, trades unionists and religious dissenters. In time, he would become an unremitting critic of the whole economic and social order of his day. The ravages of industrial production, the worship of stocks and shares, class divisions and futile social conventions, the contempt for manual labour, materialism, the pretensions of modern science, and much more, became targets of his restless pen.

But during these years of struggle to make a life for himself, the heart had remained unsatisfied; the hunger for love that had hunted him down since childhood unfulfilled. Without a close affectional tie his life was incomplete, his powers crippled, his energies misspent. The idiotic social reserve and pretence which he had continued to practice; his denial and ignoring of the obvious facts of the heart and of sex, all contributed to a feeling of desolation.

"I can hardly bear even now to think of all that early life – to think that until about the age of 35 – I never met with anything like a real satisfaction of the heart".[39] In desperation,

---

37   Edward Carpenter, *My Days and Dreams*. p. 200.
38   Ibid. p. 201.
39   Edward Carpenter, *My Days and Dreams*, early draft, (SA, MS 200).

on one occasion he had gone to Paris to see if he might make a discovery there, but the commercial samples of the boulevards, "tho' some of them deeply interested me, were nothing for my need; and I came back to England feeling hopeless and tired out".[40] But there may have been other, more satisfying, encounters. He had written in *Towards Democracy*: "I enter the young prostitute's chamber, where he is arranging the photographs of fashionable beauties and favourite companions and stay with him; we are at ease and understand each other".[41]

He was not thirty-five, but forty-one, when he found the first real satisfaction of the heart that he longed for when, early in 1886, he became involved in setting up a socialist club in Sheffield. Among the little band of workers was twenty-six-year-old George Hukin, a handsome self-employed razor grinder. Hukin is lovingly pictured in Carpenter's poem, *In the Stone-floored Workshop*, depicting men dressed in rough clothes, with clogs on their feet and yellow-splashed faces, bent over their grinding-wheels. From the gloom, his work done, emerges,

a figure with dusty cap and
Light curls escaping from under it, large dove-grey eyes and
Dutch-featured face of tears and laughter,
(So subtle, so rare, so finished a product,)
A man who understands and accepts all human life and character,
Keen and swift of brain, heart tender and true, and low voice,
Ringing so clear,
And my dear comrade.[42]

---

40 Edward Carpenter, *My Days and Dreams*, early draft, SA, MS 200.
41 Edward Carpenter, *Towards Democracy*, XLV.
42 Ibid. p.217.

George was a widower already courting his soon to be second wife, Fannie. Whatever his intimacy with men had been, he had not rejected the advances of the strikingly-handsome Carpenter, and the friendship quickly became intense. He was soon 'your faithful Chips', and George his 'dear Pippin'. In the beginning, Hukin was over-awed and struggled to bridge the gulf between them, confessing:

I would rather withdraw from, than approach any nearer to you. I feel so mean and little beside you! Altogether unworthy of your friendship. It is not your fault that I feel so. I know you have always tried to put me at my ease, to make me feel at home with you – sorry I cannot (sic) come nearer to you. How I should like to yet I feel I can't… Forgive me calling you Mr. I know I've offended you often by doing so. I won't do so again I assure you. [43]

In Brighton, 'distributing relics' after the sale of the old family house, Carpenter was cheered to receive an endearing letter from a more confident George:

You don't know how tempted I feel to come down and join you at Brighton. A thousand thanks for your kind letter. It is so good of you to love me so. I don't think I ever felt as happy in my life as I have felt lately. And I'm sure I love you more than any other friend I have in the world.[44]

The relationship quickly became physical: "He generally stays the night with me on Saturdays – either at Millthorpe, or at my quarters in Sheffield".[45] As bed-sharing was not uncommon within working-class families living in overcrowded

---

43   Hukin to Carpenter, 8 July 1886, SA MS 262/1.
44   Hukin to Carpenter, 28 October 1886, SA MS 262/5.
45   Carpenter to Oates, 20 December 1886, SA MS 351/3.

conditions, Hukin's sleeping with Carpenter would not have been seen as unusual, and in the male-dominated society in which he had been raised, physical contact between men "was neither frowned upon nor unusual", probably leading Hukin to "a casual acceptance of sex and companionship between men in private" that did not conflict with sexuality expressed through marriage and fatherhood.[46]

Hukin was Carpenter's physical ideal, and almost certainly this was his first consummated love affair. Soon he was spending a great deal of time with George: "He is staying here for a day or two and tomorrow he and I are going for a 2 or 3 days' walk among the Derbyshire Hills... His love is so disinterested and so tender. I hardly dare think it true".[47]

Over Christmas, they spent a week together in London. Back in Sheffield, Hukin could not wait to tell him:

I think on the whole these have been the happiest Xmas holidays I ever remember, dear old Chips, I don't know what I'd do without you, you are the dearest old Chips on earth. Longing to see you in Sheffield again. Your Dearest Pippin. [48]

But the relationship, on which Carpenter seemed to be placing so much store, was fated. His effusiveness had first entranced and then smothered Hukin, who could no longer keep his intention towards Fannie to himself. In May, Carpenter was on holiday in Acqui, when Hukin wrote to tell him that he had asked her to marry him. Struggling to accept his loss, he forced himself to write a consoling letter. A relieved George responded: "Your letter has cheered us both up wonderfully...

46 Helen Smith, *Masculinity, Class and Same-Sex Desire in Industrial England, 1895-1957*, (Palgrave Macmillan, 2015), p. 70.
47 Carpenter to Oates, 10 April 1887, SA MS 351/38.
48 Hukin to Carpenter, 7 January 1887, SA MS 362/7.

I feel as if quite a load has been taken off me and I hope none of us will ever feel so weighed down again".[49]

A flurry of letters from Carpenter followed, which brought a confused response from the clearly emotionally-torn George:

> I should like to be with you for just an hour! It seems so very quiet and lonely in this room without you here. I miss you much more than I thought I should and I don't find it so nice, sleeping alone, as I used to think it was... Oh how often I had wanted to tell you about it ever since that first night I slept with you at Millthorpe. You don't know how miserable I have felt all along, just because I wanted to tell you, and yet somehow I was afraid to.[50]

Carpenter, in replying, may have lapsed into self-indulgence. It induced a despairing reply from George:

> I feel very miserable just now... I think about you and love you more than ever. But I can't bear to think that you are so unhappy, and know that I am the cause of it all... I sometimes feel that I can never bring anything but unhappiness to either you or Fannie and then I feel so miserable that I would like to die. Perhaps it would be best. Then your wound might heal the sooner and Fannie might forget all about me then. At least, I can't feel as I feel now and live much longer... I don't care what becomes of me, so long as you and Fannie are happy.[51]

It is impossible to know whether George was on the verge of

49   Hukin to Carpenter, 15 May 1887, SA MS 362/9.
50   Hukin to Carpenter, 21 May 1887, SA MS 262/10.
51   Hukin to Carpenter, 24 May 1887, SA MS 362/11.

taking his own life, but his letter brought a reassuring response from a worried Carpenter:

> I have been reading yours of the 24th over more than once and cannot say all I would about it, ah the pain I have put you to, and your goodness. But I will not doubt you any more, or Fannie I will not really dear George. I will be happy for your sakes as you tell me to be and as I can be now.[52]

The company of handsome Italian men did little to mollify him:

> I got on pretty well with my Italian youth Francesco from Sarona to Genoa but we were both awfully silent walked for miles without saying a word… I feel my sexual nature swimming. I have been like a monk for the last few weeks![53]

In his head, he had accepted the finality of the situation, telling George:

> I do hope now you will be happy. I almost wish you had done me some wrong. I would so gladly forgive you but after all I think you have done the best for us all three… Love and blessings on you and looking forward ever so to seeing you.[54]

George told him, "You are so good to forgive me for all the pain I've caused you… you must stay as long as you can and get quite well and strong before you come back".[55] He needed little prompting: "I am glad of an excuse to stay a day or two

---

52   Carpenter to Hukin, Whit-Monday 1887, SA MS 361/3.
53   Carpenter to Hukin, 1 June 1887, SA MS 361/4.
54   Carpenter to Hukin, I June 1887, SA MS 362/13.
55   Ibid.

more as I feel so much better now as if I was getting quite strong again, better than I have felt for a year or two." But it was not easy to stop thinking about George: "I could have sworn you were somewhere about George... I was walking through the fields, and you came ever so close to me". And Fannie was now writing to him: "Another letter from Fannie yesterday... so good of her".[56]

On his return to Millthorpe, he told Charles Oates:

The little pain in the hidden chamber has come back again on seeing *her* (Fannie), but it is curious how almost entirely *physical* it is. Mentally I feel easy-minded and hardly distressed. She seems to draw off a little – or perhaps it is my own reflection in her that I see – but he is very affectionate, as much so as ever. The position is a little difficult for me; but I feel ever so much stronger now.[57]

Little is revealed in *My Days and Dreams* of how special Hukin was in Carpenter's life. It is another George, George Merrill,[58] who is invariably named as the individual who occupied the central place in his affections. With Merrill, 'friend and factotum', so described by Edith Ellis, who Carpenter will not meet until 1891, he will enjoy a loving domestic relationship spanning over thirty years. But his attachment to Hukin was of a different order: George Merrill lived in his affections, Hukin lived in his heart. It was his death, in 1917, that broke Carpenter's strongest link with the North.

The deep attachment that existed between them, long after their brief romance ended, is revealed in Carpenter's tenderly beautiful poem *Philoläus to Diocles*. It contains the lines:

---

56 Carpenter to Hukin, 3 June 1887, SA MS 351/5.
57 Carpenter to Oates, 19 December 1887, SA MS 351/43.
58 See chapter nine.

All the sweet noons and moons we have spent together;
All the glad interchange of laughter and love,
And thoughts, so grave, or fanciful:
What can compare with these, or what surpass them?
All the unbroken faith and steadfast reliance, nigh twenty
years twining the roots of life far down;
And not a mistrustful hour between us, or moment of
anger...[59]

The affair with Hukin brought home to Carpenter how finding his kind of love would be a life-long struggle, a "fierce and frightful waging for a mate and the mockery of women always thrust in the way..."[60] After George married, he seemed unable to let go and their physical relationship lingered for a time, after which Carpenter became involved sexually with other men in his socialist circle. This was "a startling break with conventional sexual relationships. They were crossing the divides of class, gender and monogamy all at once in the midst of intense political activity, faction fights and anarchist trials".[61]

Finding working-class men with same-sex desires was consoling. For the first time, Whitman's comradely love seemed real, but there was a need for solidarity, as he told Charles Oates, himself homosexual:

We are going to form by degrees a body of friends who will be tied together by the strongest general bond and also by personal attachment and that we shall help each other immensely by the mutual support we shall be able to give each other. The knowledge that there are others

---

59   Edward Carpenter, *Towards Democracy*, p. 413.
60   Carpenter to Oates, 27 August 1887, SA MS 351/42.
61   Sheila Rowbotham, in Sheila Rowbotham and Jeffrey Weeks, *Socialism and the New Life: The Personal and Sexual Politics of Edward Carpenter and Havelock Ellis*, (Pluto Press, 1977), p. 81.

in the same position as oneself will remove that sense of loneliness when plunged in the society of the philistines which is almost unbearable.[62]

He had cultivated friendships with a number of young Cambridge men, among them Charles Ashbee, Roger Fry, Goldsworthy Lowes Dickinson and Charles Headlam, all to distinguish themselves in later life. After a visit by Carpenter, Ashbee, then in his final year as an undergraduate, confided in his journal:

> He unfolded to me a wonderful idea of his of a new free-masonry, a comradeship in the life of men which might be based on our little Cambridge circle of friendships. Are we to be the nucleus out of which the new Society is to be organised?[63]

It seemed that they might be attached, "by throwing all the class and cultural barriers into the melting pot of Democracy",[64] but Carpenter, only fleetingly visualised "a community of men, separate and separated from the rest of British masculinity," united by their same-sex desires.[65] Such a homosexual freemasonry would surface in England in the 1890s,[66] but by this time Carpenter had moved decisively away from clandestine association towards an open defence of same-sex love: one in which the homosexual was to have "a fitting place and sphere of usefulness in the general scheme of society".[67]

---

62   Carpenter to Oates, 19 December 1887, (SA, MS 351/43).
63   Ashbee Papers, Kings College Cambridge.
64   Chushichi Tsuzuki, *Edward Carpenter, Prophet of Human Fellowship* (Cambridge U.P., 1980), p. 68.
65   Sean Brady, *Masculinity and Male Homosexuality in Britain,* (Palgrave Macmillan, 2005) *1861-1913*, p. 202.
66   The Order of Chaeronia, founded by George Cecil Ives (1867-1950).
67   Edward Carpenter, *The Intermediate Sex*, (Allen & Unwin, 1908), p. 14.

*

Given Ellis's high regard for Whitman, Carpenter's *Towards Democracy*, with its free-verse form, seemed to be a palpable imitation of *Leaves of Grass,* but when he came across a copy in a bookseller's penny-box and was able to read it at his leisure, he recanted his hasty judgement. Although *Whitmanesque* in form, it was a genuinely original book, full of "inspiring and beautiful and consoling things". Its fusion of personal testament, trenchant social criticism, and democratic ideals, appealed to Ellis's "youthful impulse of revolt against the existing social order".[68]

He wrote to Carpenter to express the "great delight and help" that reading it had given him.[69] He soon found that their intellectual sympathies ran deep, telling Olive Schreiner, "I found this letter from Carpenter. Send it back. I have never felt such a longing for anyone's friendship as for Carpenter's. I feel so near to him. He could never say anything which wouldn't be mine too."[70] When he learned of Carpenter's homosexuality it did not shock him, "though I had never before known personally anyone of that sexual temperament".[71] In turn, Carpenter was fortified to find in Ellis, "a champion of the sexual invert's right to existence".[72] In 1885, for both, writing about human sexuality was a decade away, but the years between, during which their friendship flourished, were important in influencing the form that this would take.

It was Ellis who brought Olive Schreiner and Carpenter

---

68   Havelock Ellis, *My Life*, p. 163.
69   Ellis to Carpenter, 12 March 1885, SA MS 357/1.
70   Ellis to Schreiner, in *My Other Self, The Letters of Olive Schreiner and Havelock Ellis*, ed. Y.C. Draznin, (Peter Lang, 1992), p. 378.
71   *Edward Carpenter, In Appreciation*, ed. Gilbert Beith, (George Allen & Unwin, 1931), p. 48.
72   Edward Carpenter, *My Days and Dreams*, p. 7.

together: he loaned her his copy of *Towards Democracy*, another chance happening that was to prove to be so important for Carpenter. She told Ellis. "What a splendid fellow Carpenter must be. I have just been reading his article in *Today*. It expresses what I feel so exactly that I seem to feel as if I had written it myself."[73] It was after a meeting of the New Lifers, when a few attenders were gathered together, that Carpenter noticed "a charming girl-face, of *riant* Italian type, smiling across to me".[74] It was the beginning of a close, loving, and for Carpenter life-influencing friendship that would last until Schreiner's death in 1920. Both had been introspective children, who grew into troubled adults preoccupied with their personal liberation. At the very time of their first meeting, he had fallen in love with George Hukin, and it was she who, setting aside her own romantic entanglements, helped him through the dark days that followed when the relationship ended. She would see only one future for them:

> Edward you must write much. Make your life consist in that. You and I must have no personality. We must die whilst yet we live… We must work, and every time our heart pains us work – till the agony gets still.[75]

*

At Sparkes Creek, the precocious Ellis had read early volumes of John Addington Symonds's *Renaissance in Italy*. In 1885, in a wide-ranging review of the current state of literary criticism in England, he singled out Symonds for his catholicity and

---

73 Schreiner to Ellis, 12 May 1885, *The Letters of Olive Schreiner*, ed. S.C. Cronwright-Schreiner, (Fisher Unwin, 1924), p. 19.
74 Edward Carpenter, *My Days and Dreams*, p. 226.
75 Schreiner to Carpenter, 16 April 1888, SA MS 358/21.

freedom from "the limitations of the specialist critic".[76] Shut up in Davos, Symonds was unaware of the article until Ellis, eager to make a name for himself in the literary world, sent him a copy. It raised Symonds's spirits:

> But for your kind thought of sending it, I should probably in this benighted place have missed it altogether. To do that would have been a misfortune; for I regard this as a very sincere and penetrative piece of work... What you say about myself gratifies me. It is the first word spoken clearly, which shows that anybody has taken my drift in criticism, and understood what I have always been aiming at.[77]

At the time, Ellis did not appreciate how important his article, and subsequent friendship, was for Symonds, forced through ill-health to live for years away from England. "There are some things in my life & the hardest is the necessity of living, in that magic castle of the snows, so far away from people. I feel that deprivation far more than the withdrawal from libraries, pictures, music."[78] Such isolation was enough to extinguish all intellectual activity in an individual notable for his sparkling conversation. Always with high expectations for himself, in a very revealing follow-up letter to Ellis he confessed that he had not made the mark on the world that he aspired to. "I blush to talk so much about myself. Let me however add but this: that words like yours, the sense that a man like you finds something in me, will be of steady service

---

76   Havelock Ellis, *The Present Position of English Criticism*, Time, December, 1885.

77   Symonds to Ellis, 7 December 1885, *The Letters of John Addington Symonds*, 3 vols., ed. Schueller & Peters, (Wayne State U.P., 1967-1969), vol. 111, p. 98.

78   Symonds to Arthur Galton,18 October 1889, *Letters* vol. 111, p. 393.

in the future – if life is given me to work yet with purpose."[79] The following year, Ellis received a commission to edit a series on Elizabethan dramatists and invited Symonds to contribute. It strengthened a growing friendship, but Symonds could not then have foreseen that it would not be literary criticism but the subject of homosexuality that would bring them closest.

*

Descended from six generations of Puritans, Symonds's father, Dr John Addington Symonds, was the *rara avis* of his line, having freed himself from strict evangelical orthodoxy and joined the ranks of the intellectually-progressive. He prospered, and by the time his namesake was born in Bristol, on 5th October 1840, he had risen to become one of the most fashionable physicians of his day. His professional, literary and political interests brought the family within the sphere of the celebrated and the influential.

His mother having died when he was aged four, it was during long carriage drives across the Somerset downs with his father that a strong paternal influence worked upon the young Symonds. Grasping that his father's character and many-sided culture marked him out from the ordinary run of medical men, he came to look upon him with reverence, as "an eagle born in the hencoop".[80] Immersed in a milieu of high culture and elevated expectations, living in the shadow of such a father made him painfully aware of his own deficiencies. Although conscious of the advantages that he enjoyed through the attention of the distinguished individuals who passed through his father's house, he regarded himself as a sickly, physically insignificant boy, with an ill-sounding name and nothing in

79 Symonds to Ellis, 16 December 1885, Letters, vol. 111, p. 103.
80 Phyllis Grosskurth, *The Memoirs of John Addington Symonds*, ed. (Random House, 1984), p. 53.

his family's circumstances that might carry him effortlessly forward to fame and fortune. Like his father, he would have to work for his place in the world and win what he wanted by his own efforts. "I vowed to raise myself, somehow or other, to eminence of some sort".[81]

With an inborn repugnance for sordid things, the brutality and lust that he found at Harrow School repelled him. "Here and there one could not avoid seeing acts of onanism, mutual masturbation, the sports of naked boys in bed together. There was no refinement, no sentiment, no passion; nothing but animal lust …"[82] Every boy of good looks had a female name, and was recognized either as a public prostitute or as some bigger fellow's 'bitch'. His own etherealized daydreaming about boys seemed to belong to another world. In his seventeenth year he read Plato's *Symposium*, in which he found the sanction for the love that was ruling him. It confirmed his passion for his own sex, delivered him from the horrors of Harrow, and filled his head with a vision of ideal love. His erotic dreams of brawny sailors seen about the streets of Bristol were replaced in his fancy by an Adonis, whom he yearned after as an adorable object of passionate love. The image of Venus only brought into sharp relief the overwhelming attraction of male adolescents, encountered in the form of a chaste cathedral chorister, from whom he stole his first, unforgettable, kiss. He revealed his infatuation to his enlightened father, only to be made painfully aware of its prohibition, and the danger that a liaison with the son of a draper posed for himself and the family's social standing. Nothing remained but to relegate his longings to the sphere of the imagination.

Not quite eighteen years old, in the autumn of 1858 he entered Balliol College, Oxford. The fusion of religion and homoeroticism lingered there in the wake of the Tractarian

---

81 *Memoirs*, p. 81.
82 Ibid. p. 94.

movement,[83] whilst reforms to the Greats curriculum had opened students' eyes to Hellenic paederasty.[84] Amid the distractions of study and polite society, the tread of love assumed a new intensity. The battle between the tyranny of the flesh and the aspirations of the spirit was constant: his life dominated by the discord between his spontaneous appetite for the male and his ingrained respect for social convention.

He gained a first-class degree, the best in his year he was told, and with a host of influential and congenial friends in the university, he saw his own calling there. Elected to a probationary fellowship at Magdalen College, his prospects looked bright. "I do not see why we should expect unhappiness in the future," he confided to his sister Charlotte.[85] But, within weeks, the expectation of an agreeable don's life was dashed by a scandal. He had struck up a friendship with a good-looking undergraduate from another college: "We soon became intimate and I discovered that he shared my Arcadian tastes."[86] But the relationship spelled danger when his flirtatious friend began chasing after Magdalen choristers, and to protect himself Symonds broke off the association. Feeling slighted, his lover took his revenge by revealing incriminating letters received from Symonds, and by claiming that he had encouraged him in his amorous adventures.

Symonds was exonerated, but two effusive love letters were strongly condemned by the Magdalen fellows. It was a severe blow to his self-esteem. "My name is soiled with an unbearable suspicion; my usefulness to the college is destroyed, and Oxford is made an impossibility,"[87] he confided

---

83 A movement within the Church of England, out of which Anglo-Catholicism developed.
84 See Linda Dowling, *Hellenism and Homosexuality in Victorian Oxford*, (Cornell University Press, 1994).
85 Symonds to Charlotte Symonds, October 5, 1862, *Letters*, vol. 1, p. 361.
86 Phyllis Grosskurth, *Memoirs p.* 117. 'Arcadian' meant homosexual.
87 Ibid. p. 132.

in his diary. The effect of the attack on his character could not be easily shaken off and unhappiness and physical weakness soon made college work impossible. There were the first signs of the debilitating disease of the lungs that would afflict him for the rest of his life. Early in 1864, the painful decision was made to give up Oxford. It was, he afterwards recalled, "[A] stunning crushing blow, under which my whole nature quivered and from which I thought I could not recover... mingled with regret at the sense of a life that could not again be taken up..."[88]

With his father's encouragement, he made a pretence of studying law but became convinced that what intellectual powers he possessed were not suited to it. "The history of literature is what I feel drawn to, and to this I should willingly devote my life," he told his old tutor Benjamin Jowett, asking, "Is it prudent for me to give up a profession and to choose literature...? Am I flying too high if I consecrate myself to study?"[89] Jowett counselled him to stick to the law; however a few months later ill-health brought his studies to an end. To reduce his sexual arousal he was cauterized through the urethra, and was sent by his father to see the Queen's surgeon, who recommended a hired mistress or early marriage.

Such a course ran counter to his deepest instincts, shutting him out "from passion and ideal love, neither of which had been indulged, although my whole being panted for them."[90] But long before the Magdalen incident, he had felt the necessity of growing into a *normal* man; to be at one with those he loved and honoured. To be married was the foundation of the Victorian ideal of masculinity, deeply embedded in the social fabric. Through marriage, a man entered a world of

88 Symonds to unknown recipient, 16 November 1868, *Letters,* vol. 111, p. 850.
89 Symonds to Benjamin Jowett, September 1865, *Letters*, vol. 1, p. 568.
90 Phyllis Grosskurth, *Memoirs*, p. 152.

defined familial responsibilities and sanctioned associations.[91]
In the summer of 1863, when staying at a small inn in Mirren,
Switzerland, Frederick North[92] arrived with his two daughters.
The vivacity of the younger woman, Catherine, grew upon
him and once back home he entered the family's social circle
and set out to woo her. The following year, he followed the
family to Switzerland and at Pontresena, whilst walking in the
mountains with Catherine, he found a romantic setting and
proposed. In little more than four months they were married.
Having shrunk alike from the prostitute and the soldier, he
had never performed a sexual act and was pleased to find that
he was potent. Within a year the first of four daughters was
born.

Successful intercourse did not diminish his appetite for
the male. Living at the time off Hyde Park, after a sleepless
night he would stroll to the Serpentine to feast his eyes
upon the youths bathing there. One evening, returning
home from his club, he was accosted by a young Grenadier
Guardsman. A nervous man of fashion in dress clothes, he
found himself walking side by side with a strapping fellow
in a scarlet uniform, exuding physical magnetism. Following
a few commonplace remarks, the soldier abruptly made a
proposal and mentioned a house nearby to which they could
go. Although aroused, Symonds lost his nerve and broke
away from the soldier, "with a passionate mixture of repulsion
and fascination." What the soldier offered was not what he
then desired, but the thrill of his first sexual contact with a
working-class man had stirred him deeply and it taught him
something about himself. His lingering regret at not accepting
the soldier's offer was mixed with a sense of deliverance from

---

91   See Sean Brady's *Masculinity and Male Homosexuality in Britain,*
     1861-1913. (Palgrave Macmillan, 2005).
92   Frederick North, Member of Parliament for Hastings and a descendant
     of Prime Minister Lord North.

danger, but the encounter had stirred a desire, the like of which he had not before experienced. It was a turning point: "The longing left was partly a fresh seeking after comradeship and partly an animal desire the like of which I had not before experienced".[93]

For several years after giving up the law, he led a nomadic life, with a number of long stays on the European continent. Enforced idleness through ill health gave time for a great deal of reading and his sojourns, especially in Italy, provided opportunities to plan literary projects and to gather material, laying foundations that would in time bear fruit, with a succession of well-received books, articles and reviews in leading literary journals. One enterprise, a study of Walt Whitman, might never have seen the light of day if, only weeks after Carpenter's discovery, he had not also come across Rosetti's collection.

He had scanned it for poems celebrating male comradeship, and was audacious enough to query with Rossetti the omission of poems from the 1860 *Calamus* cluster, in which the opening poem (later given the title *In Paths Untrodden)* was Whitman's 'coming out': the song of a lover of his own sex. They would never meet, but Symonds wrote a month before the poet's death: "Brought up in the purple of aristocratic school and university, provided with more money than is good for a young man ... I might have been a mere English gentleman, had not I read *Leaves of Grass* in time".[94] When Rossetti sent him a piece of Whitman's handwriting he told a friend: "I wd (sic) as soon have this as that of Shakespeare or Plato or Dante."[95]

The discovery of Whitman's *Calamus* cycle aroused in him a determination to write a history of paederastia in ancient Greece: to provide "a theoretical demonstration of the

---

93   Phyllis Grosskurth, *Memoirs*, pp. 186-7.
94   Symonds to Horace Traubel, 27 February 1892, *Letters*, vol. 111, p. 667.
95   Symonds to Graham Dakyns, 22 August 1868, *Letters*, vol. 1, p. 837.

chivalrous enthusiasm which seemed to me to be implicit in comradeship."[96] His mind brimming with classical learning, he wanted to explain how the Greeks felt about sexual passion; to show how it was connected with their sense of beauty, and how it influenced their institutions.

Intent on revealing what he believed to be the core of Whitman's poetry, during a correspondence spanning twenty years he will attempt to prise from him an admission that his was a new poetic voice proclaiming the joys of same-sex love. He will pore for hours over the pages of *Calamus*, "burning for a revelation of your more developed meaning, panting to ask – is that what you would indicate...? Shall I ever be permitted to question you & learn from you?"[97] But Whitman had presented his man-loving poems in the context of the reunification of the American nation, and any imputation of carnality would have been highly damaging to his reputation. He had told Carpenter that there were truths that it was necessary "to envelop or wrap up", likening himself to a furtive old hen secreting away her eggs.[98]

After years of travelling throughout Europe, Symonds had begun to crave Switzerland, where his poor constitution seemed particularly adapted to the Alpine air. In 1877, he saw Davos for the first time, set in "a bare bleak Alpine valley, 5,200 feet above civilisation".[99] Instinct told him that it was a place where he might regain his health, for after long sojourns abroad he found the English climate impossible. Three years later, in September 1880, plagued by constant bouts of ill health, on the advice of his doctors the family left England. Symonds was sorrowful, believing that he was

---

96   Phyllis Grosskurth, *Memoirs*, p. 189.
97   7 February 1872, in Horace Traubel, *With Walt Whitman in Camden*, (Small, Maynard and Co, 1906), vol. 1, pp. 74-6.
98   Edward Carpenter, *Days with Walt Whitman*, p. 43.
99   Symonds to Edmund Gosse, 8 November 1877, *Letters*, vol. 11, p. 498.

"on the threshold of perhaps enduring exile."[100] They had a house built at Davos Platz, with large wooden balconies on the south and west sides to enable Symonds to get as much sun as possible.

There is little doubt that the suppression of his homosexuality, time and again brought him to a state of nervous collapse, but we do not agree with Brady, that his emigration was a selfish act, "to assuage the intense anxieties" that he had about his sexuality, and the difficulties that this created for him in England.[101] Like Carpenter, he felt liberated in the freer sexual climate of southern Europe,[102] but the move abroad caused a major domestic upheaval. Clifton Hill House, inherited from his father, had to be given up, and furniture and thousands of books disposed of. He would later fret over having imposed such a constraining life upon his family, and from time to time a return to England, if not for himself then for his wife and children, was seriously considered. His enforced isolation constantly dragged him down: "Climate is good; but solitude from all society congenial to my work is pernicious... I am weak to bear the isolation of absorbing intellectual occupations mitigated by peasants."[103]

In June 1882 during a visit to England, active disease was found in his right, hitherto untouched, lung and his health once again became an absorbing preoccupation. Three doctors spoke gravely of his condition and would not let him stay in England a day longer. He was concerned enough to tell Horatio Brown[104] that he had made him his literary executor. Back in Davos he anticipated the worst:

---

100 Symonds to Graham Dakyns, 8 June 1880, *Letters*, vol. 11, p. 637.
101 Brady, *Masculinity and Male Homosexuality in Britain*, p. 83.
102 See Robert Aldrich, *The Seduction of the Mediterranean*, Writing Art and Homosexual Fantasy, (Routledge 1993).
103 Symonds to Henry Sidgwick, 5 April 1895, Letters, vol. 111, p. 43.
104 Horatio Forbes Brown (1854-1926), historian and life-long friend.

If I am doomed to decline now, I can at least say that in the five years since I came here dying, I have had a very wonderful Indian summer of experience. The colours of my life have been even richer, my personal emotions even more glowing... It seems a phase of my disease that I should grow in youth and spiritual intensity inversely to my physical decay.[105]

Writing became his solace, although it had to be accomplished under extraordinary difficulties. Away from great libraries, books had to be sent from England, making it "a ruinous indulgence to study in Davos with any completeness."[106] The exception was the writing of his *Modern Problem,* which could not have been undertaken without the availability of works on homosexuality by continental writers, which were virtually unobtainable in England. It was not until 1892 that an English translation of Richard Krafft-Ebing's influential *Psychopathia Sexualis* was available: a book always open to being banned as obscene.[107] Symonds had been in Davos for nine years before he began reading any of the work of continental sexual theorists, so gaining access to this material did not figure in his decision to leave England.

In 1883, within months of the appearance of Carpenter's *Towards Democracy,* Symonds completed and privately published his study of homosexual love in Hellas, a work that can be traced back to lectures he gave on the Greek poets at Clifton College fifteen years earlier. It was given the innocuous title, A *Problem in Greek Ethics.* Only ten copies were printed and given to those closest to him. In the single

---

105 Symonds to Brown, 30 June 1882, *Letters,* vol. 11, p. 757.
106 Symonds to T.S. Perry, 15 July 1883, *Letters,* vol.11, p. 832.
107 Brady argues that the absence of such literature in England at this time was part of a 'culture of resistance' to the circulation of works on homosexuality.

letter on the monograph to be found in his correspondence at this time, he told an American friend that it was, "the most learned" of his writings:

> The Essay on Greek Manners wh (sic) *I* told you I had printed privately is an attempt to analyse the social conditions & philosophical conceptions out of wh (sic) Plato's theory of love is set forth in the Phaedrus & Symposium... You will understand from this description the reasons why I do not wish to give this study publicity. Unfortunately the English public is almost devoid of scientific curiosity.[108]

Soon after its appearance, he was sent a copy of Carpenter's *Towards Democracy* by his close friend Henry Sidgwick.[109] The first edition did not carry Carpenter's name but its authorship had become known among his old Cambridge circle, which had included Sidgwick. Symonds's first reaction to the work was similar to that of Ellis: "It interests me, so far as I have read," he told Sidgwick, but added that he found it, "too palpably a copy of W.W."[110]

In Symonds's brief letter there is no allusion to the book's muted homosexual theme, let alone recognition that it might be a trumpet call for the right of the homosexual to exist. If he later read *Towards Democracy* from cover to cover, he would not have missed a number of homoerotic passages. He had a life-long preoccupation with detecting signs of a homosexual sensibility; a positive inclination or a skilfully disguised passion for the male body. It is unlikely that he would have overlooked the following:

---

108 Symonds to T.S. Perry, 22 March 1884, *Letters*, vol. 11, p. 894.
109 Henry Sidgwick became Knightsbridge Professor of Philosophy at Cambridge that year.
110 Symonds to Sidgwick, 4 December 1883, *Letters*, vol. 11, p. 862.

In the shadow of the thicket I lie spreading my fevered limbs to the cool breeze, bruising their unslacked passion against the stony earth – in the cool shadow I lie and gaze at his face I know so well.[111]

All this day we will go together … The night ever insatiate of love we will sleep together, and rise early and go forward again in the morning … we shall not desire to come to the end of the journey, nor consider what the end may be: the end of all things shall be with Us.[112]

…where the young man dreams all night of the face of his new-found friend and the kisses of his lips …[113]

From the time of his youth, Symonds had an infatuation with the young male body. He kept a collection of photographs and drawings of nude youths, which he was in the habit of exchanging with his acquaintances among the English boy-loving Uranian poets. Over ten years of adolescence and early manhood he had done everything in his power to sophisticate his sexual feelings; to throw off his enthrallment with "young lads", sealing his vow with the decisive act of marriage. But, fight it as he did, he could not shake off these idealistic, ultimately erotic desires. His infatuation was shared by his closest and most intimate life-long friend, Graham Dakyns, a master at Clifton College. Their many letters to each other contain frequent allusions to Clifton College boys: "Remember that Clifton is a terrible enchantress, and her sweet things are poisonous" Symonds warned.[114] It was at Dakyns' dinner table, in December 1868, that Symonds first set eyes on 'Norman'[115], an appealing sixth-former who was to

111 Edward Carpenter, *Towards Democracy*, LV.
112 Ibid. L1X.
113 Ibid. L1V.
114 Symonds to Graham Dakyns, 24 May 1865, *Letters*, vol. 1, p. 397.
115 Edward Norman Peter Moor (1851-95).

have a decisive influence on his sexual ideals and behaviour. It was Symonds's most difficult entanglement, and in recounting his sexual history he thought it important enough to devote a whole chapter to it.

Face to face with an adolescent in "the beauty-bloom of ladhood",[116] in order to approach him, he solicited an invitation to lecture to the sixth form on the Greek poets, and deliberately engaged in an *amour*, "tinged with unmistakable sensuality".[117] But he was courting danger, for his interest in the youth had not gone unnoticed: "A little shadow overcast us yesterday. His aunt at Clifton doubts about me."[118] On the eve of Norman's departure for Oxford, Symonds's idealised homosexual life culminated in the arms of a modern ephebe, at a time when his mind was dominated by the Greek ideal of the intimate bond between man and youth. But what he was searching for he did not find. "Of physical closeness I have as much as I can want. Of spiritual closeness I get little," he wrote in his diary.[119] He was naive in seeking an ideal love with a youth, "conscious of his fascination, but not attachable".[120] He learned how valueless was mere physical intimacy without "truly passionate or spiritual closeness".[121]

Reading Whitman encouraged him to invigorate his sexual feelings; to overcome his infatuation with young lads and to absorb Whitman's conception of *comradeship*: "My desires grew manlier, more defined, more direct, more daring by contact with *Calamus*".[122] In his years away from England, he would find tranquillity through taking his sexual pleasures with simple, healthy young working men,

116 Phyllis Grosskurth, *Memoirs*, p. 210.
117 Ibid. p. 194.
118 Symonds to Dakyns, I May 1869, *Letters*, vol. 11, p. 65.
119 Phyllis Grosskurth, *Memoirs*, p. 207.
120 Ibid. p. 206.
121 Ibid. p. 207.
122 Ibid. p.189.

but indulgence in libertine pleasure always offended him. In Venice and Rome, he rubbed shoulders with individuals who, as Algernon Swinburne teased, were more drawn to the blue of the gondolier's stockings than that of the Venetian sky. The unsentimental pursuit of sexual gratification by two of his aristocratic friends, the poet Roden Noel and the sculptor Lord Ronald Gower, shocked him. From his time at Harrow, right down to advanced manhood, the idea of a "divine almost mystic sensuality" had persisted in his mind, side by side with a marked repugnance for sexual avarice.[123]

If, beyond the censorious gaze of his English circle, on many occasions he found sexual pleasure with complete strangers, he tried always not to treat his partners as instruments of lust: "To pay a man to go to bed with me, to get an hour's gratification out of him at such a price, and then never to see him again, was always abhorrent to my nature."[124] He craved physical gratification, but only if it was offered freely, without coercion.

It was in Venice, in the spring of 1881, that his resolve was tested, when a strikingly handsome twenty-three-year-old gondolier, Angelo Fusato, was pointed out to him. In Symonds's words, it was "love at first sight".[125]

Black broad-brimmed hat thrown back upon his matted *zazzera* of dark hair. – Great fiery grey eyes, gazing intently, with compulsive effluence of electricity – the wild glance of a Triton. – Short blond moustache; dazzling teeth; skin bronzed but showing white and delicate through open front and sleeves of lilac shirt. – The dashing sparkle of this splendour… fixed and fascinated me.[126]

123 .Phyllis Grosskurth, *Memoirs*, p. 62.
124 Ibid. p. 277.
125 Ibid. p. 272.
126 Ibid. p. 271.

The image of Angelo burned into his brain and kept him awake at nights, wondering how he might make him part of his life. Impulsively, he sought him out and arranged an assignation. Angelo would have classed him with other men for whose caprices he had sold his beauty, and the purpose of their meeting would have been clear to him. But, in his loneliness, Symonds sought more than fleeting passion; more than possession of his powerful and radiant manhood. As Angelo lay, "mother-naked white as lilies" upon the bed, he refused what was so freely offered. He craved love, not transient sex.

Unable to bear the strain of Angelo's attraction, he left Venice the next day, and throughout the summer thought, and poetised, incessantly about him. Determined to somehow place his passion on a solid footing, he returned to Venice in the autumn. Angelo was then in the service of a French general, but was persuaded to become Symonds's gondolier, with a fixed wage and allowances. To his friends, he was *ill matto*, the mad-cap, poor by circumstances, determined to have money and indifferent to how it came to him. Symonds did not disappoint, presenting him with a gondola and giving him a good deal of money, which enabled him to marry the girl he was living with and set up house.

Angelo soon became a feature of the family for the Symonds girls, adding romance to outings in their "beautiful new gondola with our coat of arms in gold at the back of the seat."[127] Of Angelo, another daughter recalled: "The curious devotion of this only half-tamed creature was something very remarkable in its strength and constancy. He was wonderfully handsome…"[128]

---

127 Katherine Furze, *Hearts and Pomegranates*, The Story of Forty-Five Years, 1875-1920, (Peter Davis, 1940), p. 46.

128 Margaret Symonds, (Mrs. W Vaughan), *Out of the Past,* A Memoir of John Addington Symonds, (T Fisher Unwin, 1908), p. 240.

Symonds closed his eyes to the deep anomaly of a relationship with so much passion on his part and indulgence on Angelo's. Throughout life, he never ceased to struggle to moralise "the sexual flower of comradeship" that had driven his long interrogation of Whitman. His reflections on his bond with Angelo are overlaid by the need to justify a physical relationship with a man, secure in his heterosexuality, who accepted such comradeship, and for whom "it did not signify" if such a relationship was monogamous and protected by prudence on both sides. And Symonds felt, once persuaded of its permanence and its freedom from *volgivaga Venus* (love that prowls at large), Angelo's friends understood and accepted the bond between them.

Life with Angelo, which lasted until Symonds's death, was an important chapter. Had it not been for his homosexuality, he would never have come to know and appreciate a human being so far removed from him in "position, education, national quality and physique."[129] But Angelo could never have given him what he always longed for. Only months before his death he would whisper to his daughter Margaret of a life-long, "numbing paralyzing pain at the heart."[130] He feared that he would pass out of the world without experiencing "the highest happiness of mortals, an ardent love reciprocated with ardour."[131]

129 Phyllis Grosskurth, *Memoirs*, p. 275.
130 Symonds to Margaret Symonds, 4 November 1892, *Letters*, vol. 111, p. 772.
131 Phyllis Grosskurth, *Memoirs*, p.190.

My Best Work,
My Least Presentable

In April 1890, proud of his first book The New Spirit,[1] Ellis sent Symonds a copy. The centenary of the French Revolution had given him the idea of defining the "spirit" of his own age, to be found in the work of literary figures who described life as it was, stripped of make-believe. Symonds was pleased to find that Ellis counted Whitman among such realists. Frustrated by the poet's evasive responses to his questions on the meaning of comradeship, he saw an opportunity to quiz Ellis. It was their first exchange on the subject of homosexuality.

> I wish you had said more about "Calamus": or, if you have formed an opinion, that you would tell me what you think. In many ways Whitman clearly regards his doctrine of Comradeship as what he might call "spinal". Yet he nowhere makes it clear whether he means to advocate anything approaching its Greek form, or whether he regards that as simply monstrous. I have tried but have not succeeded in drawing an explicit utterance upon the subject from him. But I felt that until my mind is made up on this important aspect of his prophecy, I am unable to

---

1   Havelock Ellis, *The New Spirit*, (George Bell and Sons, 1890).

judge him in relation to the ethical and social problems…
In one word, does Whitman imagine that there is lurking in manly love the stuff of a new spiritual energy, the liberation of which would prove of benefit to society? And if so, is he willing to accept, condone or ignore the physical aspects of the passion? [2]

In a chapter seized upon by prurient critics, Ellis had written in *The New Spirit* that Whitman "finds the roots of the most universal love in the intimate and physical love of comrades and lovers", and made reference to one of the most homoerotic poems in the first edition of *Leaves of Grass*,[3] although he later claimed to have passed over the homosexual strain in Whitman as being "negligible".[4] Three months later, Symonds once again quizzed Whitman, by drawing his attention to Ellis's book, and suggesting that he, too, "expresses some perplexity" about the doctrine of manly love.[5] Symonds thought he had detected Ellis's commitment to the study of human sexuality when he had asked of Whitman: "Why should the sweetening breath of science be guarded from this spot?"[6] But he did not tell him that he was writing a monograph on homosexuality in contemporary English life, which had been incubated five years earlier.[7]

In the early 1880s, there had been a long campaign against child prostitution led, among others, by the social reformer Josephine Butler. When, in the summer of 1885, William

---

2   Symonds to Ellis, May 6 1890, *Letters*, vol. 111, p. 458.
3   Havelock Ellis, *The New Spirit*, p.122.
4   Havelock Ellis, *My Life*, (Heinemann, 1940), p. 263.
5   Symonds to Whitman, August 3, 1890, Letters, vol.111, p. 481.
6   Havelock Ellis, *The New Spirit,* p. 27.
7   John Addington Symonds, *A Problem in Modern Ethics*, being an *Inquiry into the Phenomenon of Sexual Inversion*. (Privately printed, London 1891). All references are to number 62 of an edition of 100 copies printed in 1896. It is referred to throughout as the *Modern Problem*.

Stead, the thirty-six-year-old editor of the *Pall Mall Gazette*, showed how easy it was to procure young girls for sex by 'abducting' the thirteen-year-old daughter of an East End chimney sweep, there was a huge public outcry. Although his action was intended purely to expose this traffic, the law took a different view and Stead found himself serving a short prison sentence, whilst legislation was hastily prepared to, *inter alia,* raise the age of female consent to sexual intercourse from thirteen to sixteen. The draft legislation went before the House of Commons on August 6 1885.

Had Henry Labouchère perished under the wheels of a carriage as he made his way to the Chamber that day, Symonds's future, and the course of homosexual law reform in England, would certainly have been different. As it was, by the end of discussion on the proposed legislation he had succeeded in having a five-line clause inserted into a bill that was intended *only* to control female prostitution. It read:

"Any male person who, in public or private, commits, or is a party to the commission of, or procures or attempts to procure the commission by any male person, of any act of gross indecency with another male person, shall be guilty of a misdemeanour, and being convicted thereof, shall be liable, at the discretion of the court, to be imprisoned for any term not exceeding one year with or without hard labour."[8]

In London, extensive female prostitution was the most visible manifestation of unrestrained male lust, but members strolling to the House that evening, had they

---

8   Criminal Law Amendment Act, 1885. The Labouchère amendment became section 11, 'Outrages on Public Decency', with the maximum term of imprisonment increased to two years, with or without hard labour. It did not replace the 1861 Offences against the Person Act, which retained buggery as a criminal offence.

cared to look, could not have avoided seeing young males plying the same trade in the bustling Haymarket, or the seductive soldier-prostitute parading in all his finery along London's leafy park-walks. Only the previous year, an extensive homosexual ring had been uncovered in Dublin Castle, the seat of the British Government in Ireland, when harsh sentences for sodomy were handed down. The wide-spread homosexuality among boys in public schools experienced by Symonds, and its diffusion into the upper reaches of society, had also become a fixation. In a depleted House of Commons, late at night, it did not take much to persuade members that this was an opportunity to extend the law on sex between men.

The amendment was entirely the result of Labouchère's initiative and was included in the bill after the Speaker, when questioned on its relevance to the legislation, ruled that it was in order. At the time, the government appeared to have no plan to introduce further legislation on homosexual behaviour and its non-involvement would seem to negate the 1885 Act as an intended instrument of state policy on sex between men, and a legal 'categorization' of the male homosexual.[9] But, although the government had not initiated the amendment, it did not block it, thus unwittingly recognising and bringing to public attention the widespread existence of sexual relations between men, distinct from the 'unnatural' offence of buggery buried in Section 61 of the 1861 Offences against the Person Act. The recognition of acts of gross indecency between men inevitably weakened any culture of resistance against the acknowledgement of homosexuality.[10] Going forward,

---

9   An issue of much debate among historians but too broad to be rehearsed here.
10   The central argument of Sean Brady in his *Masculinity and Male Homosexuality in Britain, 1861-1913, (Palgrave Macmillan, 2005).*

the availability of this new legislation to prosecute a hitherto legally-unrecognised male sexual offence opened a window on the homosexual underworld.

The clause was not a model of drafting precision. The introduction of the catch-all term 'gross indecency' made any intimate behaviour between males potentially a criminal offence, leaving the scope of the offence to be defined entirely by decisions of the courts. More fundamentally, the amendment made gross indecency an offence, whether committed in a public or a private place. The practice, under the buggery Acts, had always been to prosecute homosexual acts *wherever* committed, but to incorporate this in legislation marked a significant change in the reach of the law. It came at a time when the sovereignty of the individual over self-regarding actions was being asserted. John Stuart Mill's influential essay[11] had given impetus to the argument that the remit of the state was to protect its citizens in the public realm, not to act as a moral censor over the behaviour of consenting adults in private, who, as Symonds expressed it, should be "allowed to dispose as they like of their own persons."[12] In France, under the *Code Napoléon*, sexual relations between consenting males that did not involve violence, protected minors and did not outrage public decency, had been legal since 1792. By1889, when Italy introduced a similar law, the Netherlands, Belgium and Spain had all introduced comparable legislation.[13]

Labouchére was not known to be a scourge of homosexuals. A friend of Oscar Wilde, rich, a philanderer and frequenter of brothels, he moved in theatrical circles, living with the actress Henrietta Hudson before marrying her. He

---

11 John Stuart Mill, *On Liberty*, 1859.
12 Symonds, *A Problem in Modern Ethics,* chapter X/1X.
13 Whilst homosexual acts that took place in private between men over the age of twenty-one were decriminalised in England in 1967, Scotland had to wait until 1980, and Northern Ireland until 1982.

never gave a clear explanation for his action, but stung by the hostility expressed by some of his enlightened friends, claimed to have taken the wording for the amendment, *mutatis mutandis,* from the French *Code Napoléon* of 1802. If so, he had misread it, for the code did not prohibit consensual sex between adult men in private. After Oscar Wilde's conviction under the Act, he showed himself to be much less sympathetic towards homosexuals than in his earlier protestations. In his first draft of the clause he had made the maximum sentence seven years, but had been advised by government ministers that, as convictions in such cases were always difficult, the maximum sentence should be two years.

Symonds was obsessional about English sexual hypocrisy that condemned homosexuality but tolerated child prostitution. When he heard of Labouchère's intervention, he was incensed that a purity campaign had led to the reinforcement of the law on homosexual acts: "I will not tell you what I think about Stead's action: beyond this, that I regard his present sentence as too easy, & that I should like to see his instigatrix, Mrs J. E. Butler in prison too."[14] This last barbed remark hid a story: before turning to the rescue of fallen women, Butler had devoted her energies to reviving the wavering Christian faith of young men. When an undergraduate, Symonds had come under her influence at a time when he was attempting to stimulate romantic feelings for women. Butler, he wrote at the time, represented "the noblest womanhood I had ever met," but she did not alter his sexual feelings for the male.[15]

In the midst of the Labouchère furore, he became involved in the controversy surrounding the publication of the final volume of Sir Richard Burton's unexpurgated translation of

---

14 Symonds to Gosse, December 23, 1885, *Letters*, vol. 111, p. 106.
15 Horatio F. Brown, *John Addington Symonds*, (Smith Elder & Co., 1895), p. 124.

The Arabian Nights' Entertainments.[16] He defended it in a letter to *The Academy*, as he told Burton, against "those middle-class Censors of Morals who are seeking to discredit it."[17] The volume included the scandalising *Terminal Essay* on homosexuality and it was probably its hostile reception that prompted Symonds to spring to Burton's defence. But it was a warning of the opposition that he was likely to encounter if he called for a change in the law.

Two years earlier, using material gathered when preparing his *Studies of the Greek Poets*,[18] he had printed ten copies of a long essay, A *Problem in Greek Ethics*,[19] which was passed around under the strictest secrecy. It was an examination of the practice of paederastia in ancient Greece. Addressing it especially to medical psychologists and jurists, he wanted to offer a different perspective from the one usually adopted by writers on forensic medicine. Their neglect of cultural history in the examination of homosexuality troubled him deeply and he set out to show that, within the refined civilizations of a small number of Greek city states, homosexual relationships between aristocratic youths and men had been recognised and utilized for the benefit of the individual and society. Dorian boy-love was a feature of a distinctive social system, to be clearly distinguished from "effeminacies, brutalities and gross sensualities."[20] He marshalled a wide range of historical and literary material to illustrate the forms that it had taken; its relationship to Greek aesthetic values and, importantly, the ethical attitude of the Greeks towards it. He hoped that by writing about what was

---

16   Sir Richard Burton, *The Book of the Thousand Nights and a Night*, 1885.
17   Symonds to Burton, October 24, 1885, *Letters*, vol. 111, p. 90.
18   John Addington Symonds, *Studies of the Greek Poets*, (Smith Elder & Co., 1873-76).
19   John Addington Symonds, *A Problem in Greek Ethics:* An Inquiry into the Phenomenon of Sexual Inversion, *1883.* Referred to throughout as the *Greek Problem.*
20   Ibid. p. 19.

an aspect of one of the most brilliant periods of human history, and a relationship that some Greeks thought to be superior to heterosexual love, he might mitigate Victorian hostility.

During 1890, between bouts of debilitating illness, he struggled with the *Modern Problem*, complaining to Edmund Gosse how the burden of his homosexuality had engaged such a large portion of his nervous energy and mental powers, when they were most needed "for tranquil study and patient labour at art". It had broken his health, and for what? "It seems to me not only sad & tragic, but preposterous & ludicrous that this waste should have to be incurred by one man after another, when the right ethic of the subject lies in a nutshell".[21] It drove him on.

He had not included Burton in the circulation of the *Greek Problem and* thought to send him his last copy, at the same time telling him about his new monograph. Burton urged him to publish his work, whilst disclosing that he was preparing a general history of "*le Vice*". Symonds, who had found gaps in the *Terminal Essay*, politely suggested two writers whose work he might look at.[22] Burton then invited him to visit him in Trieste. In conversation, Symonds had found him to be "a perfect mine of curious knowledge about human nature & one of the very few men who talk without reserve & with abundance of information upon its strangest problems".[23] But the trip had to be deferred and the frank talk that he looked forward to never took place, as Burton died in October of that year.

If Burton had lived, there would have been a lively exchange on the 'general theory', developed in the *Terminal Essay*. In the *Modern Problem*, Symonds will recognise that Burton had assembled a large number of ethnological facts,

21   Symonds to Gosse, 28 February, 1890, *Letters*, vol. 111, p. 447.
22   Karl Ulrichs and Richard Craft-Ebbing.
23   Symonds to Dakyns, September 24, 1890, *Letters*, vol. 111, p. 500.

but believed, as he would write, that he had "no notion of the complicated psychology of Urnings" to be found in the medical and legal literature.[24] And, much to Symonds's regret, Burton seemed to assume that homosexuality meant *only* the practice of sodomy. More significantly, the novelty of the *Terminal Essay* lay in Burton's claim that the prevalence of homosexuality could be explained by geographical and climatic conditions, leading him to propose the existence of what he called a 'Sotadic Zone'. Symonds regarded this as no more than "a curious and interesting generalisation". It could not account for the existence of homosexual practices in regions lying outside the zone.[25] It was more scientific to conjecture that the phenomenon was universal, whilst its practice was tolerated only in certain parts of the world, suggesting that It could not be regarded as specifically geographical and climatic. Interestingly, Burton had also conjectured that, in cultures within the zone, there could be found individuals in whom there was a blending of the masculine and feminine temperament, but did not offer any explanation for what others would describe as a *third* sex.

In July, Oscar Wilde sent him a copy of his scandalising novel *Dorian Gray*. When an undergraduate, Wilde had written his first literary review on a chapter from Symonds's *The Greek Poets*, but they were never more than acquaintances. He grumbled to Horatio Brown, "I resent the unhealthy, scented, mystic, congested touch which a man of this sort has on moral problems".[26] Wilde's manner of treating such an important subject would not help the case for legal reform, instead, as he told Gosse, could only "confirm the prejudices of the vulgar".[27]

---

24 John Addington Symonds, *Modern Problem*, p. 78. 'Urning' was a term coined by Karl Ulrichs.
25 Ibid. p. 79.
26 Symonds to Horatio Brown, July 22, 1890, *Letters*, vol. 111, p. 477.
27 Symonds to Gosse, July 22, 1890, *Letters*, vol. 111, p. 478.

He would later repeat his objection to Wilde's "touch upon moral psychological problems" to another friend. *Dorian Gray* would reinforce the prejudice that "aesthetics are inseparable from unhealthiness" and that an interest in art implied "some corruption in its votaries".[28] He would not live to see that it was this very connection that would trip Wilde up five years later.

When the monograph was nearing completion, Gosse suggested printers, but Symonds hesitated, telling him, "It is a matter in which I must move very cautiously." He seemed unclear in his mind what he should do with it, but would only seek a printer, "if I do not abandon the idea of privately printing altogether".[29]

In November, he told Gosse that he had decided on this form of printing and sent him proofs, to show what line he was taking, but said little more. What he told his daughter Madge the following month suggests that he had still been toying with the idea of a conventional publication but had stepped back:

> If I were to publish it now, it would create a great sensation. Society would ring with it. But the time is not right for the launching of A Problem in Modern Ethics on the world. The MS. lies on my table for retouches; & then will go to slumber in a box of precious writings, my best work, my least presentable, until its day of Doom.[30]

But it would not be put in the box immediately. The time might not be right for an orthodox publication, but it could still be shown to close friends and others, for comment. Fifty copies were made in the form of a manuscript with a wide

---

28   Symonds to Arthur Galton, July 24, 1890, *Letters*, vol. 111, p. 479.
29   Symonds to Gosse, 22 July 1890, *Letters*, vol. 111, p. 478.
30   Symonds to Margaret Symonds, December 6, 1890, MS UBSC.

margin on each one-sided page for written remarks. Given the proportion of the monograph assigned to an examination of the medico-psychological literature surrounding homosexuality, and his suggestions for legislative reform, he could also draw on his late father's contacts in these professions.

When responses began to come in they included a dozen 'confessions' from individuals leading furtive homosexual lives. Edmund Gosse, reliving his own youth, expressed a common theme:

> The position of a young person so tormented is really that of a man buried alive and conscious, but deprived of speech. He is doomed by his own timidity and ignorance to a repression which amounts to death.[31]

Only now did Gosse, a friend for fifteen years, feel able to reveal his own early struggle with homosexual passion:

> Years ago I wanted to write to you about all this, and withdrew through cowardice. I have had a very fortunate life, but there has been this obstinate twist in it! I have reached a quieter time, some beginnings of that Sophoclean period when the wild beast dies. He is not dead, but tamer; I understand him and the trick of his claws.[32]

People had handed the manuscript around and he was surprised by how "highly respectable" persons felt towards a subject which, in society, they would only mention as unmentionable. And he was taken aback by how much they

---

31 Edmund Gosse to Symonds, March 5 1891, quoted in Phyllis
     Grosskurth, *John Addington Symonds*, (Longmans, 1964), p. 282.
32 Edmund Gosse to Symonds, 24 February 1891, MS UBSC.

knew about the subject, and how much they accepted it as a fact of human nature.

Sifting through the replies, he got the impression that if the law could be amended "without discussion", the majority of unprejudiced people would accept the change with equanimity. What was dreaded was "a public raking up of the question".[33] His respondents were enlightened individuals but a furore would be inevitable once it became a public legislative issue. A judge in favour of amending the law was down-to-earth, telling him that "there is no one who cares to take the matter up".[34]

But the support for reform made him more confident in the justice of his cause, and more daring in his intentions. He planned to revise and enlarge the monograph and produce a new version. And now, only a few months after telling his daughter Margaret that it would slumber in a box of precious writings, he told Graham Dakyns, "I am almost minded to print it in a PUBLISHED vol: together with my older essays on Greek Morals & some supplementary papers".[35] Although he was destined never to live again in England, this change of mind should not be attributed to his exile, which placed him beyond the reach of the English law.[36] He was at the end of his tether and emboldened to speak out, as he wrote bitterly to Gosse, in order that the mental turmoil that had overwhelmed him throughout his life should not continue to be borne "by one man after another".[37]

The monograph was written in a climate of deep hostility towards homosexuality in England. Christian morality, laid down at a time when theology was in the ascendant, was

---

33 Symonds to Gosse, 23 February 1891, *Letters*, vol. 111, p. 533.
34 Ibid.
35 Symonds to Dakyns, May 20 1891, *Letters*, vol.111, p.578.
36 As argued by Arthur Calder-Marshall, in *Havelock Ellis, a biography*, (Rupert Hart Davis,1959), p.156.
37 Symonds to Gosse, 23 February 1891, *Letters*, vol. 111, p.533.

the most intractable influence on public opinion. Its edict was absolute: "No delicate distinctions, no anthropological investigations, no psychological analysis, and no spirit of toleration."[38] Generally, writers on forensic medicine looked upon inverted sexuality with hostility, if not disgust, rather than with scientific impartiality. There was a common emphasis on morbidity; on exposing the supposed inherent defects, physiological and psychological, of those addicted to homosexual practices. And, as physicians, they held sway in the courts as expert witnesses in criminal trials involving homosexual crimes.

He had given the monograph the title, *A Problem in Modern Ethics*, to run in tandem with the *Greek Problem* and, as a precaution against possible prosecution for publishing an obscene book, it was addressed "especially to Medical Psychologists and Jurists". It broke ground as the first open discussion of homosexuality that focussed on the predicament of the sexually-inverted in England. Although written to help to establish a case for the decriminalisation of homosexuality between consenting adults in private, 'Suggestions Upon Legislation' took up just fourteen succinct concluding paragraphs in a work running to over one hundred and thirty pages. His objective was broad: to engage critically with current ideas on the nature of homosexuality, and for the monograph to be received, not as a polemic, but as a well-researched contribution to a subject which, with the development of forensic medicine in Europe over the previous forty years, was receiving increasing attention. The core of the monograph was a 'deconstruction' of the then leading theories on the nature and causes of homosexuality, combined with a powerful argument for its partial decriminalisation. Its style, he told Gosse, was intentionally "arid & severe".[39]

38   John Addington Symonds, *Modern Problem*, p. 5.
39   Symonds to Gosse, 23 November 1890, *Letters*, vol. 111, p. 519.

His fire was directed principally towards the hostile 'medico-forensic' and 'medico-psychological' theories, which he claimed were full of "dangerous errors". Recent scientific investigations showed clearly that, in a large proportion of persons, inverted sexuality was innate and could not be "diverted" into normal channels:

> The problem is too delicate, too complicated, also too natural and simple, to be solved by hereditary disease and self-abuse. When we shift the ground from acquired to inborn sexual inversion, its puzzling character will become still more apparent. We shall hardly be able to resist the conclusion that theories of disease are incompetent to explain the phenomenon in modern Europe. Medical writers abandon the phenomenon in savage races, in classical antiquity, and in the sotadic zone. They strive to isolate it as an abnormal and specifically morbid exception in our civilisation. But facts tend to show that it is a recurring impulse of humanity, natural to some people, adopted by others, and in the majority of cases compatible with an otherwise normal and healthy temperament.[40]

The passion had not altered but the way of regarding it, morally and legally, had changed. But a scientific investigator "ought not to take changes of public opinion into account when he is analysing a psychological peculiarity".[41]

It is hardly surprising that a quarter of the monograph is devoted to the ideas of Karl Heinrich Ulrichs,[42] who Symonds recognises as the first to challenge the morbidity argument, thereby changing the whole debate about the

---

40   John Addington Symonds, *Modern Problem*, pp. 51-52.
41   Ibid. p. 34.
42   Karl Heinrich Ulrichs (1825-1895).

nature of homosexuality. In 1864, this obscure Hanoverian jurist, under the pseudonym Numa Numantius, published the first of a series of booklets on the *Riddle of Love Between Men*.[43] In it, he claimed that homosexual desire was the result of an abnormal development of the embryo, which influenced the function of the psyche in determining the direction of the sexual drive. In this restricted sense, not all individuals were born completely male or female. Of course, Ulrichs only speculated: he could not explain why or how this occurred. What gripped Symonds, and led him to assiduously read all eleven of Ulrichs's booklets, was the realisation that a new phase in the understanding of homosexuality had been opened up; one offering a credible scientific explanation that challenged the idea that it was a pathological condition.[44]

He also recognised that Ulrichs was the first to pose a fundamental legal question: whether any society had the right to punish individuals who were sent into the world with homosexual instincts. The sexually-inverted had a right to satisfy their sex drive in the manner that came most naturally to them. The expression of the same-sex drive between consenting adults in private should only be open to legal sanction if it involved the seduction of minors, was achieved by force or threat, or offended public decency. In his eleventh booklet, *Araxes*, Ulrichs penned the first comprehensive, strikingly modern, statement of homosexual rights, opening with the claim:

The Urning too is a person. He too, therefore has inalienable rights. His sexual orientation is a right

---

43 *Forschungen über das Rätsel der mann-männlichen Liebe*. He went on to publish eleven booklets, the seventh and subsequent booklets appearing under his own name.

44 This judgement has lasted: see Hubert Kennedy, *Karl Heinrich Ulrichs First Theorist of Homosexuality*, in *Science and Homosexualties*, ed. Vernon Rosario, (Routledge, 1996).

established by nature. Legislators have no right to veto nature; no right to persecute nature in the course of its work; no right to torture living creatures who are subject to those drives nature gave them.[45]

Although Ulrichs demolished utilitarian arguments justifying the repression of homosexual practices, this was subordinate to his claim that individuals had 'natural rights'. Symonds passed over this claim without comment, probably believing that natural law and natural rights theories had finally been despatched by Bentham.[46] Interestingly, although not published during Bentham's lifetime, Symonds may have known of his essay, *Offences Against One's Self*.[47] Written around 1785, Bentham advocated the decriminalisation of sodomy, then a capital offence, making the essay the first known argument for homosexual law reform in England.

Ulrichs's theory of the homosexual drive separated sex physiology from sex psychology, thus challenging the assumption that the physiology of the individual determined sexual feelings. If sexually-inverted males with normal genitalia were not physically attracted to women, physiology could not be the determinant of sexual orientation: the sexual drive had to be controlled by the psyche. This led him to conclude that such individuals, in so far as the sexual drive was concerned, possessed female psyches. A female 'sex-love' could reside in a male body, *anima muliebris virili corpore inclusa*, and likewise, a male sex-love in a female body. Individuals with normal male sexual organs, but a sexual drive towards the same sex, were

---

45 *The Riddle of "Man-Manly Love*, translated by Michael A Lombardi-Nash, (Buffalo N.Y. Prometheus Books, 1994) vol. 2, pp. 604-605.
46 Jeremy Bentham (1784-1832), English philosopher, jurist and social reformer.
47 Jeremy Bentham, *Deontology and the Science of Morality* ed. John Bowring (Longman, 1834), reproduced in the *Journal of Homosexuality*, 1978, vol. 3:4 and vol. 4:1.

neither fully men nor fully women, leading him to assert that the sexually-inverted constituted a third sex, das *dritte geschlecht*. And it followed that there had to be a fourth sex made up of women who possessed a normal female sexual anatomy but a male sex-drive. In both cases, there was discordance between body and mind, stemming from the abnormal development of the embryo.

The idea of homosexuals as a third sex was never an entailment of Ulrichs's initial hypothesis, and when it was underpinned by *feminisation* it became highly controversial, as it suggested that all homosexuals experienced a gender identity that was inconsistent with their physiological sex. The third sex claim will be carried forward in Germany by Magnus Hirschfeld, and in England by Carpenter, with negative consequences, as we argue in chapter ten.

Setting aside this issue, Ulrichs had other 'firsts'. Because they had male genitalia, both society and the legal system took the sexual orientation of those charged under anti-homosexual laws to be heterosexual, and their homosexual acts signs of debauchery. The possibility that there were males who differed from heterosexuals in their psychic natures was scientifically ground-breaking. The phenomenon of same-sex love might now be explored by studying the development of the embryo, and, for the first time, a class of persons could be identified and named. Before this bold idea, only non-gendered sexual acts had been recognised, not persons with definable sexual natures.

Ulrichs took it as axiomatic that sexual love for a man must be a feminine drive. Gender inversion was psychological; but simply arguing that the unobservable psychologically-determined sex drive was feminine would hardly convince, and, initially, he argued that *a*ll homosexuals could be identified by manifest female characteristics and gender non-conformity in childhood. He drew on his own childhood, focussing on what he considered to be his feminine nature: his desire to be dressed as a girl and his partiality for girlish activities and a girl's playthings. This feminine element in his nature, he believed, was a consequence of his sexual love-drive. The body of the homosexual, he claimed, also displayed feminine traits, with some specifically male features, body shape, voice, beard, deportment, being absent; but many males who were sexually-inverted did not report such feminine behaviour in childhood and regarded their bodies and behaviour as masculine.

Those who knew Ulrichs well, did not regard him as feminine. He was, for his times, seen as conventionally gendered. But he was acquainted with homosexuals who called themselves sisters and gave themselves female names and this reinforced his view. And the idea of the *feminisation* of homosexuals had historical credence in the subculture of 'mollies', where feminine dress, the assumption of female roles in homosexual relationships and mock marriages were common. But nothing in these behaviours necessarily denoted gender inversion.

The personal characteristics and sexual tastes of the individuals inhabiting the homosexual underworld in large European cities during this period, did not support Ulrichs's claim of feminisation. It was contradicted by the diversity of individuals with a same-sex preference. There were men who loved women and men alike; there were men who loved other men, tenderly and sentimentally, but desired women sexually. And it was abundantly clear that there were individuals who were homosexual but who possessed all the physical and many of the intellectual and emotional characteristics of men who were not inverted sexually. On the other hand, there were clearly many men who possessed the kinds of feminine characteristics described by Ulrichs who were not feminine in the psychic sense because they were not attracted to men sexually.

Although Symonds credited Ulrichs with being the first to offer a scientific explanation for sexual inversion, he regarded the idea that he belonged to a sex apart as "extraordinary". He did not find in himself anything which justified the theory of a female psyche. In character, behaviour, tastes and habits, he felt that he was more masculine than many of the men he knew who adored women. He had no feminine feeling for the males who aroused his desire. As he saw it, the anomaly of his position was that he admired the physical beauty of men more than of women, derived more pleasure from their contact, and was "stirred to sexual sensations exclusively by persons of the male sex".[48] Given that the masculine-feminine dualism was essential to the bourgeois self-image, Symonds would, in any case, have naturally resisted such a characterisation. Moreover, forensic medicine, at least since Lombroso,[49] had also stereotyped the homosexual as physiologically marked in appearance and this Symonds strongly resisted. But he recognized that Ulrichs's core idea of a third sex, no matter how deficient, did have strategic significance. The new focus on the phenomenon as an embryological abnormality, rather than a pathological condition, was a step-change in the understanding of the sexually-inverted.

But, no matter how powerful as a possible scientific explanation for his own sexual nature, Symonds remained sceptical that Ulrichs's psychological hypothesis removed, once and for all, the consideration of other possible causal factors. And, even though it was now becoming accepted that in a large number of cases homosexuality was congenital, Ulrichs ignored the frequency of acquired homosexuality, especially its prevalence among schoolboys, prisoners, and sailors and soldiers deprived of female contact. He also shut his eyes "to the force of fashion and depravity". He had claimed

---

48 Grosskurth, *Memoirs,* pp. 64-65.
49 Cesare Lombroso (1835-1909) Italian criminologist and physician who introduced the concept of criminal atavism.

too much by overlooking "all other aspects of the question".[50] In his *Memoirs*, he would repeat his view that his 'abnormality' could not be explained by either those who regarded it as a pathological condition or Ulrichs's theory. Any explanation had to be sought "far deeper in the mystery of sex, and in the variety of type exhibited by nature".[51] But he supported Ulrichs's attempt to distinguish homosexual 'types', the first to do so. He saw himself as a *Mittel Urning*, one whose emotions were directed towards the male sex during adolescence and early manhood, but did not have an effeminate passion for robust adults or a predilection for young boys.

The fundamental issue, taken up in the final chapter of the monograph, is that of the justice, and effectiveness, of the criminalisation of sexual relations between males under English law. [52] Those who supported the existing law had to prove that discrimination was justified, either on grounds of serious injury to the person or serious danger to society. Symonds held that 'temperate' indulgence of 'abnormal' sexuality was no more injurious to the individual than a similar indulgence of normal sexuality. And the law did not interfere with various forms of 'sterile' intercourse between men and women:

> It would not be easy to maintain that a curate begetting his fourteenth baby on the body of a worn-out wife is a more elevating object of mental contemplation than Harmodius in the embrace of Aristogeiton, or that a young man sleeping with a prostitute picked up in the Haymarket is cleaner than his brother sleeping with a soldier picked up in the Park.[53]

---

50 John Addington Symonds, *Modern Problem*, pp. 98-99.
51 Grosskurth, *Memoirs*, p. 65.
52 Women were deemed not able to commit sodomy, and sexual relations between women were not covered by the 1885 Criminal Law Amendment Act.
53 John Addington Symonds, *Modern Problem*, pp. 109-110.

The idea that so-called 'unnatural inclinations', if tolerated, would be acquired by whole nations was not credible. Under the *Code Napoleon* in France, and incorporated in the Italian *Nuovo Codice Penale*, in 1889, homosexuality was tolerated under the same restrictions as normal sexuality, and there was no evidence, Symonds claimed, that it had led to an increase in homosexual practices. But where it remained a criminal offence, as in England, it was an incitement to blackmail.

Reliving his own youth, he also complained that in England, higher education was an open contradiction to the law, resting as it did on the study of the Greek and Latin classics; a literature impregnated with paederastia. This had become a point of contention with Benjamin Jowett. When staying with him in Davos, working on the proofs for a new edition of his translations of Plato's Dialogues, he mentioned that he was considering adding an essay on Greek love, which he believed to be devoid of sensuality and purely 'figurative'. Later, when learning that Jowett had abandoned the idea, Symonds felt the need to write a long letter explaining why the study of Plato was injurious to young men who were attracted to their own sex. If a nobler-minded youth sought a spiritual transfiguration for his sexual desires, others found in Plato the encouragement of their "furtively cherished dreams" of physical consummation. Plato was sweet poison to such a youth, but what was an institutionalised element of Hellenic life was utterly rejected by English society. To make Plato a textbook in a nation that repudiated Greek love, was to place in a youth's hands a literature, "pregnant with the stuff that condemns him".[54]

---

54 Symonds to Benjamin Jowett, February 1, 1889, *Letters*, vol. 111, p. 354.

A Fateful Collaboration

As Symonds was completing his *Modern Problem*, Dr Daniel Hack Tuke,[1] an intimate friend of his father and joint-editor of the prestigious Journal of Mental Science, came to stay with him at Davos. He tried to engage the stern old Quaker on the subject of sexual inversion, "but I found that he preferred to discourse on hypnotism".[2] It was now over a year since he had exchanged views with Ellis on Whitman and homosexuality. At the time, he had made him a gift of his *Essays Speculative and Suggestive*,[3] and in a belated letter of thanks, Ellis surprised him:

> I was interested to hear from my friend, Dr Tuke, and others that you are thoroughly working out the question of Greek love in modern life from the moral side. Whenever you are in London I hope I may have the opportunity of talking over this question with you. I am not sure that I should altogether agree with you, but the question is one that constantly forces itself on one's attention.[4]

---

1   Daniel Hack Tuke, (1827-1895), was a specialist in mental diseases and the father of Henry Scott Tuke, painter of Cornish fisher-boys.
2   Symonds to Edmund Gosse, 15 November 1890, *Letters*, vol. 111, p. 517.
3   John Addington Symonds, *Essays Speculative and Suggestive*, (Chapman and Hall, 1890).
4   Ellis to Symonds, 10 July 1891, BUSC DM 109/23.

Tuke, who was in regular contact with Ellis, may have shown him his copy of the *Modern Problem,* but had at least discussed it with him. Tuke was fully aware of Symonds's purpose in writing the monograph, touched upon when he stayed with him. How else do we make sense of Ellis's remark that he was not sure that he would "altogether agree" with Symonds, if he had no knowledge of Symonds's purpose in writing the *Modern Problem?* The use of the phrase, "from the moral side", makes it clear that it was the issue of legislative reform that he understood Symonds to be concerned with. The late Phyllis Grosskurth suggested that there was "abundant evidence" that Ellis was seriously contemplating a book on homosexuality before the summer of 1892,[5] and that his letter was an early overture to their subsequent collaboration on *Sexual inversion,* therefore rebutting Ellis's claim that the book was all down to Symonds.[6] But in the preface to the first English edition of the book, and in his autobiography, Ellis will make clear that it was only after an approach by Symonds that he seriously took up the idea of a book on homosexuality.[7]

Replying to Ellis's letter, Symonds, recalling Tuke's obduracy when he attempted to discuss homosexuality with him, regretted that he shrank from entertaining the question in any practical sense. This was a disappointment shared by Ellis, who later cited a review by Tuke of Albert Moll's[8] "able book *Die konträre Sexualempfindung*", in which "he wraps a wet blanket around it with inverted eyes".[9] Tuke's attitude towards the subject fully reflected the English

5   Phyllis Grosskurth, *Havelock Ellis*, A Biography, (Allen Lane, 1980), p. 173.
6   Phyllis Grosskurth, John *Addington Symonds*, (Longmans, 1964), p. 286.
7   Havelock Ellis and John Addington Symonds, *Studies in the Psychology of Sex*, vol. 1, *Sexual inversion*, (Wilson and MacMillan, 1897), p. ix.
8   Albert Moll (1862-1939), German psychiatrist.
9   Ellis to Symonds, 1 July 1892, UBSC, DM 109/3.

medical profession's long history of stubbornly rejecting any consideration of homosexuality; of resisting its inclusion in its medical lexicon.[10]

Symonds stressed to Ellis that, for England, the issue of homosexuality was now a legislative one: "France and Italy stand in glaring contrast to England and Germany".[11] He neatly summarised the two prongs of his attack in the *Modern Problem*, declaring that "the medical and forensic authorities who are taking it up, seem quite ignorant both of history and fact", and "[t]heir pathological hypothesis will certainly not stand the test of accumulated experience."[12] He went on:

> I do not believe that you and I would disagree at bottom about the ethical views. But we cannot discuss this on paper without knowing more about our principles and sympathies. After all, the phenomenon is there, and for England is a very serious one. It ought to be scientifically, historically, impartially investigated, instead of being left to Labby's inexpansible legislation.[13]

At this time, Ellis was unware of Symonds's "principles and sympathies", but Symonds must have regarded him as a possible supporter of legislative reform, whilst Ellis may have been influenced by Symonds's insistence that the subject of homosexuality required scientific investigation, making him more inclined to undertake such a study. But, it should be noted that, for Ellis, it was axiomatic that the normal expression of the sexual instinct should always be studied before the so-

---

10 See chapter five of Sean Brady's *Masculinity and Male Homosexuality in Britain, 1861-1913*.
11 Symonds to Ellis, July 1891, *Letters*, vol. 111, p. 587. Consensual sex between adult males in private had been legalised in France in 1791 and in Italy in 1889.
12 Symonds to Ellis, July (undated) 1891, *Letters*, vol.111, p.587.
13 Ibid. p. 587. The reference is to the Labouchére clause.

called *abnormal*. There had to be a strong reason for reversing this order.

Aware that Symonds was writing a life of Michelangelo, he mentioned an essay by Cesare Lombroso[14] on the artist's reputed homosexuality, which Symonds was exploring. Ellis had recently published his second book, *The Criminal,* and, by return, Symonds was fulsome in his praise for a work "combining so much knowledge of authorities with originality…"[15] He had alighted upon Ellis's principal strength: the skill of meticulously surveying others' findings and drawing insightful conclusions from them. They were warming to each other; Ellis had sent him a photograph of himself "in the hope that it may induce you to send me one of yours which I should sincerely value".[16] Symonds duly reciprocated, regretting that his was "not as nice as Hollyer's of you".[17]

A year passed, and in June 1892, as Symonds was preparing for what was to be his last visit to England, he was struck by a deep foreboding of death, sharing his fear with his closest daughter, Margaret:

> I do not think I should have written so candidly to you as I have done under this cover, were I not starting soon for a journey to England with this Fear upon me… And I say now to you what I say to no one else. Think well of me when all is over. I have been a very unhappy man, as you will find out if you read the history of my life. But I have tried to be a brave one & to work.
>
> And before I go hence & see the lovely earth no longer

14 Cesare Lombroso (1835-1909), Italian criminologist and physician who introduced the idea of criminal atavism.

15 Symonds to Ellis, 21 August 1891, HRC.

16 Ellis to Symonds, 10 July 1891, HRC.

17 Symonds to Ellis, July 1891, *Letters*, vol. 111, p. 587. The reference is to Frederick Hollyer (1838-1933), a renowned photographer of the day.

I want to do so much still. I want to write my history of Graubünden, to publish my work on Sexual Aberrations, & to get my Autobiography finished.[18]

It was eighteen months since he had told her that the *Modern Problem* would never see the light of day; months during which his health had become more precarious, with frequent debilitating episodes of lung congestion. If it was to happen, he could delay no longer over the publication of his work on "sexual aberrations".

Some years earlier, a young Arthur Symons,[19] had made him a gift of his first book. They kept up a regular correspondence and their friendship deepened after Symons joined him as an editor for Ellis's Elizabethan dramatists' series. In June, he wrote to thank Symons for a favourable review. Aware that he had recently written an article on Paul Verlaine, and perhaps recalling Verlaine's affair with Arthur Rimbaud, he suddenly interposed: "Apropos Verlaine, will you ask Havelock Ellis if he will take a book from me on 'Sexual inversion' for his Science Series?"[20] He had decided that the prestigious series, of which Ellis was now the general editor, would carry the right imprimatur for a book on homosexuality, restrict its circulation to the medical and legal professions, and give protection against possible prosecution as an obscene publication. He told Symons that to make a book, his two monographs could be combined, adding that, "Sir Richard Burton in the year before his death was very urgent on me to publish these treatises. But I cannot see my way at present to doing so".[21] Ellis might provide a way forward.

---

18 Symonds to Margaret Symonds, 8 July 1892, *Letters*, vol. 111, p. 711. Graubünden was the Canton that included Davos Platz.
19 Arthur William Symons, (1865-1945), poet and modernist critic.
20 Symonds to Arthur Symons, 13 June 1892, *Letters*, vol. 111, p. 690.
21 Ibid.

Following their earlier exchange on Whitman's 'comradeship', and after learning of his *Modern Problem*, Ellis must have had an inkling of why Symonds was so interested in the subject. Naturally, he had always been guarded about his sexuality, even with long-standing friends such as Symons. Now, poised to embark on a course of action that was likely to make his personal interest in the subject clear, it was a time for candour. He hoped to see Symons when in London: "You are so good to me and so understanding of the real man who has "never spoken out" yet, that I should like to tell you some things about myself wh (sic) cannot well be written".[22]

Symons was close to Ellis, often holidaying with him, and at one time sharing lodgings. He passed on Symonds's request during an outing to watch a company of acrobats at the famous Vauxhall Empire music hall; an apt prelude to the period of mental gymnastics that was to follow. Ellis responded promptly, surprising Symonds by telling him that, only days before Symons had spoken to him, he had "some idea of writing" to him about the subject on which they had exchanged letters a year earlier. He explained: "My attention has been frequently drawn to it of late, partly through finding how it exists to a greater or less (sic) extent in many persons whom I know, or know of, and whom I most love and respect".[23] His claim to know "many persons" who were homosexual was surely implausible, as in a climate of extreme social intolerance individuals would be most reluctant to reveal their sexuality. Moreover, the excessively shy Ellis is most unlikely to have been intimate enough with any male to learn of such a secret. But there was an explosive truth hidden in his exaggerated statement.

Six months earlier, he had married Edith Lees, two years

22   Symonds to Arthur Symonds, 13 June 1892, *Letters*, vol. 111, p. 690..
23   Ellis to Symonds, 18 June 1892, BUSC DM 109/30.

his junior, who he had met in 1887 through the Fellowship of the New Life. A relationship sprang up that moved slowly from cordiality to "sympathetic comradeship".[24] As they became increasingly intimate, they wrote and talked endlessly about what kind of future, if any, they might have together, and if so, what sort of union would suit two individuals who jealously guarded their "independent spiritual lives".[25]

> It may seem to some that the spirit in which we approached marriage was not that passionate and irresistible spirit of absolute acceptance which seems to them the ideal. Yet we both cherished ideals, and we seriously strove to mould our marriage as near to the ideal as our own natures and the circumstances permitted. It was certainly not a union of unrestrainable passion; I, though I failed yet clearly to realise why, was conscious of no inevitably passionate sexual attraction to her, and she, also without clearly realising why, had never felt genuinely passionate sexual attraction for any man.[26]

Several men had been in love with Edith and made offers of marriage, but her own feelings were not involved. Whatever passionate attractions she had experienced were for women. During their long 'courtship' she had told him of the sentimental and sometimes passionate attraction which, from early school life, she had experienced for girl-friends, some possessing a slight but definite "sensuous character".[27] At the time, Ellis had not found in Edith any of the masculine traits commonly associated with lesbianism, but had no real understanding of inborn sexual inversion: "I was not yet able to

---

24 Havelock Ellis, *My Life*, p. 218.
25 Ibid. p. 249.
26 Ibid. p. 233.
27 Ibid. p. 263.

detect all those subtle traits of an opposite sexual temperament as surely planted in her from the beginning..."[28]

From the day of their marriage, there was an understanding that, given their different personalities and interests, it was to be a relationship requiring regular time apart. "Edith was as warm an advocate of independence and frequent separation as I was".[29] Through such interludes apart, each hoped to escape a marriage of romantic illusions. But out of separation sprang heartbreak for Ellis. Shortly after their marriage, they took a cottage in Carbis, Cornwall, where Edith settled whilst Ellis remained, for most of his time, in London. Alone, highly sociable by nature and used to hosts of visitors, she invited a female friend, 'Claire', who she had known from girlhood, to stay. Sometime later, out of the blue, a letter arrived from Edith, telling Ellis, in a direct and spontaneous way, that she had developed a passionate attachment for 'Claire'. It was a severe shock. The relationship had only a fleeting and shallow sexual colouring, but he was now conscious of a flaw in the ideal of marriage that he had so far cherished, and felt a secret wound of the heart. The full reaction to Edith's disclosure came a few months later:

> I restlessly paced up and down my study at Paddington with heart aching over letters from Carbis... the realisation, as rightly or wrongly it seemed to me, that this new absorption in another person was leading unconsciously to a diminution in the signs of tenderness in her love towards me.[30]

Ellis's agitated state of mind, at the very time that a serious discussion on homosexuality was opening up with Symonds, has not been recognised as the critical factor in the subsequent unfolding of events. Edith's revelation triggered a need

---

28 Havelock Ellis. *My Life,* p. 263.
29 Ibid. p. 265.
30 Ibid., p. 263.

to understand her nature; to explore a sexuality that now challenged his masculinity and blighted his marriage. Chris Nottingham has taken a different view on Ellis's motivation, suggesting that, by undertaking a study of homosexuality, "there could be no more emphatic way to shock the conventional, rally the progressive, demonstrate solidarity with the oppressed, and celebrate a commitment to the higher transcendental love".[31] This disregards Ellis's judgement that, in the then climate, it was a subject best passed over, although the relation of sexual inversion to the law was something that could be investigated. Replying to Symonds's book request, he told him that he was going to write a paper on this subject for a forthcoming congress on criminal anthropology.[32] He had probably seen an opportunity, after his earlier exchange with Symonds on "the moral side" of homosexuality, to make himself known by writing about it himself.

Replying to Symonds's request, Ellis said that he would like to take a book from him, but it might not be suitable for the Contemporary Science Series. Aware that he was coming to England, he suggested that they should meet to talk things over. Symonds's daughter Katherine recalled that he was heartened to find in Ellis a man "to whom he could write freely and be sure of finding sympathy for his efforts to get attention for the problem which he felt to be of vital urgency and importance to his country as well as to many individual human beings".[33]

In his next letter to Ellis, Symonds abruptly put aside his proposal to publish his own work and raised the possibility that they might write a book together. No reason was given for

---

31 Chris Nottingham, *The Pursuit of Serenity*, (Amsterdam University Press, 1999), p. 69.
32 Ellis to Symonds, 18 June1892, BUSC DM 109/30.
33 Katherine Furze, *Hearts and Pomegranates*, (London: Peter Davies, 1940), pp.106-7.

this sudden change of mind, but he must have concluded that his severe criticism of the views of continental physicians and psychologists in the *Modern Problem* could be easily set aside as those of a known homosexual, and also a layman. He would later tell Carpenter: "I need somebody of medical importance to collaborate with. Alone I could make but little effect – the effect of an eccentric."[34] In putting his idea to Ellis, he wanted to make the strongest case for a collaborative work, and ended up drafting two letters, only one of which was sent. The one not sent did eventually come into Ellis's possession. In it, Symonds explained why there was a need for an English book on homosexuality at this particular time:

> It is, I think, one of the psychological subjects which require an open treatment now, because of crude legal disabilities under which abnormal natures lie, & also because of the extraordinary light which this eccentricity of nature throws upon previous conceptions of sex. The whole subject is a *terra incognita*; and must be explored in its physiological & sociological relations.[35]

He wanted to send him his two monographs, as a basis for discussion when he came to England:

> We might strike out some way of collaboration, which would enable me to place at your disposal a vast number of facts & critical conclusions collected by me through a lifetime. I have always taken great interest in the topic; & I am certain it is me which will soon engage the attention of the world. The great thing is to handle it in a large historical & philosophical spirit. This it has not yet had.[36]

---

34 Symonds to Carpenter, 29 December 1892, *Letters*, vol. 111, p. 797.
35 Symonds to Ellis, 20 June 1892, HRC.
36 Symonds to Ellis, 20 June 1892, *Letters*, vol. 111, p. 693.

The editors of Symonds's collected letters treated this letter as a draft for the second letter, which was more substantial. In it, the possibility of their jointly-authoring "an impartial and really scientific survey of the matter" was raised. Such a work, he suggested, "might come from two men better than from one, in the present state of public opinion".[37] After proposing that his own contribution could consist of an historical analysis, "which I am sure must form a basis for the study", he flattered Ellis: "You are more competent than I am to criticize the crudest modern medical and forensic-medical theories, but I might be of use to you here by placing at your disposition what I have already done in 'getting up' the material, and in collecting data of fresh cases."[38] Stressing that he did not want to be "aggressive or polemical", he entered a caveat: "We should have to agree together about the *legal* aspects of the subject. I should not like to promulgate any book, which did not show the absurdity and injustice of the English law". And, it would increase understanding of homosexuality if cultural history was combined with science. It was "absolutely necessary" to connect those two investigations in any comprehensive handling of the subject. Physicians were wrong in diagnosing as morbid, "what was the leading emotion of the best and noblest men of Hellas".[39]

Having made his position quite clear on this central issue, Symonds then wrote:

I am almost certain that this matter will very soon attract a great deal of attention; and that it is a field in which pioneers may not only do excellent service to humanity, but also win the laurels of investigators and truth-seekers... If you do not feel able to collaborate with me, I shall probably

---

37   Symonds to Ellis, 20 june 1892, *Letters*, vol. 111, p. 693..
38   Ibid.
39   Ibid.

proceed to some form of solitary publication, and I should certainly give my name to anything I produced. [40]

Ellis delayed his answer, as he said, in order to mull over the proposal. What might he have been thinking? He saw himself as an 'investigator and truth seeker' poised to undertake his life's work, but might the laurels in England now fall to Symonds? In the preface to the first English edition of *Sexual Inversion* he will write pointedly: "If I had rejected the proposed collaboration, he intended ultimately to publish a book on his own account".[41] When he responded he was positive: "So far as I can see, there is no real difficulty in the way, and I should be very willing to cooperate with you on the same lines – we shall be able to come to a definite decision when we meet".[42] However, he did not think that such a book could be included in the Contemporary Science Series: "Several of the volumes approach various forbidden topics as nearly as it is desirable, and I am inclined to agree with the publisher that there is too much at stake to involve the Series in any really risky pioneering experiment".[43] To include the subject of homosexuality would be a step too far.

In a few short months, a further twenty-two letters will be exchanged on collaboration: fifteen from Symonds to Ellis and seven from Ellis to Symonds.[44] These focus on issues on which they had to agree at the outset, and on working out a structure for the book and a division of labour. They also

40 Symonds to Ellis, 20 June 1892, HRC.
41 Havelock Ellis and John Addington Symonds, *Sexual Inversion* (Wilson and Macmillan, 1897), p. xi.
42 Ellis to Symonds, 1 July 1892, BUSC DM 109/30.
43 Ibid. One publication was probably *The Evolution of Sex* by P. Geddes and J. A. Thompson, (Walter Scott, 1890).
44 The complete extant correspondence between Ellis and Symonds on collaboration can be found in Sean Brady's *John Addington Symonds (1840-1893) and Homosexuality, A Critical Edition of Sources.* (Palgrave Macmillan, 2012).

exchange views on the ideas and findings of several prominent European writers on homosexuality likely to figure in the book, and the need to acquire autobiographical profiles of English homosexuals. The letters also explore, in a more discursive manner, various issues and topics. Here, we focus on the core, critical, exchanges.

For the first time, Symonds learned of the programme of research into human sexuality that Ellis was planning. He told him that, for over fifteen years, he had been preparing to deal with "questions of sex psychology & sex ethics (though by no means especially with sex inversion). I have not written, partly because I think it is a mistake to begin by identifying oneself with these questions, and still more because I have not felt qualified to do so".[45]

Clearly, homosexuality was not to be a topic of special interest, but what he says is not without ambiguity. Would the "mistake" be, to begin by identifying himself with homosexuality or with questions of sex psychology and sex ethics? It was probably the latter that he did not yet feel "qualified" to undertake. He was immersed in his study of the secondary sexual characteristics in man and woman, which, in a sense, were not sexual. This was a clearing of the ground before embarking upon his major work; and a way of introducing himself to his peers by publishing pieces in the British Medical Journal.[46] "When this is done, I shall feel free to attack primary sex questions & had planned a book on sex psychology which should contain at least one chapter on inversion, especially with its genus in normal persons".[47] He was no doubt thinking of Edith.

There is sufficient in these remarks to reach the conclusion that, when Symonds approached him, Ellis was not ready to

---

45   Ellis to Symonds, 1 July 1892, BUSC DM 109/30.
46   Havelock Ellis, *Man and Woman*, (Walter Scott, 1894).
47   Ellis to Symonds, 1 July 1892, BUSC DM 109/30.

begin his study of human sexuality (the work on secondary sexual characteristics would not be finished until 1894), and certainly not to launch it with a book on homosexuality. But, following Edith's revelation, he found himself in a different place. It is notable how he ends this letter: "Many thanks for congratulations on marriage. My wife – I may say in this connection – is most anxious I should collaborate in the book, and can supply cases of inversion in women from among her own friends".[48] But making a connection between Edith and female homosexuality must have puzzled Symonds.

Ellis will write in the preface to the first English edition of *Sexual Inversion*:

> It was not my intention to publish a study of an abnormal manifestation of the sexual instinct before discussing its normal manifestations. It has happened, however, that this part of my work is ready first, and, since I thus gain a longer period to develop the central part of my subject, I do not regret the change of plan.[49]

It was, he wrote, Symonds who had proposed that they should collaborate on a book, and he had "willingly entered into correspondence with him".[50] But exactly what underlay this willingness could not be revealed.

In his letter of 1st July, Ellis wrote: "So far as I can see at present, we should not differ on any important point".[51] Symonds was pleased:

> [N]ow that you have met me so kindly, I look forward to discussing the subject with you and seeing whether

48 Ellis to Symonds, 1 June 1892, BUSC DM 109/30..
49 Havelock Ellis and John Addington Symonds, *Sexual Inversion*, (Wilson and Macmillan, 1897) p. xi.
50 Ibid. p. xi.
51 Ellis to Symonds, 1 July 1892, BUSC DM 109/30.

anything can be done. I feel that, in a matter of this sort, two names, and two men of different sorts would be stronger as attracting public opinion than any one alone of any sort, and also would be more likely to get a wide and serious attention.[52]

The issue of morbidity, and the significance of homosexuality among the Greeks, had been briefly touched upon; two areas where agreement would be essential. Symonds doubted that sexual inversion was ever and by itself morbid, although it could often co-exist with morbidity. The theory, if more humane, he regarded as no less false than that of sin or vice. On the question of Hellenic homosexuality, he believed that no survey of sexual inversion was worth anything "without an impartial consideration of its place in Greek Life".[53] As only so much progress could be made through an exchange of letters, it was important to meet when he was in London in July.

In January of that year, Horace Traubel[54] had sent letters to Whitman's English friends reporting on the poet's declining health.[55] Carpenter sent his on to Symonds who, in acknowledging it, recalled his first reading of *Towards Democracy*. "I think I know you somewhat & had long felt towards you as one who has been able to simplify his life. Am I right?" Something in Carpenter's letter must have touched him: "Thank you for your kind words. I respond with the greetings of a sincere comrade and herzlich grüssend (greetings from the heart), as we say here".[56]

A little later Carpenter sent him a copy of the enlarged third edition of *Towards Democracy*. Like Ellis, Symonds

---

52   Symonds to Ellis, 7 July 1892, *Letters*, vol. 111, p. 709.

53   Ibid.

54   Horace Traubel (1858-1919), friend, literary executor and compiler of *Walt Whitman in Camden*.

55   Whitman died two months later on 26 March 1892.

56   Symonds to Carpenter, 23 January 1892, *Letters*, vol. 111, p. 653.

recanted his first reaction to the work, regretting that its form was likely to make a careless reader lay it aside as "a mere sub-species of *Leaves of Grass*". But it was "a thoroughly personal, a specifically English" interpretation of Whitman's leading ideas, which would do much to diffuse his thinking.[57]

On 19th July he left for England to deliver his address at Oxford on the Italian renaissance, intending to stay for several weeks and make a round of visits to relatives and friends. He told Carpenter of his plans and hoped that they could meet, but on arrival could not recall his address and had to get it from Carpenter's friend, the Whitman admirer Dr John Johnston.[58] Eventually they arranged to meet in Brighton, where Symonds would be staying with their mutual friend, Roden Noel.[59] When Symonds mentioned his project with Ellis, Noel, who also knew him, told him that he could not find a more open-minded person with whom to collaborate. After Carpenter arrived, with three Whitman devotees in the house, the question of whether comradeship sanctioned physical intimacy between men, uppermost in Symonds's mind, would almost certainly have been talked over. Symonds had tried, unsuccessfully, to get Carpenter's views on the question two years earlier, knowing that he had twice visited Whitman. Now, face to face for the first time, he recalled hearing him spoken of as "faddy", as a supporter of idiosyncratic causes, but, as he told Johnston, he found him "strong and distinguished enough to cover a few fads"[60] Carpenter learned of Symonds's monographs on homosexuality and his determination to confront the 1885 Criminal Law Amendment Act. In a little more than half a year, he will begin to write his own pamphlets

---

57 Symonds to Carpenter, 20 March 1892, *Letters*, vol. 111, p. 674.
58 Johnston was a member of an informal literary society established in Bolton in 1885, devoted, *inter alia*, to the study of Whitman.
59 Roden Noel (1834-1894), English poet.
60 Symonds to Johnston, 21 January 1893, *Letters*, vol. 111, p. 809.

on sexuality, including one on homosexuality. With such interests in common, before parting they agreed to meet again.

Symonds returned to London, to find a note at his club from Ellis about their meeting. But after nine weeks in an uncongenial climate rushing all over the country he was exhausted. He scribbled a short reply, telling him that he feared his health might break down if he remained in England a moment longer. He cancelled all his London engagements, including one with Edmund Gosse, and left for Davos the next day, telling Ellis, fatefully, "I suppose there is no hurry about it".[61] Phyllis Grosskurth set a hare running by suggesting that Symonds gave no priority to meeting Ellis, unable to fit him in between "dukes and hairdressers"[62] but on arriving in England, as he had planned, he went straight to Oxford for his address, and then travelled on to Stratford-upon-Avon for the unveiling of his friend Lord Ronald Gower's sculpture of Hamlet.[63] From there he continued north, then into Scotland, before travelling back down to the southwest, where, among others, he visited Leslie Stephen.[64] He then retraced his steps, calling on Tennyson at Blackdown in West Sussex, one of the last to see him alive, then travelling along the coast to meet Carpenter and Roden Noel in Brighton, where talk would have fine-tuned his thinking prior to meeting Ellis. Below, we surmise what might have occurred had the meeting taken place, but there is no reason to believe that he intentionally avoided it. He probably thought that Ellis, a keen traveller, could be easily persuaded to come out to Davos.

Back home, he received Ellis's comments on the *Modern*

61   Symonds to Ellis, 21 September 1892, *Letters*, vol. 111, p. 749.
62   Phyllis Grosskurth, *John Addington Symonds*, (Longmans 1964), p.290.
63   Lord Ronald Gower (1845-1916), politician, sculptor and writer.
64   Leslie Stephen (1832-1904) English author and critic; father of Virginia Woolf and Venessa Bell. Symonds may have mentioned his intended meeting with Carpenter in Brighton, as Stephen had held the clerical fellowship at Trinity Hall, Cambridge, immediately before him.

Problem, which were mildly critical.[65] In particular, Ellis was concerned about its tone, in places, stressing the importance of maintaining scientific objectivity. Symonds took the point, but perhaps conceded too much. "I never regarded myself as really competent to deal with the psychology of this matter, and my sense of a great injustice having been done by law and social opinion has made me less judicial than the treatment requires".[66] But, whatever its tone, as Ellis later made clear, he recognised the large amount of "scientific inquisition" in the *Modern Problem,* and wanted to draw on it for the 'medical' chapters of the book.

Symonds's over-hasty concession on the value of the *Modern Problem* led him to narrow his possible contribution: "If it comes to collaboration, probably the best method would be for me to make myself responsible for the historical essay on Greek love. This, according to my own view of the topic, is an important part of the enquiry". He could not stress enough his view that it was a mistake to treat sexual abnormality as a disease, "face to face with the facts of ancient Greek society".[67] In June, he had insisted that an historical analysis "must form a basis for the study".[68] This insistence had been repeated again in July: an understanding of ancient Greek life was "indispensable to the study of inversion". No survey was "worth anything" without an impartial consideration of its place in Greek life.[69]

For Symonds, the importance of Greek paederasty was that it was socially-sanctioned and structured, a part of the *rites de passage* for aristocratic young men. It was the most elevated

---

65 Ellis's letter has not survived. Here, and in other places where an Ellis letter has not survived, his concerns are identified through Symonds's responses.
66 Symonds to Ellis, 2 October 1892, *Letters*, vol. 111, p. 755.
67 Ibid.
68 Symonds to Ellis, 20 June 1892, *Letters*, vol. 111, p. 693.
69 Symonds to Ellis, 7 July 1892, *Letters*, vol. 111, p. 709.

testimony to the non-pathological nature of homosexuality. Establishing this was a priority: indeed, in his eyes, the essential foundation for any rational discussion of the subject. He was proposing a defence of homosexuality that would combine authoritative scientific findings with ethnography: an objective examination of the physiological and psychological bases of sexual inversion with accounts of homosexuality in societies which accorded it both moral worth and social usefulness. As we argue later, in the understanding of homosexuality there was never a dichotomy in Symonds's mind between ethnography and psychology.

Ellis proposed to sketch out a plan for the book, and how the work might be divided between them. In the meantime, more views were exchanged on the ideas of continental physicians, with Symonds persistently contesting "the purely psychiatrical theory" of sexual inversion: "With the progress of scientific analysis & speculation, the assumed morbidity of sexual perversion is thus being gradually excluded. Its abnormality or divergence from the average, will remain self-evident".[70] He could not wait to meet and talk to Ellis about homosexuality, as he knew it: "I have a considerable experience, & been able to study the phenomena of sexual perversion in the great world – i.e. not from the point of view of the consulting room or the police court, or the coteries of 'tantes' [sic] – to, I believe, an exceptional extent". [71]

Ellis's plan for the book reached Symonds in the middle of November.[72] He seemed reassured by the clear statement that their objective was "primarily a study of a psychological anomaly". He thought this was "exactly right".[73] He had been concerned that Ellis might insist on presenting it as a psychiatric

---

70   Symonds to Ellis, 3 November 1892. HRC.
71   Ibid.
72   This letter has not survived.
73   Symonds to Ellis, 1 December 1892, *Letters*, vol. 111, p. 787.

disorder, which would have brought the collaboration to an abrupt end: "We must come to some fundamental agreement about neuroses". He did not deny that sexual inverts were frequently neurotic: "I only doubt whether neurosis can be regarded as the cause of sexual inversion", he had earlier told Ellis.[74] Uppermost was his concern that Ellis would not be able to accept that sexual inverts were perfectly normal individuals whose self-repression, feelings of abnormality and self-loathing were largely a result of the widespread prevalence of the idea that it *was* a sickness. Again, he had made the point earlier: "I think sex-inverts can only be called abnormal, in so far as they are in a minority, i.e. form exceptions to the large rule of sex. I doubt, from what I have observed in the matter, that sexual inversion is ever and by itself morbid. It may often of course co-exist with morbidity..."[75] His own self-worth was entirely bound up with this question.

In presenting a case for the acceptance of homosexuality as a congenital abnormality, Symonds recognised that it would not be possible to avoid the fact that, as in ancient Greece, it might be a matter of preference, "rendering the argument *ad legislatores* complicated".[76] The case for a change in the law could be undermined if homosexuality was seen as either freely chosen or an acquired behaviour, which partly explains Ellis's antipathy to Symonds's *Greek Problem*. But there is no evidence that he deliberately played down the significance of cases of acquired homosexuality, in order not to blunt the book's "political focus".[77] Ellis deferred to Albert Moll, in reaching the conclusion that cases of acquired inversion were rare, for he had no evidence of his

74   Symonds to Ellis, 29 September 1892, *Letters*, vol. 111, p. 753.
75   Symonds to Ellis, 7 July 1892, *Letters*, vol. 111, p. 709.
76   Symonds to Ellis, 1 December 1892, *Letters*, vol. 111, p. 787.
77   As suggested by Ivan Crozier, in *Sexual Inversion, Havelock Ellis and John Addington Symonds*, A Critical Edition, (Palgrave Macmillan, 1908), p. 43.

own, given that all his cases were examples of congenital homosexuality.[78]

Symonds accepted with good grace that Ellis had assigned the main chapters on psychological analysis to himself, but, importantly, had allocated the writing of the book's conclusions to him. Yet, even now, there was still a residual doubt as to whether they could succeed in producing a book together. But if they did, again professing his "want of scientific equipment", Ellis's name should go first and his second on the title page. And, although ideally it should be placed with one of the medical publishers he was undecided, wanting the subject "to come under the notice of laymen".[79] On the question of a publisher, Ellis endorsed Symonds's preference for one that was "both medico-scientific and general", as the purely medical publishers made a very narrow appeal. But he could not tell "how far publishers would be shy of the book".[80]

It so happened that laymen were being made aware of the subject, for in December a widely-reported prosecution of a number of men for homosexual offences took place in Bolton, under the 1885 Act.[81] Symonds wrote to a friend: "[T]ell me all you can about the affair… I am interested in watching the exact working of Labouchère's clause".[82] The next day he wrote in similar vein to another friend in Bolton, asking for "exact information".[83]

In his response to Symonds's last letter, the main issue that Ellis took up was that of morbidity which, all along, was

---

78 Havelock Ellis, *Studies in the Psychology of Sex*, vol. 1, *Sexual Inversion*, (Wilson and Macmillan, 1897), p. 41.
79 Symonds to Ellis, 1 December 1892, *Letters*, vol. 111, p. 787.
80 Ellis to Symonds, 21 December 1892, BUSC DM, 109/30.
81 See Helen Smith's *Masculinity Class and Same-Sex Desire in Industrial England 1895-1957*, (Palgrave Macmillan, 2015).
82 Symonds to Charles Kains-Jackson, 18 December 1892, *Letters*, vol. 111, p.790.
83 Symonds to J.W. Wallace, 19 December 1892, *Letters*, vol. 111, p.792.

going to be a make or break one. To overcome this possible "serious difficulty" between them, they had to compromise: to recognise that the issue of causation was a complex one. On his part, Ellis accepted that the movement of scientific opinion was towards Symonds's position, and he would want to avoid "any assumption of the necessity of psychopathic conditions" although, in his view, there could be little doubt that the sexually-inverted were often neurotic persons. And Symonds had admitted previously that where there was a marked aversion to the opposite sex, a "horror feminae", there might be a psychopathic explanation. Furthermore, it would be "bad policy" to put themselves in opposition to the medical psychologists who had studied the question most carefully. This was a point not lost on Ellis, setting out to establish his credentials among his medical peers. In the current climate, removing the homosexual question completely from the field of pathology would be difficult. It was best to recognise that it was impossible "to attach great importance to any one theory of causation".[84] The way forward was to present the evidence, fairly, on the basis of what specific cases revealed.

Wayne Koestenbaum has argued that, in determining the division of labour, Ellis was intent on "depriving" Symonds of a voice,[85] but all the evidence refutes this claim. In his provisional sketch of responsibilities, Ellis reserved the chapters on the nature of sexual inversion for himself because, as he said, quite reasonably, it was there that the reader would expect to find "the more medical writer". But he fully recognised the value and importance of the large amount of original material to be found in the *Modern Problem*, especially when set against, as he freely admitted, his then own more limited understanding of homosexuality:

---

84   Ellis to Symonds, 21 December 1892, BUSC DM, 109/30.
85   Wayne Koestenbaum, *Double Talk, The Erotics of Male Literary Collaboration*, (New York 1994), p. 44.

I should wish to work in all your material and not to make any serious statements to which you object. So that while I should be finally responsible for the form of these chs., (sic) the joint-authorship would clearly appear in them. [86]

He would repeat his appreciation of what Symonds could bring to the book in his next letter:

It seems to me that my contribution of fresh material to the book will be a very humble one compared to yours. [87]

And in his penultimate letter to Symonds he wrote:

I am anxious in the important chapters on the nature of sex inversion to prepare a statement which shall represent the views of both writers… [88]

Finally, in the preface to the first English edition, which was published after Symonds's death but under both their names, and in which his input mostly appeared as fragmentary appendices, Ellis made clear that, had their collaboration not been cut short, Symonds's contributions "would otherwise have been fitted into the body of the book". These were "not purely literary" but embodied "a large amount of scientific inquisition".[89]

Symonds was reassured by Ellis's responses:

I think that we may now consider that all important disagreement on the fundamental points is at an end. I

---

86   Ellis to Symonds, 21 December 1892, BUSC DM, 109/30.
87   Ellis to Symonds, 3 January 1893, BUSC DM, 109/30.
88   Ellis to Symonds, 19 February 1893, BUSC DM 109/30.
89   Ivan Crozier, ed. *Sexual Inversion, Havelock Ellis and John Addington Symonds*, A Critical Edition, ed. Ivan Crozier, (Palgrave Macmillan, 2008) p. 93.

most emphatically approve of the attitude you wish to take with regard to medical psychologists. Nor did I ever deny that sexual inverts are frequently neurotic. I only doubt whether neurosis can be regarded as the cause of sexual inversion.[90]

Shifting the debate from neuropathology to physiology and psychology was Symonds's most important objective, and Ellis seemed to be on his side, having described sexual inversion as a "sport"; meaning an aberration, maybe due to imperfect sexual differentiation. Symonds agreed: "My feeling upon the point is that sexual inversion will eventually be regarded as a comparatively rare but quite natural and not morbid deflection from the common rule, due to mental imaginative aesthetical emotional peculiarities of the individual in whom it occurs".[91]

In response to another point in Ellis's letter, he was, again, quick to claim that he could bring to their work a knowledge of the homosexual world far beyond Ellis's reach:

I doubt very much whether the North Italians are more homosexual than the Germans for example. They regard the South Italians as essentially different in this respect from themselves. A male prostitute whom I once saw at Naples told me that he was a Venetian, but had come to Naples because at Venice he only found custom with Englishmen, Swedes and Russians, whereas at Naples he could live in excellent Italian society and be abundantly supported.

---

90 Symonds to Ellis, 29 December 1892, (HRC). This letter is incorrectly dated 29 September 1892 in Schueller and Peters, *Collected Letters,* vol. 111, p. 753.
91 Ibid.

And he would have a good deal to say about inversion in Switzerland, where "it plays a prominent part".[92]

For whatever reason, when he met Carpenter in Brighton, Symonds had not told him about writing a book with Ellis. Perhaps he did not want it to be known until all hurdles to collaboration had been overcome. But, as he was again writing to Ellis, a letter arrived from Carpenter revealing that Ellis had told him about it. Now he would be able to seek Carpenter's views on the critical issues that he hoped had finally been thrashed out with Ellis. It would be too strong to claim that Symonds was the catalyst for Carpenter's decision to write about homosexuality, but their discussion in Brighton would have played a part, and his imminent involvement in the project would have provided a further impetus.

In December, Ellis wrote to Carpenter:

In conjunction with J A Symonds I am arranging to write a book on sexual inversion, including the Greek form of psychic abnormality and that felt and advocated by Whitman. Symonds has given much study to the subject, both in old Greek & in modern times (has himself printed pamphlets about the matter), & feels very strongly about it. I have been independently attracted to it, partly through realising how widespread it is, partly through realising also, how outrageously severe the law is in this country (compared with others), & how easily the law can touch a perfectly beautiful form of inversion.

We want to obtain sympathetic recognition for sexual inversion as a psychic abnormality which may be regarded as the highest ideal, & to clear away many vulgar errors – preparing the way, if possible, for a change in the law.[93]

---

92   Symonds to Ellis, 29 December 1892, (HRC)..
93   Ellis to Carpenter, 17 December 1892, SA MS 357/5.

This is an important letter. Firstly, it reveals that Ellis held to an *ideal* of homosexual love. Secondly, it sheds light on a contentious question: was the book, as well as contributing to the understanding of homosexuality to have a political purpose?

Two phrases reveal his attitude towards homosexuality: "… how easily the law can touch a perfectly beautiful form of inversion", and this psychic abnormality, "… may be regarded as the highest ideal". In his struggle to come to terms with Edith's emotional involvement with another woman, homosexuality is depicted as a spiritual, non-physical form of same-sex loving. He will apply this ideal to the male homosexual, for when the inversion is deep-seated, the individual should strive, to "refine and spiritualise" his sexual impulse and hold before his eyes "the ideal of chastity".[94] In respect of the book's objectives, his wish is to gain "sympathetic recognition" for homosexuality as a "psychic abnormality", by removing "many vulgar errors", and, "preparing the way, if possible, for a change in the law". From the outset, Symonds had firmly linked the writing of the book to challenging the "crude legal liabilities" to which homosexuals in England were subjected, and had made clear to Ellis that he would not want to collaborate on a book that did not show "the absurdity and injustice of the English law".[95]

In his last letter to Symonds, Ellis outlined a strategy for engaging the reader that would meet his own demand for impartiality and Symonds's wish that the book should help to bring about a change in the English law:

It seems to me that the most effective way of treating matters would be to avoid so far as possible in the body of the book any insistence on the social bearing of inversion, on its "criminal" character. When the reader has thus been

94 Havelock Ellis, *Sexual Inversion*, p. 147.
95 Symonds to Ellis, 20 June 1892, HRC.

led to a sympathetic or at all events intelligent point of view, the existing state of social feeling as crystallised in law, etc. can be clearly and more effectively set forth. [96]

This is exactly how Ellis finally structured the book. Following his account of the nature of homosexuality, in the final chapter he reviewed the existing legal position and its social consequences, showing, as Symonds had expressed it, "the absurdity and injustice of the English law", but very clearly leaving it to his readers to draw their own conclusions from the facts. He was not opposed to the change to the 1885 Criminal Law Amendment Act that Symonds wanted, which would make homosexual acts that took place in private non-criminal, but simply observed that, with this restriction removed, the English law would be "in harmony with the most enlightened European legislation". [97]

As Chris Nottingham has suggested, it is difficult to evaluate the scientific status of Ellis's work because of ambiguity in his use of the term, but he clearly had a strong commitment to the *utilitarian* function of science "as a body of applicable knowledge which must by reason and of necessity become the basis of understanding society and developing the agenda of modern government". [98] Grosskurth's assessment, that Ellis's aim was "to dispel myth, puncture prejudice, and to present as factual a report of the real situation as possible", accords with this view. [99] But an earlier biographer's opinion was that Ellis largely wrote "moral and educational books disguised as science". [100] We hold

96 Ellis to Symonds, 3 March 1893, BUSC DM 109/31.
97 Ellis, *Sexual Inversion*, p. 151.
98 Chris Nottingham, *The Pursuit of Serenity: Havelock Ellis and the New Politics*, (Amsterdam University Press, 1999), p. 144.
99 Phyllis Grosskurth, *Havelock Ellis, A biography*, (Allen Lane, 1980), p. 185.
100 Arthur Calder- Marshall, *Havelock Ellis, A biography*, (Rupert Hart-Davis, 1959), p. 154.

that Ellis never wanted *Sexual Inversion* to be seen as openly advocating a change in the law, which would have destroyed, at once, any reputation that he hoped to build as a detached observer of human sexuality. At every opportunity during their written exchanges he had cautioned Symonds against harming the book's scientific integrity by taking a partisan position on the legal status of homosexual acts. Years later, when he distanced himself from the book, he admitted that, had Symonds lived, its significance would have been "greatly discounted by the fact that one of the writers was known to many as personally concerned in the question of homosexuality".[101] This strengthens our view that he never intended, as claimed by Ivor Crozier, that the book should stand as "a politically-motivated sexological text,"[102] although its findings, as he had told Carpenter, might help those who argued for its partial decriminalisation in England. If Ellis had legal reform as an objective, then Symonds's vested interest, rather than hindering this objective, might well have strengthened the book's impact.

Ellis felt sure that Carpenter would be supportive and hoped that he could provide "notes or suggestions" which would help them: "Nothing of the kind has yet been published, at least in England, & I cannot help feeling that the book will do much good. We are both resolved to put our names to it, but of course every care will be taken with regard to those who help us with material".[103] Carpenter agreed to help where he could and met Ellis to discuss it. Afterwards, he told Symonds: "He has promised to write notes of his own observations and experiences, & also to obtain, if possible, autobiographical notes of others".[104] When Symonds later drew up a questionnaire,

---

101 Havelock Ellis, *My Life*, p. 296.
102 Ivan Crozier, Sexual Inversion, *Havelock Ellis and John Addington Symonds*, p. 59.
103 Ellis to Carpenter, 17 December 1892, SA MS, 357/5.
104 Ellis to Symonds, 18 January 1893, (HRC).

based on one constructed by Krafft-Ebing, Carpenter utilized it among his friends and was able to provide his own and several autobiographical histories. Ellis was learning all the time: "I was interested to hear he (Carpenter) finds homosexuality fairly common among the English working classes, as you do at Venice, etc., and in much the same way – the men marrying simply as matter of course but forming romantic attachments with persons of their own sex".[105]

Symonds's friendship with Carpenter was growing. In October 1890, Carpenter had embarked on a spiritual odyssey to Ceylon and India to meet Ponambulam Arunachalam, a special Ceylonese friend from his Cambridge days, and had just published *From Adam's Peak to Elephanta,* an account of his life-changing experiences there.[106] He sent Symonds a copy and his wife read it aloud to him: "We both of us are quite enthusiastic about its style & its feeling. Some passages are very beautiful".[107]

It has been argued by Sean Brady that Carpenter fled to the East to escape the dominant masculine culture in England, and that oriental mysticism, "indirectly, facilitated his sexual propensities", in the face of the alien "inversion theories of sex psychologists".[108] Brady's claim appears to rest solely on the view of Parminder Bakshi, that the book is imbued with homoerotic desire, and that Carpenter's interest in the East was entrenched in the nineteenth-century convention of homosexual orientalism.[109] But a careful reading reveals very

105 Ellis to Symonds, 18 January 1893, (HRC)..

106 Edward Carpenter, *From Adam's Peak to Elephanta*, (Swan Sonnenschein, 1892).

107 Symonds to Carpenter, 10 January 1893, *Letters*, vol. 111, p. 803.

108 Sean Brady, *Masculinity and Male Homosexuality in Britain, 1861-1913*, p. 159.

109 Parminder Kaur Bakshi*, Homosexuality and Orientalism: Edward Carpenter's Journey to the East,* in Brown, ed. *Edward Carpenter and Late Victorian Radicalism*, (Cass, 1990).

little linking Carpenter to a tradition of homosexual literature in which the Orient is represented as a region free of the constraints of Western sexual taboos, and an Elysium for the English homosexual adventurer. Bakshi places Carpenter in this tradition, charging him with "sexual colonialism" in his treatment of Ceylon and India. Yet it is difficult to find any confirmation in the book of a "powerful personal erotic subtext".[110] Carpenter's descriptions of semi-naked boys and men are taken as evidence of a homoerotic fixation, and he supposedly portrays Ceylonese and Indian males as "free of emotional constraints… and potentially available for sexual liaisons".[111] The further claim that he had a sexual relationship with a Singhalese man is a tenuous one.

Arunachalam had long entreated Carpenter to visit him and learn more of the ancient religious mysteries and esoteric philosophy of India, which, after reading the *Bhagavat Gita,* had already saturated his mind when he wrote *Towards Democracy.* His time spent there was not a search for an alternative affirmation of his homosexuality, denied him in the West, or an enlargement of the sexual freedom that he, and other English homosexuals, enjoyed in Southern Europe and North Africa. The importance of his journey was, essentially, metaphysical.

The visit to the East in some sense completed the circle of my experiences. It took two or three years for its results to soak and settle into my mind; but by that time I felt that my general attitude towards the world was not likely to change much, and that it only remained to secure and define what I had got hold of and to get it decently built out if possible into actual life and utterance.[112]

---

110 Parminder Kaur Bakshi, *Orientalism and Homosexuality.* p. 175.
111 Ibid. p. 163.
112 Edward Carpenter, *My Days and Dreams*, p.145.

The book, as well as being, as Carpenter had intended and Symonds had found, a charming account of his odyssey, was also a witty parody of British colonial India. In return for the gift, Symonds sent Carpenter his own "last little book", pointing out that it included an essay on Antique and Platonic ideals of love.[113] And he suggested that Carpenter should read *South Sea Idylls*, Charles Warren Stoddard's homoerotic tales of life among the natives of the South Pacific Islands: "If you cannot get a copy, let me hear, & I will send you mine".[114]

He was eager to talk about the book with Ellis. He still felt that he was too inclined to stick to the "neuropathic" explanation, although he was "whittling" it away to a minimum, and he certainly agreed with Ellis that it would not be wise to break off completely from this well-established line of analysis. But he considered that each new book published on the subject diluted the claim that sexual inversion was a neurotic disease. He repeated to Carpenter his claim that it was necessary to introduce a new feature into the discussion, by giving a complete account of homosexual love in ancient Greece:

All the foreign investigators from Moreau & Casper to Moll are totally ignorant of Greek Customs. Yet it is here that the phenomenon has to be studied from a different point of view from that of Psycho-pathology. Here we are forced to recognize that one of the foremost races in civilization not only tolerated passionate comradeship, but also utilized it for high social and military purpose".[115]

---

113 John Addington Symonds, *In The Key of the Blue,* (Matthews and Lane, 1893).
114 Symonds to Carpenter, 29 December 1892, *Letters*, vol.111, p. 797.
115 Ibid.

He was sending Carpenter one of the two remaining copies of his *Greek Problem*. There would be much to talk about when they met.

They were now sufficiently at ease with each other to talk frankly about homosexuality. Referring to the practice of fellatio, was it possible, Carpenter asked, that the absorption of semen transferred one man's virility to another? Symonds responded:

> You raise a very interesting question with regard to physiological grounds for this passion. I have no doubt myself that the absorption of semen implies a real modification of the physique of the person who absorbs it, & that, in these homosexual relations, this constitutes an important basis for subsequent conditions – both spiritual and corporeal. It is a pity that we cannot write freely on the topic. But when we meet, I will communicate to you facts which prove beyond all doubt to my mind that the most beneficent results as regards health and nervous energy, accrue from the sexual relation between men: also, that when they are carried on with true affection, through a period of years, both comrades become united in a way which would be otherwise quite inexplicable.[116]

Returning to the subject in a later letter, Symonds wondered whether Carpenter had been reading a work by Silvo Venturi, published the previous year.[117] Venturi had injected male semen into the blood of insane patients and suggested that it acted on the nervous system. Symonds had asked Ellis whether this was something worth considering, given the frequent claims of inverts, "that they derived a peculiar bien-étre & refreshment

---

116 Symonds to Carpenter, 29 December 1892, *Letters*, vol. 111, p. 797..
117 Silvo Venturi, *Le Degerazioni Psico-Sexuali, (Psycho-Sexual Degeneration)*, 1892.

from fellatio & passive paedicatio".[118] And he told Carpenter: "[It] has this peculiarity that it tackles the problem you raised. It is so strange to find this (otherwise tedious & stupid book) tonight under my hand (but the only one in which I have seen the subject treated) – so strange that I think you must have been reading it or something similar. – Let me hear if this or any other literary work put you on the track".[119]

Carpenter encouraged Symonds to press on with the book, praising Ellis for his special qualities. Symonds agreed: "What you say about H Ellis in conversation is just what R[oden] Noel told me. In correspondence I find him full, eager, open-minded, and scientifically conscientious: the sort of man I think, to lead our joint inquiry." Carpenter was now preparing his notes for Ellis, which Symonds wanted to see first: "[O]f course, H.E. will see the bulk of them. But you might feel it more appropriate to let me have things wh (sic) you would not care to submit to him. This is only a suggestion arising from my desire to lose nothing you may have to say".[120]

For nearly twenty years, Symonds had engaged in a protracted correspondence with Whitman, always asking in round-about ways a single question: did comradeship between males sanction physical love-making? In August 1890, he had made his final attempt to prise an answer out of the poet. After the efflorescence of the 1860 *Calamus* cluster of poems, homoeroticism had become muted in subsequent collections, and it is reasonable to suppose that Whitman did not want his large poetic output to be narrowed down to a justification of male-on-male sex. After all, he had presented his man-loving poems in the context of the reunification of the American nation, and the imputation of carnality, long voiced by some

118 Symonds to Ellis, 31 January 1893, HRC.
119 Symonds to Carpenter, 29 January 1893, *Letters*, vol. 111, p. 810.
120 Symonds to Carpenter, 21 January 1893, *Letters*, vol. 111, p .808.

in his own country, would have been highly damaging to his European reputation. To protect himself, he had to respond to Symonds's persistent badgering. For a number of his English admirers he was a prophet of homosexual emancipation, but he could not associate himself with this sentiment by authorising such a reading of his work. If this was his reasoning, was it not time to fashion a defensive fiction about his past sexual life"? On 19th August 1890, he despatched a letter to Symonds, thought to be the only statement that he ever made on his attitude towards homosexuality:

Abt the question on Calamus pieces &c: they quite daze me. L of G. is only rightly to be construed by and within its own atmosphere and essential character – all of its pages & pieces so coming strictly under that – that the Calamus part has even allow'd the possibility of such a construction as mentioned is terrible – I am fain to hope that the pages themselves are not to be even mentioned for such gratuitous and quite at the same time undream'd and unrech'd possibility of morbid inferences – wh' are disavowed by me and seem damnable. My life, young manhood, mid-age, times South, &c: have all been jolly, bodily and probably open to criticism... Tho always unmarried I have had six children – two are dead – One living Southern grandchild, fine boy, who writes to me occasionally. Circumstances connected with their benefit and fortune have separated me from intimate relations.[121]

Placed in the context of the long inquisition that he had been subjected to by an obsessional Symonds, had Whitman simply

---

121 *The Correspondence of Walt Whitman*, ed. Edwin Haviland Miller, 6 vols., (New York University Press, 1961-77), vol. 5, pp. 72-73.

made it up to spite him? Was it, as has been suggested, "an enormous lie?"[122]

Symonds's study of Whitman was now in the hands of the printer and he copied out for Carpenter the poet's letter of protestation: "I feel sure he would not have written it, when he first published *Calamus*. I think he was afraid of being used to lend his influence to "Sods" [sodomites]. Did not quite trust me perhaps".[123] In *Sexual Inversion* Ellis will recognise that homosexuality might be an important psychological key to understanding Whitman's personality, but is adamant that his work should not be treated as merely that of an "invert". Carpenter agreed, and advised him that it would be a mistake to give weight to the letter, especially as it was "in hopeless conflict" with the *Calamus* poems. When, years later, he read a paper on Whitman he told his audience that there was no doubt in his mind that the poems gave expression to "what we would now call the homosexual passion – which passion, although at the time ignored and unacknowledged by the world, was burning fiercely within him... spiritual and emotional of course, but well rooted in the physical and sexual also".[124] Symonds had, unwisely, attempted to drive Whitman into a confession of his real nature, but had simply aroused his resistance and caused him to hedge more than ever. If Whitman had "made allowance for possibilities in that direction... he knew that the moment he said such a thing he would have the whole American Press at his heels, snarling and slandering, and distorting his words in every possible way".[125]

Early in February 1893, Symonds sent Carpenter a copy

122 Charley Shively, *Calamus Lovers, Walt Whitman's Working Class Comarados*, (Gay Sunshine Press, 1987), p. 27.

123 Symonds to Carpenter, 21 January 1893, *Letters*, vol. 111, p. 808.

124 Edward Carpenter, *Some Friends of Walt Whitman*, read before the British Society for the Study of Sex Psychology in 1922, and published by the Society (no. 13) in 1924.

125 Ibid.

of his *Modern Problem*, with the caution, "It does not represent my views completely, since I have read and thought a great deal during the last two years".[126] But cut off in Davos, barring the occasional visit of one or two of his knowing friends, there was nobody with whom he could discuss the subject. Whenever it was to take place, he knew that he would have to be well-prepared for his first meeting with Ells, and would greatly benefit from Carpenter's advice. He had found the notes on inversion that he had sent him "very interesting & valuable" although, for whatever reason, Ellis would take a different view. They were for Symonds's use, but given the timing, may have been a first draft of, or notes for, his own *Homogenic Love* pamphlet, which would be published the following year.[127] For Symonds, the notes raised all sorts of important questions: "I do so much wish that we could meet & exchange thoughts in quiet somewhere before the book on sexual inversion is begun".[128]

He would want to cast a critical eye over what Ellis wrote. One clash is certainly foreshadowed by Symonds's claim, in the same letter to Carpenter, that Ulrichs "must be regarded as the real originator of a scientific handling of the phenomenon". As we note later, this was not Ellis's view. Although in the jointly-authored edition of *Sexual Inversion* he would include an appendix on Ulrichs from Symonds's *Modern Problem*, he discounted Ulrichs's work on the ground that, being homosexual, he could not possibly *be* objective. Again, in his *Modern Problem* Symonds had mounted a polemic against Krafft-Ebing's claim that homosexuality was the outcome of an "hereditary taint", of impaired health in ancestors.[129] In one of his letters to Carpenter, Symonds had commented on the

---

126 Symonds to Carpenter, 7 February 1893, *Letters*, vol.111, p. 814.
127 Sheila Rowbotham, *Edward Carpenter, A Life of Liberty and Love*, (Verso, 2008), p. 188.
128 Symonds to Carpenter, 7 February 1893, *Letters*, vol. 111, p. 814.
129 Richard Krafft-Ebing, (1840-1902), Austro-German physician and author of the authoritative *Psychopathia Sexualis*.

case of an invert, mentioned by Carpenter, who was the only boy in a family of six girls. He wondered whether "cases of this sort do not support Ulrichs's physiological hypothesis: as though the combination of the parents tended to female sexuality in the differentiation of the offspring, so that when a male came he was feminine in character".[130] On the other hand, he knew of inverts in families where males and females were "pretty equally distributed". But this could be a fruitful line of research to counter the idea of an hereditary taint: "I wish the medical psychologists would study the phenomenon from this point of view. If only it had fallen into the hands of Fr[ancis] Galton".[131] As we argue later, Ellis would see in eugenics the means of eliminating unwanted characteristics in the human population, of which sexual inversion might be considered to be one. On these and other matters, knowing Ellis's regard for him, it would be advantageous to have Carpenter on his side. He asked from Davos: "[C]ould you not come out and stay with me in the early summer here, or could you come to Venice and stay with me in May? I have a little house at Venice, wh (sic) is delightful for two people." He added: "In April I want to be in Rome."[132]

The previous day Symonds had received a copy of Carpenter's *Civilisation: Its Cause and Cure*. This collection of previously-published papers included his *Defence of Criminals,* with its endorsement of "male friendship carried over into the region of love"; a passion exemplified by the heroic Theban legion, the "sacred band", into which no man might enter without his lover. This brief discussion of comradely love foreshadowed the obstacles Carpenter would have to surmount as he set out to defend a passion which "the modern

---

130 Symonds to Carpenter, 5 February 1893, *Letters*, vol. 111, p. 813.
131 Francis Galton (1822-1911), pioneer of eugenics and a friend of Symonds's father.
132 Symonds to Carpenter, 7 February 1893, *Letters*, vol. 111, p. 814.

world scarcely recognises… or if it recognises, does so chiefly to condemn it".[133] Symonds had not had time to do more than glance through the book, but had alighted upon these "firmly and delicately touched" passages".[134]

When Symonds wrote to Ellis on 12th February 1893, to report on progress, it was to "My Dear Ellis".[135] As collaborators, it was time to drop the Mr. Since they last exchanged letters, he had framed a set of questions, that he had asked friends and acquaintances who he knew to be homosexual, to use in outlining their sexual histories, taking pointers from Krafft-Ebbing and Ulrichs. He now had sixteen autobiographical accounts by "English Inverts", which he was sending to Ellis, vouching for their genuineness. These "candid and uninspired" records were quite different from those collected by physicians from reformatories and prisons. All could be used with profit in Ellis's part of the book and, if possible, he would acquire more.

He had revised the *Greek Problem*, which would need to be worked into "the scheme of the whole book". It had also been agreed that, on the historical side, there should be an account of homosexuality from the Greek, through the Roman and mediaeval periods to modern times, but which, because of limited space, would have to be done superficially. Later, it was agreed that there should also be a selection of a few "unchallengeable eminent Inverts" in history, although he wondered, without accessible records, what useful psychological conclusions could be drawn. Perhaps the best that could be done was to draw up a list of those in whom the aberration was "fairly ascertained".[136]

---

133 Edward Carpenter, *Civilisation: Its Cause and Cure*. (Swan Sonnenchein, 1889), p. 819.
134 Symonds to Carpenter, 13 February, *Letters*, vol. 111, p. 818.
135 Symonds to Ellis, 12 February 1893, *Letters*, vol. 111, p. 816.
136 Symonds to Ellis, 22 February 1893, *Letters*, vol. 111, p. 820.

He now wanted to know whether Ellis had begun to write his parts of the book, wishing their work to proceed in tandem. He had lots of other things to do and would willingly postpone work on the book, but did not want to get behind. Replying, Ellis again raised the issue of its 'tone': "You will, I think, agree that we should adopt a rather austere style in this book, avoiding as far as possible a literary or artistic attitude towards the question, appealing to the reason rather than the emotions. For this reason, some passages in your *Modern Problem* ought, I think, to be omitted". He thought that all the confessions Symonds had provided were worth publishing, although he intended, "for various obvious reasons", to make a number of modifications and omissions. Personal histories, carefully edited to ensure anonymity and dispassionately analysed, had to form the empirical foundation of the work.[137] Symonds agreed. Unless the book was strictly analytical, it would not get "a fair hearing from the English". He repeated his earlier concession, that Ellis was free to work over anything that he used from the *Modern Problem* to "erase its bias and eliminate its literary quality".[138]

It seemed that they had now reached sufficient agreement on fundamentals for the project to go ahead. Symonds would provide the ethnographical and historical material and as many case histories as he could acquire, whilst Ellis would be responsible for the purely 'medical' chapters, but which would incorporate material from the *Modern Problem*. It was agreed that the *Greek Problem*, with certain enlargements suggested by Ellis (notably, a section dealing with inversion in women among the Greeks, at Edith's suggestion), would form one chapter of the book. Both were occupied with other work, so it suited them that the main pressure to write would not come for several months.

In Rome, on Sunday 16th April 1893, Symonds took to his

---

137 Ellis to Symonds, 19 February 1893, HRC.
138 Symonds to Ellis, 22 February 1893, *Letters*, vol. 111, p. 820.

bed with what appeared to be a touch of influenza, then about in the city. But by Tuesday, pneumonia had settled in both lungs, leading to gradual paralysis. Aware that he might not recover, he asked his daughter Margaret for pencil and paper and wrote a barely legible note to his wife Catherine, who was herself ill in Venice:

> There is something I ought to tell you, and being ill at Rome I take this occasion. If I do not see you again in this life you remember that I made H F Brown depository of my books. I wish that legacy to cover all written Mss Diaries Letters & other matters found in my books cupboard, with the exception of business papers. I do this because I have written things you could not like to read, but which I have always felt justified useful for society. Brown will consult & publish nothing without your consent.[139]

He sealed it, and on the cover drew his initials and the trefoil of his seal. Before he drifted into semi-consciousness, he asked for the small book of prayers that had belonged to his mother. Having little remembrance of her, it had gone with him on all life's journeys, and now lay under his hand. It was carnival time in Rome and the streets were thronged with noisy revellers; fireworks lighting the evening sky and dancing across the ceiling of the room where he lay subdued, talking to himself in a faint voice. On Wednesday morning, he was peaceful but scarcely breathing, and as the end neared those around him saw a face ravaged by illness throughout life grow visibly more youthful. At noon, aged fifty-two, on a serene summer-like day, he slipped away before Catherine could reach Rome. A plot was secured for him in the English cemetery of Cains Cestins, close to the grave of Shelley. Benjamin Jowett, soon

---

139 *The Letters of John Addington Symonds*, vol. 111, p. 839.

to follow his old pupil in death, was asked to compose the epitaph for his tombstone.

On the very day of his passing, his long-projected study of Whitman was published. Having failed to prise from him an admission that the *Calamus* cycle of poems was suffused with homoeroticism, he had not let go. His pronouncement from the grave was that the Good Grey Poet had "omitted to perceive, that there are inevitable points of contact between sexual anomaly and his doctrine of comradeship".[140]

Had Carpenter accepted Symonds's invitation to visit him in Davos or Venice, he may well have altered his plans to be in Rome, and had he lived we can only speculate on what might have transpired when he finally met Ellis. In their letters, they had seemingly thrashed out all possible disagreements on issues that each regarded as sticking points, but their very different personalities may well have clashed: Symonds, sophisticated and worldly, Ellis, "shy, awkward, reserved".[141] Perhaps feeling intimidated by such a confident forceful character who "talks better than he writes,"[142] Ellis may have quickly concluded that a book with Symonds would, after all, be very difficult to achieve. Or might Symonds have withdrawn from the project after failing to get final agreement on the structure of the book or the treatment of issues that he believed were non-negotiable? And Ellis might have concluded that the task of incorporating the large amount of facts and critical conclusions that had been amassed by Symonds in the *Modern Problem* was too daunting.

In scope, depth and originality, the *Modern Problem* was a superior work to the more derivative *Sexual Inversion*, but the claim by Joseph Bristow that it was Symonds's work that

---

140 John Addington Symonds, *Walt Whitman: a study*, (J.C. Nimmo, 1893).
141 Havelock Ellis, *My Life*, p. 256.
142 Symonds to Margaret Symonds, 20 December 1890, *Letters*, vol. 111, p. 526.

provided the foundation upon which Ellis built his profile as an expert in the field is clearly wrong.[143] Ellis, in the end, described his time spent on the topic of homosexuality as a "toilsome excursion", which delayed his entry into the wider field of sexual science.[144] The foundation on which he was to establish himself was laid later, as we indicate below. More controversially, Bristow seeks to build a case for an irreconcilable gulf between the two men, by drawing a distinction between Symonds's 'history' and Ellis's 'heredity'. But the lengthy written exchanges between the two men, when considering the book's structure and the allocation of responsibilities for specific areas, show that Symonds was as eager to enter the debate on the validity of existing physiological and psychological explanations for homosexuality, as to bring forward historical and ethnological facts to broaden understanding of the phenomenon. The *Modern Problem* was well-balanced in this regard. And although, as we note in chapter eight, Ellis believed that heredity could have a role in the aetiology of homosexuality, Symonds nowhere discounted this.

Clearly, their long-term aims were not the same, but they were not irreconcilable. Ellis wanted to build a reputation in the emerging field of the scientific study of human sexuality. He fully accepted that the criminalisation of homosexuality imposed a heavy penal burden and a severe social stigma on individuals, rendering the subject in special need, as he had told Carpenter, of "elucidation and discussion". In keeping with his humanistic outlook, he thought that this would be helpful to law reformers, and believed that, except under certain special circumstances, neither sodomy nor gross indecency ought to be penal offences. But legal reform was

---

143 Joseph Bristow, *Symonds's History, Ellis's Heredity*, in *Sexology in Culture*, eds. Bland and Doan (Polity Press 1988) p. 80.
144 Ellis, *Sexual Inversion*, p. 158.

not what motivated him.[145] From the first stirrings at Sparkes Creek, there was a single-minded focus on *understanding* human sexuality, and locating his work within the mainstream of European investigations. As he insisted after the personally distressing prosecution of *Sexual Inversion*, he saw himself as an "impartial student", dedicated to "the critical and dispassionate investigation of complicated problems".[146] Political campaigns, whether for the freedom to publish or the freedom to express one's sexuality, he would leave to others.

Symonds was entirely focussed on legislative reform. The *Modern Problem* was, first and foremost, a political tract aimed at helping to bring about a modification in the law. And, because he believed that there was an historical bias in current writing on homosexuality, he insisted that its cultural dimensions, its 'normality' found across time and across societies, should be given an integral place in the book. Revealing the psychological and physiological factors underlying homosexuality was essential, and the first task of the book. The claim that Symonds rejected "scientific theories of inversion" is not sustainable.[147] His critique of such theories was not a denial of science, but alone such findings would not be sufficient to challenge the English mind-set on homosexuality. He believed that a greater understanding of the pervasiveness of homosexuality would help to 'humanise' the Victorian mind. This sentiment was certainly shared by Ellis, but he worried that, as its prevalence did not *explain* homosexuality, too great an emphasis would

---

145 A contrary view is offered by Crozier, who argues that a 'political aim' was present in all Ellis's writing on sex. See his *Sexual Inversion, Havelock Ellis and John Addington Symonds,* (Palgrave Macmillan, 2008), p. 29.

146 Havelock Ellis, *A Note on the Bedborough Trial,* (The University Press, London).

147 Brady, *Masculinity and Male Homosexuality in Britain, 1861-1913,* (Palgrave Macmillan, 2005), p.161.

undermine the book as a contribution to the scientific literature. Yet it would be wrong to see Ellis as opposed to the introduction of historical and cultural material, when it came to understanding homosexual *behaviour*, as a sociological phenomenon, and although never prescriptive he invariably pointed out the social implications of his findings.

It is fair to ask whether, after Symonds's death, Ellis was justified in going on to publish the German and first English editions of *Sexual Inversion* as their joint work. As we argue in chapter eight, Symonds would never have accepted much of what Ellis wrote in the book's Conclusions, a task that had originally been allocated to him.

Grosskurth suggested that Ellis was "relieved to see the end of the collaboration",[148] because of his unease over possible incompatibilities of style, and nervousness over how seriously the book would be taken, once it became widely known that Symonds was himself an 'invert'. But she did not provide an explanation for *why* he carried on with the book. Years later, he put forward a number of reasons why collaboration was always going to be problematic. He said that he would have found joint-authorship with Symonds, or any other person for that matter, difficult. In the early days of his friendship with Olive Schreiner they had considered writing a paper together, but soon realised that it was impossible: "A highly individual writer cannot write in association with another writer, all the less if they are both highly individual".[149] He had raised this very issue at the start of his written exchanges with Symonds: "Collaboration is difficult, as a whole not worth the trouble of attempting, but in this case the advantages to be gained seem quite enough to make it worthwhile to smooth over the difficulties",[150] although he did not spell out what these advantages were.

---

148 Phyllis Grosskurth, *Havelock Ellis*, p. 179.
149 Havelock Ellis, *My Life*, p. 295.
150 Ellis to Symonds, 21 December 1892, BUSC DM 109/30.

In recounting events, he was emphatic that it had not been his intention to launch himself on the world as a writer on human sexuality with a volume on homosexuality. If Symonds had not approached him, he implied, he would not have devoted a whole volume to the subject, but he makes no mention of the decisive role of Edith Ellis in encouraging him to work with Symonds. It was her intervention that explains why Ellis was prepared to begin work on an *abnormal* manifestation of the sexual instinct, when, in the large scheme of research then taking shape in his mind, any treatment of *abnormal* sexual behaviour would, as he stated, follow on from the treatment of its "normal manifestations".[151]

There was another, more fundamental, reason for not going ahead. As a subject, Ellis knew that homosexuality could not possibly serve as the foundation for the comprehensive study of human sexuality that he was planning. Following the completion of *Man and Woman*, his examination of the sexual impulse proper would begin with an analysis of its egocentric manifestations, which he labelled *auto-eroticism*. This, together with *The Evolution of Modesty* and *The Phenomena of Sexual Periodicity*, he presented as "the necessary *prolegomena*" to the analysis of the sexual instinct.[152] Tellingly, these studies subsequently became volume one of his series of books, whilst *Sexual Inversion* was relegated to volume two.

Ellis's immediate explanation for publishing the book as a joint enterprise was that he did so out of loyalty to Symonds. But there was no obvious moral obligation to do so, as before Symonds's death, they had not agreed anything other than a provisional division of labour. In truth, there were three options open to him: to abandon the project altogether and

---

151 Ellis, *Sexual inversion,* p. xi.
152 Havelock Ellis, *Studies in the Psychology of Sex: The Evolution of Modesty; Phenomenon of Sexual Periodicity; Auto Eroticism*, (Leipzig & Philadelphia University Press and F.A. David, 1900).

treat homosexuality, as he had intended, as a topic under *abnormal* manifestations of the sexual instinct, but without a whole book being devoted to it; to publish a volume containing only the 'medical' chapters that he was responsible for, or to publish a book with limited textual references to Symonds, together with stand-alone pieces provided by him. This is what he chose to do in the German and first English editions.

In reaching a fair judgement on Ellis's motives and actions, it should also be recognised that there was a strong financial consideration behind his decision to go ahead with the book. He was frequently impecunious, "rarely free from some degree of worry over money".[153] He had to live off the fruits of his pen, which was seldom still. His industriousness at this time was remarkable: he was hurrying to finish his *Man and Woman*, and ongoing there was a translation of Zola's *Germinal* (for which he was paid £50), a significant collection of essays, on Nietzsche, Casanova, Zola and Saint Francis, together with regular pieces for journals and book reviews. It is understandable that he did not put aside the material on homosexuality that he had laboured over, but wished to make use of it to boost his income. In the three years following Symonds's death, he had seven articles published on homosexuality in American, German and Italian medical, legal, scientific, and psychological journals. The earliest was a survey of the study of homosexuality, published in 1894.[154] In it, he made the claim that he put forward as the principal justification for his book: that homosexuality had to be studied among the general population, not just the special populations open to the physician and lawyer. To go on to publish a book bringing together the material in these articles was the obvious next step.

---

153 Havelock Ellis, *My Life*, p. 227.
154 Havelock Ellis, *The Study of Sexual Inversion,* American Medico-Legal Journal, April 1894, vol. 12, pp. 148-157.

A Defence of Erotic Life

In late-Victorian England, the bourgeois recognition of the value of personal autonomy, increasingly, made individual feeling, not religious, moral or social strictures, a basis of choice in personal matters. Following Mill's influential essay[1] sanctioning a sphere of privacy for the satisfaction of individual desires, the expression of the sexual instinct assumed a new importance in the definition of the modern self. As such, homosexual passion could not be denied legitimacy as an element of personal self-fulfilment and happiness. Rather than continuing to collide with the dominant culture, possessors of a homosexual sensibility now sought acceptance within it.[2]

The detachment of sex from the dogma of procreation also marked the acceptance that women were sexual beings; that sexual pleasure was not the exclusive entitlement of the inseminating male. That the female was not to be denied orgasmic satisfaction was a view being cautiously advanced in the 1880s. In 1884, Dr Elizabeth Blackwell, one of the first women to be admitted to the medical profession, questioned the prevalent dogma of female sexual passivity, and suggested that physical sex was an even larger factor in the life of the

---

1   John Stuart Mill, *On Liberty*, (John W Parker & Son, 1859).
2   Michael Bronski, *Culture Clash: The Making of Gay Sensibility*, (South End Press, 1984).

woman, married or unmarried, than in the life of the man. There was "nothing necessarily evil in physical pleasure" nor was it "the special act necessary for parentage".[3]

But giving sexual desire autonomy was a threat to marriage and the family and not all women endorsed such a detachment, and the prominence being given to their sexuality. There were those, even feminist reformers, who regarded women as more spiritual than physical in nature. A female clamouring to sever her sexual drive from procreation, and a male directing his sexual drive towards his own sex were regarded as equally abnormal, and dangerous.

Other cultural changes also presented a challenge to Victorian sexual codes, neatly summarised by Fraser Harrison:

Male supremacy, the fundamental principle on which mid-Victorian sexual conventions were founded, was vigorously challenged; the fraudulence of the moral double standard was exposed; submissiveness ceased to be the universally accepted hallmark of femininity; the increasing use of contraceptive techniques decisively reduced the middle-class birth rate and the size of the average family; the awe in which fathers had previously been held was diminished and wives were released from the hitherto inescapable round of pregnancy and childbirth.[4]

In 1893, soon after Symonds's death, Carpenter began to write a number of pamphlets on "sex-questions", although not questions that lay strictly in the domain of sexology, those "fanciful divisions and dissections of human nature".[5] From

---

3   Elizabeth Blackwell, *The Human Element in Sex*, (J.A. Churchill, 1884).
4   Fraser Harrison, *The Dark Angel: Aspects of Victorian Sexuality.* (Fontana, 1979), p. 4.
5   Edward Carpenter, *The Drama of Love and Death: A Study of Human Evolution and Transfiguration.* (George Allen, 1912), p. 81.

the very beginning, his purpose in writing on human sexuality *was* ethical: to challenge deeply entrenched attitude*s* to the expression of the "sex-passion". Same-sex love, if personally the most urgent, was only one dimension of human sexuality. Of the few men who at this time supported the reform of sexual codes, Carpenter was the most open in addressing specific problems underlying relationships between the sexes and, at a deeper level, the modes of expression of the sexual instinct.

The individual who, above all, influenced Carpenter's new direction was Olive Schreiner. The brooding discontent that she harboured at having been born a female in a world in which women were subordinated, excluded, silenced, propelled her towards men who would treat her, not as a woman but as an equal and a fellow-worker, without her sex ever intruding. The awareness of how much more life would have given her as a man was never far from the surface. She would complain: "I wish I was a man that I might be friends with all of you, but you know my sex must always divide".[6] And again: "I shall never be a man and a brother among you men that I love so, but I have my work".[7] Her search for love, not found in an indifferent mother and a neglectful father, was overlaid by a need for the protection of an all-loving, all-wise, male figure, whom she seemed to find in Carpenter. And, even if the gender divide could never be closed, Carpenter was one of the two men, the other was the freethinker and socialist Karl Pearson,[8] with whom she had a brief emotional involvement, who, she believed, saw her "as a worker and not as a woman".[9]

---

6   Schreiner to Carpenter, 1 April 1887, SA MS. 359/4.
7   Schreiner to Carpenter, 10 January 1889, SA MS. 359/34.
8   Karl Pearson (1857-1936), English mathematician and founder of the progressive Men and Women's Club.
9   Richard Rive, ed. *Olive Schreiner Letters*, vol. 1, 1871-1899 (OUP, 1988), p. 122.

From the very beginning of her involvement in English radical politics, the 'woman question' was the compelling passion of her life, and one that went far beyond the modest demands of the suffragettes. She had told Ellis soon after they met: "The question of women having the vote and independence and education, is only part of the question, there lies something deeper".[10] What lay deeper in her mind was the universal spectacle of female servitude: a condition which women could only begin to overcome if they gained autonomy over their own bodies and were freed from both oppressive male sexuality and socially-enforced procreation.

In the summer of 1893, Schreiner spent several months in a cottage close to Carpenter's home in Millthorpe. Two other women friends also visited over the summer and with three 'advanced' women around, inevitably, there was talk that touched on women's issues. Carpenter had, by now, come to see these as so important that he had been trying, without success, to persuade one of his woman friends "to take the subject up".[11] He knew that such issues ought to be dealt with by a woman, but he was no more successful in his search that summer.

Schreiner, since the publication of *The Story of an African Farm*, was temperamentally inclined to use art for the exploration of women's issues. "The question of sex is so very complex, and you cannot treat it adequately at all unless you show its complexity".[12] In moments of exasperation she was inclined to leave the sex question, "and turn to the other problems which are always drawing me". But she could not turn away from the work that she felt to be her own, although it would "be as if a great iron weight had rolled off me if I had once said what I have to say". [13] She would go on to craft novels

10   Schreiner to Ellis, 12 May 1884, HRC.
11   Carpenter, *My Days and Dreams*, p.195.
12   Schreiner to Carpenter, 3 January 1887, *Olive Schreiner Letters*, ed. Rive, p.118.
13   Ibid.

in which the people of her imagination became more real than those of flesh and blood, and through them she applied her moral code. The allegorical story became her medium.

Carpenter decided that he would take on the task. We do not know what consideration he gave to this possibly personally-damaging departure from his conventional socialist writings. In his autobiographical notes, we are simply told, in a quite matter of fact way, that early in 1894 he started writing "a series of pamphlets on sex questions"; questions that at the time, were "generally tabooed, and practically not discussed at all".[14] But, undoubtedly, it dramatically changed the direction of his life and his public profile. He would have recognised the strategic advantage of establishing himself as a writer on sexual issues, before turning to the more hazardous issue of homosexuality. His known connections with women's reform groups provided a legitimising context, and as a man he could say things which, coming from a woman, might have been easily dismissed. Over the next year, he produced three inter-related pamphlets: *Sex-Love, and its Place in a Free Society*; *Woman, and Her Place in a Free Society*, and *Marriage in a Free Society*. A fourth pamphlet, *Man the Ungrown*, was also written. The first three pamphlets covered a range of issues, including, male supremacy, on which Victorian sexual conventions rested, the social degradation of women, the burden of child-bearing, motherhood and prostitution. Each had a clear, unambiguous aim: to challenge Victorian sexual orthodoxies and to initiate a discussion on the healthiness of the expression of sexual energy. They were also an attack on the prevailing economic and social subservience of women. The fourth pamphlet condemned the male attitudes that perpetuated women's 'serfdom'.

The anger that Carpenter felt towards the subjugation of

---

14   Carpenter, *My Days and Dreams*, pp. 194-195.

women was expressed in one of his most powerful political statements, which went like a dagger to the heart of Victorian 'manhood':

> ... the male bitten by it [the greed of private property] not only claimed possession of everything he could lay hands upon, but ended by enslaving and appropriating his own mate... reducing her also to a mere chattel, a slave and a plaything... shutting her more and more into the seclusion of the boudoir and the harem, or down to the drudgery of the hearth; confining her body, her mind; playing always upon her sex-nature, accentuating always that, as though she was indeed nought else but sex... arrogating to himself a masculine licence, yet revenging the least unfaithfulness on her part by casting her out into the scorned life of the prostitute; and granting her more and more but one choice in life – to be a free woman and to die, unsexed, in the gutter; or for creature-comforts and a good name to sell herself, soul and body, into life-long bondage.[15]

The first, most important pamphlet, *Sex-Love and Its Place in a Free Society*, opens the case for "the enfranchisement of the body", first proclaimed twenty years earlier in *Towards Democracy*. It is the bedrock on which many of his most important arguments rest. In it, he tackles head-on the issue of repressed sexuality: arguing that the restraints placed on the natural expression of the sex instinct are highly damaging to the proper development of the individual. As a brother to six sisters, he had witnessed at first hand the suppression of their emotional lives. There had to be a "regeneration"

---

15   Edward Carpenter, *Love's Coming of Age*, p. 36. In 1896, the papers were combined and published under this title by the Manchester Labour Press Society. All references are to the 1914 edition, published by Methuen & Co.

of ideas about sex; for it to no longer be seen as something covert, shaming, and unclean. And it had to be freed from "the damnable commercialism which buys and sells all human things", and from "the religious hypocrisy which covers and conceals" it. In the place of such repressive social attitudes should be "a healthy delight in and cultivation of the body and all its natural functions, and a determination to keep them pure and beautiful, open and sane and free…"[16]

For an individual, not to have experience of the sex passion is a form of deprivation, a stilting of growth. The separation of the spiritual and physical aspects of love, the one lauded the other condemned, cripples human health and vitality. Love cannot be confined to the emotional plane, as his own life affirmed. When physical fulfilment is denied, "the body becomes surcharged with waves of emotion – sometimes to an unhealthy and dangerous degree". But there was no common acceptance of this need, for *either* sex, but especially for women. In the social life of the future, "the state of enforced celibacy in which vast numbers of women live to-day will be looked upon as a national wrong, almost as grievous as that of prostitution…"[17] Love is, before all else, an "ethereal human yearning for personal union", and only to a lesser degree is it a desire to propagate the species.[18] This was a dangerous challenge to the Victorian belief that the single purpose of sexual intercourse *was* procreation.

The acceptance by society of what must follow when the sexual instinct is fully understood, is as important to his conception of a new womanhood as it is to his defence of same-sex love. There had to be a recognition of sexual fulfilment as a primary need, essential to human well-being, and the granting of a degree of sexual freedom. For lovers of

---

16   Edward Carpenter, *Love's Coming of Age*, p. 19.
17   Ibid. pp. 2-3.
18   Ibid. p. 21.

their own sex, it meant the acceptance of their natures and the overcoming of shame and guilt. Once attitudes were open and sane, society might be emancipated *from* sex, and come to see it as "only one very specialised factor in the full total of human love".[19]

He knew that the pamphlets would have no chance with ordinary publishers and they were printed and distributed by The Labour Press Society of Manchester, set up with financial support from Carpenter, to spread socialist ideas. They were well received, each selling three to four thousand copies, he later estimated, and of sufficiently wide interest for a German publisher to issue translations.

Although the strength of Carpenter's support for women is made abundantly clear in the pamphlets, he has been criticised for his biological essentialism: the acceptance that gender-specific roles, if always to a degree socially-constructed, were constrained by the biological differences between the sexes. But, for Carpenter, this did not rule out gender malleability, as societal norms clearly influenced gender ascription and gender roles. At the time, it was accepted that each sex possessed fixed biological characteristics, which controlled physiological drives and emotional responses. It was the nascent sciences of embryology and neurology that informed late nineteenth century thinking about gender, not gender *formation* through social conditioning and ascription. Carpenter accepted that there were biologically-determined differences, physiological, psychological and cognitive, between the sexes. Ellis's *Man and Woman*, published in the same year as these women-related essays, was an extensive study of 'secondary sexual differences' relevant to the issues surrounding gender.

Whilst he may have held a conventional view of the

---

19   Edward Carpenter, *Love's Coming of Age*, p. 19.

biological basis of gender, this did not limit his vision of women's potential. He rejected the idea that the "good woman" was no more than a child-bearer, making clear that, whilst this was a woman's "most perfect work", there was a nobler womanhood to be achieved; one which, just as Schreiner argued, required "her complete freedom as to the disposal of her sex".[20]

His separation of sex from the function of procreation has also been presented as a clever strategy to justify a homosexual erotic life. The defence of same-sex love is seen as the hidden agenda in his account of sex-love, enabling him to exonerate the homosexual "from the charge of licentiousness". Here, the implicit charge is that he used the women's cause for his own selfish purposes.[21] Others, have associated him with homosexual men of the 1890s who were supposedly intent upon preserving male dominance and male separatism: in the belief that they had more in common with heterosexual men. If homosexual 'identity-formation' depended strongly on such misogyny, then homosexual men "could not be dependable allies".[22] Carpenter was well aware that there were misogynistic homosexual men, typically men who had little or no contact with women, and who did regard relationships between men as more spiritual and purer than heterosexual relationships.

A further criticism is that he was tainted by a misogyny stemming from his 'aesthetic' preference for the male body. But he never denied how he felt towards a woman as an erotic object, which was no different from his lesbian

20   Edward Carpenter, Love's Coming of Age, p. 63.
21   Beverly Thiele, *Coming of Age: Edward Carpenter on Sex and Reproduction*, in *Edward Carpenter and Late Victorian Radicalism*, pp. 107-8.
22   Elaine Showalter, *Sexual Anarchy: Gender and Culture at the Fin de Siècle*, (Viking, 1990), p. 175.

friend Kate Salt's reaction to the male body; her "instinctive repulsion for any physical intimacy with the other sex".[23] As we have noted, in the *Modern Problem* Symonds pointed to evidence suggesting that this was a physiological not a moral response; a case of "horror feminae". And Carpenter would write:

> That men of this kind despise women is not an uncommon belief, but is hardly justified. Though naturally not inclined to 'fall in love' such men are by their nature drawn rather nearer to women, and it would seem that they often feel a singular appreciation and understanding of the emotional needs and destinies of the other sex, leading in many cases to a genuine, though what is called 'Platonic Friendship'... They are quite often the faithfulest of friends, the truest allies and most convinced defenders of women.[24]

There is little doubt that this was Schreiner's view of Carpenter. He was "the faithfulest of friends". If he had been at all misogynistic, the highly sensitive Olive would never have opened herself to him. Almost from the beginning of their friendship he was her 'beautiful boy', her 'darling', her 'big brother'. She would tell him: "Edward, I love you so dear, you have entered right into my heart".[25] A special bond had been forged between them. Schreiner was the 'new woman' in search of the 'new man', and it was the homosexual Carpenter who may have come closest to this ideal: closer than either of the progressive intellectuals, Ellis and Karl Pearson, with whom she became emotionally entangled when in England.

---

23   Kate Salt to Edward Carpenter, 17 February 1897, SA MS. 355/15.
24   Edward Carpenter, *The Intermediate Sex*, (George Allen and Unwin, 1908), p. 35.
25   Schreiner to Carpenter, 6 April 1888, SA MS 259/18.

In one of her last letters to Carpenter before returning to South Africa, she told him:

> My beautiful old Edward, I have been clinging to you these last days as a little child clings to its mother… I have been passing through much darkness and when I have looked around the world for a ray of light I have found you… go on your path Edward, my beautiful brother. Some far off day to come it will be seen what a light you were, how far before your time. [26]

---

26   Schreiner to Carpenter, 21 March 1889, SA MS 359/39.

Born Lovers of their Own Sex

With Symonds gone, Carpenter was determined to defend same-sex love, to present an elevating representation of such attachments; one that distinguished the "innate homosexual bias" from "carnal curiosity". His women-related pamphlets, although a sustained attack on Victorian sexual codes and the institution of marriage, had not attracted the attention of the censor. In January 1895, although dated 1894, he released a further pamphlet, *Homogenic Love and its Place in a Free Society*.[1] Its title demonstrated his characteristic shrewdness, in coining a new word *homogenic*. Derived entirely from the Greek, and therefore linguistically purer than homosexual, his intention was to remove undue stress on the physical side of this love. For the same reason, he will occasionally use the noun *homophile*.

These were dangerous times in which to lay down such a provocative challenge. In 1889, there had been a widely-publicised scandal surrounding a male brothel in Cleveland Street, off Tottenham Court Road in the West End of London. During an investigation into a theft at the Central Telegraph Office, a delivery boy was found in possession of a large sum of money. When

---

1   Edward Carpenter, *Homogenic Love and Its Place in a Free Society*, (Manchester Labour Press Society, 1894).

questioned, he said that he had been given it for "going to bed with gentlemen". Soon other boys were implicated and began naming prominent persons as clients of the brothel. As well as members of Parliament, Lord Arthur Somerset, a superintendent of the Royal stables, was implicated, and it was hinted that Prince Eddy, son of the Prince of Wales, was also a visitor. Other aristocrats, the Earl of Euston and Lord Arthur Clifton, were also named. Very quickly it developed into "the most elusive and mysterious affair of Queen Victoria's reign".[1]

Public alarm, stirred up by lurid newspaper accounts of this and other homosexual scandals, was not the only obstacle Carpenter faced. Coded, sometimes even explicit, homoerotic literature was being openly published at the time, with an efflorescence of poetry and prose associated with the Uranian school of poets: a close-knit group of individuals who shared an idealisation of pre-pubescent or adolescent boys, and whose verse and prose, full of literary artifice, was a cover for either sexless devotion or homosexual passion. "They wrote to sublimate their love, not to display their talents; for each other's entertainment, not for the public ear. If they could fool the world by supressing the sex of their beloved and so earn a few pennies from publishing their verse, they did so…"[2]

In 1892, John Gambril Nicholson[3] published *Love in Earnest*, a collection of sonnets, ballads and lyrics in which the sex of the love object was not disclosed but the heavily paederastic collection was a word play on the Christian name of a boy at a school where Nicholson was an assistant master. Other writers or artists of the day who were fixated on young boys or youths included Symonds's literary executor and close friend Horatio

1   Colin Simpson, *The Cleveland Street Affair*, (Weidenfeld and Nicholson, 1977), p. 3.
2   Timothy d'Arch Smith, *Love in Earnest*, (Routledge and Keegan Paul, 1970), p. xxii.
3   John Gambril Nicholson (1866-1931), English schoolmaster and quintessential Uranian poet.

Forbes Brown, William Johnson Corry, Ernest Dowson, Charles Masson Fox, and Charles Keynes-Jackson, who wrote a sonnet on a picture of Falmouth fisher-boys painted by boy-lover, Henry Scott Tuke, the son of Dr Daniel Hack Tuke. Frederick Rolfe (Baron Corvo), sent Fox photographs of naked Italian youths, together with long graphic descriptions of his love-making with compliant boys picked up in the slums of Venice.

The following year, a five guinea, highly explicit erotic novel of homosexual love, *Teleny or The Reverse of the Medal* appeared.[4] It carried no author's name, but Oscar Wilde was immediately thought to have had some part in its composition. In 1894, a new literary periodical, *The Yellow Book,*[5] was launched, with a distinctive binding and decoration by Aubrey Beardsley, whose androgynous illustrations were denounced by the prominent art critic Harry Quilter as perverted, for depicting manhood and womanhood mingled together "in a monstrous sexless amalgam".[6] The periodical was viewed with suspicion as the new trumpet-piece of the Decadents.[7] Its opening editorial proclaimed that it "would have the courage of its modernness, and not tremble at the frown of Mrs Grundy". During its three years of life, discreetly homosexual individuals, including Henry James and Edmund Gosse, contributed, but it also drew in others, such as Arnold Bennett and W B Yeats, who gave the journal an air of respectability.

---

4   *Teleny or the Reverse of the Medal*: A physiological romance of today, (Cosmopoli, 1893).
5   *The Yellow Book*: an illustrated quarterly, 1894-97, (Elkin Mathews and John Lane).
6   Richard Davenport-Hines, *Death and Punishment: attitudes to sex and sexuality in Britain since the Renaissance, (*Collins, *1990),* p. 126.
7   Seen as a transitional period between romanticism and modernism. Originating in France, in England it was chiefly applied to those associated with the Yellow Book.

In the same year, a scandalising novel, *The Green Carnation*,[8] was published anonymously in London. On the opening night of Oscar Wilde's first society comedy, *Lady Windermere's Fan, a* dozen young men had sported a carnation dyed green, already a symbol of homosexuality in Paris. It was well-known in homosexual circles that the author of the novel was Robert Hitchens, a friend of Lord Alfred Douglas[9] and on the fringes of the Wilde circle. Its principal character was seen as a thinly-disguised portrait of Wilde, which satirised him, "just within the laws of libel".[10] Its depiction of a network of men corrupting boys gave it the appearance of a manifesto for sodomites.

The novel appeared when a growing storm of scandal was beginning to swirl around Wilde and Lord Alfred Douglas. Wilde was incensed enough to write to the Pall Mall Gazette,[11] "to contradict, in the most emphatic manner" the suggestion that he was the author. It seems that he could not bear to think that such a mediocre piece of literature could be attributed to him. Vanity blinded him to the obvious danger of drawing attention to himself, ensuring that his name became more widely associated with the book.

Also in 1894, John Francis Bloxam, an Oxford undergraduate, produced a magazine, *The Chameleon*,[12] in which the subterranean theme was boy-love. The very first issue included a scandalising pederastic story, *The Priest and the Acolyte*,[13] written by Bloxam. It also carried a collection of epigrams by Wilde, *Phrases and Philosophies for the Use of the*

8   Robert Hitchens, *The Green Carnation*, (Heinemann, 1894).
9   Lord Alfred Bruce Douglas, (1870-1945), Oscar Wilde's lover.
10   *The Green Carnation*, edited with an introduction by Stanley Weintraub, (University of Nebraska Press, 1970), p. viii.
11   Pall Mall Gazette, 2 October 1894.
12   *The Chameleon*, edited by John Francis Bloxam, (Gray and Bird, 1894).
13   John Francis Bloxam, *The Priest and the Acolyte*, privately printed for presentation only, 1894.

Young.[14] It will be cited by the Marquess of Queensberry's counsel during the libel action brought against him by Wilde, as evidence of Wilde's association with a publication "calculated to subvert morality and to encourage unnatural vice".[15] Wilde had also contributed to *The Spirit Lamp*,[16] another Oxford undergraduate periodical, of which a number of issues were edited by Alfred Douglas. It appealed to "all who are interested in modern life and the new culture": a number of pieces by Symonds appeared in this short-lived journal. *The Artist and Journal of Home Culture*,[17] edited by Kains-Jackson, was a similarly innocuous-sounding publication that carried a good deal of homoerotic poetry and fiction.

The greater visibility of individuals seen as sexually 'aberrant' which these publications reinforced, drew dire warnings of cultural collapse. Weeks before Wilde went on trial the *Weekly Sun* carried a front page review of a translation of Max Nordau's *Entartung (Degeneration)*.[18] It was a scathing attack on "Egomaniacs, Decadents and Aesthetes," as sexually perverted, mentally diseased, and a grave threat to social stability, Wilde being a particular object of Nordau's scorn. The paper cited the author's views as a warning against "the tendencies and perils of the age". The homosexual was a source of contagion and, when detected, should be confined. Nordau was an admirer of the Italian criminologist Cesare

---

14 Oscar Wilde, *Phrases and Philosophies for the Use of the Young*, (Gay and Bird, 1894).

15 The Marquess of Queensberry's trial opened on 3 April 1895. After Wilde's libel action was withdrawn, he faced two trials for 'gross indecency' under the 1885 Criminal Law Amendment Act.

16 *The Spirit Lamp*. Fifteen issues appeared between 1892-1893, (Oxford, James Thornton).

17 *The Artist and Journal of Home Culture* began publication in 1880 as *The Artist*, and assumed the new title a year later. After Kains-Jackson was replaced as editor in 1894, it reverted to its founding title, ceasing publication in 1902.

18 Max Simon Nordau (1849-1923), Hungarian physician and social critic.

Lombroso,[19] who also claimed that the homosexual was a source of contagion and should be confined from youth.

After Wilde was found guilty of gross indecency, three articles appeared in a single issue of the influential *Contemporary Review*. Sir Clifford Allbutt, in *Nervous Diseases and Modern Life*, warned that it was necessary to guard against "the encroachment of peoples of lower standards and lower ethical capacities upon the seats of nations"; J. A. Noble exposed *The Fiction of Sexuality*, and Harry Quilter attacked The *Gospel of Intensity*.[20]

Such was the government's concern that the Wilde trials had opened the public's eyes to the homosexual underworld, that there was an unsuccessful attempt to criminalise the publication of details of such depravity, lest they should encourage individuals to imitate the crime. But press freedom prevailed.[21]

For Carpenter to publish an unequivocal defence of homosexuality at such a time was more than daring, it was perilous. A respectable, and respected, individual now dared to write openly on the subject, with little encoding and with an intimacy that was not tantalizing. "No word or hint of impropriety ever sullied his page... The mystery, perhaps, lay in his tact, his charm and his cunning use of words".[22] His task was a daunting one: to reveal its full psychological and emotional dimensions, showing the homosexual to be an otherwise normal person and not a simple perpetrator of aberrant sexual acts.

His earlier pamphlets were aimed at freeing women from the bondage of the Victorian hearth and marriage bed. He

---

19 Cesare Lombroso (1835-1908), physician and criminologist who introduced the theory of criminal atavism.
20 *The Contemporary Review*, number 67, 1895.
21 See Brady, *Masculinity and Male Homosexuality in Britain*, pp. 147-148.
22 Noel Annan, *Our Age: Portrait of a Generation*, (Weidenfeld and Nicholson, 1990) p. 107.

now turned to attack the harsh legal and social edicts against same-sex love. He did not ask simply for tolerance for such a love, a plea that would become a central concern of sexual liberationists in the following century. He sought public recognition of the homosexual impulse as a natural, stable variant of human sexuality. As such, the pamphlet was, he later recalled, "among the first attempts in this country to deal at all publicly" with the issue of homosexuality.[23]

Running to over fifty pages, it was couched in everyday language and, unlike Symonds's restricted monographs, was aimed at the educated reader, not the medical and legal professions. But because the subject, as he said, was surrounded by "anathemas and execrations", he was well aware that the pamphlet would almost certainly be deemed obscene were it to come to the attention of the authorities. It was not sold but "sent round pretty freely to those who I thought would be interested in the subject or able to contribute views or information upon it".[24] Three months later the Oscar Wilde scandal broke.

With Symonds's *Greek Problem* clearly in mind, the pamphlet opens with a short historical survey of such attachments to be found in widely different cultures. This is tactical: to give the reader "some idea of the place and position in the world of the particular sentiment". [25] It sets an uplifting tone and prepares the ground for a discussion of the social function and value of what he calls "the homogenic attachment". A passing reference to its "healthiness" anticipates the strong attack to come on the idea of homosexuality as morbid.

He utilises important arguments from his *Sex-Love*

23   Edward Carpenter, *My Days and Dreams,* p. 195.
24   Ibid. p. 195.
25   Edward Carpenter, *Homogenic Love and its Place in a Free Society,* (Manchester Labour Press Society, 1894), p. 12.

pamphlet, especially his definition of love as, firstly, a search for union. Whatever a person's sexual orientation, all individuals have a need to love and to be loved. Individuals for whom such ties can only be found with a person of the same sex should not be denied the fulfilment of this need. Without "a close affectional tie of some kind his life is not complete, his powers are crippled, and his energies are inadequately spent".[26] Other important earlier arguments brought forward are the separation of procreative from non-procreative sex, the distinction between the spiritual and physical sides of love, and the damage to the individual's well-being of repressed sexuality.

The foremost claim, from which all other arguments are for Carpenter entailments, is that the homosexual orientation is an *innate* biologically-determined drive. But the study of homosexuality by physicians had begun from a general assumption of morbidity: leading to the dictum that the mere failure of the sexual instinct to propagate the species was itself pathological:

> It seems a strange oversight that science, to date, has taken little interest in this matter – a desire for corporeal intimacy of some kind between persons of the same sex existing in such force and so widely it would seem almost certain that there must be some physiological basis for the desire. Until we know more than we do at present as to what the basis may be, we are necessarily unable to understand the desire itself as well as we might wish.[27]

Without an understanding of the psychology of love, the inverted sex-feeling can no more be explained than can the normal impulse. The critical question then becomes, not

---

26   *Homogenic Love and its Place in a Free Society,* p. 43.
27   Ibid. p, 32.

whether the instinct is capable of "morbid and extravagant manifestation", but whether it is capable of "a healthy and sane expression."[28] The medico-scientific investigators, whose field of research was usually in great modern cities, and who drew their cases from prisons and mental asylums, were bound to meet with cases that *were* of a morbid character. It was no wonder that the idea of disease coloured their conclusions. But more recent studies had begun to dispel the view that the passion was always associated with "distinct disease, either physical or mental".[29] Carpenter foresaw a time when such terms would finally be abandoned as descriptive of the general sentiment of love towards a person of the same sex. He judged that the two physicians then at the forefront of the study of homosexuality in Europe, Richard Krafft-Ebing[30] and Herbert Moll,[31] were the least disposed to insist upon the theory of morbidity, although both noted a marked tendency in inverts to suffer from "nervous maladies". Carpenter knew from his own experience that a nervous temperament often inflicted the sexually-inverted, but this was more often not constitutional but the effect of an unhealthy repression of sexual feelings.

It was very important to insist that individuals who are homosexual do not differ from heterosexual men in any identifiable physical or mental particular. There is "no congenital malformation, no distinct disease of body or mind".[32] The attraction, both mentally and physically, to one of the same sex is "in a vast number of cases quite instinctive, twined in the very roots of individual life and practically

---

28 *Homogenic Love and its Place in a Free Society*, p. 3.
29 Ibid. p. 27.
30 Richard Krafft-Ebing, (1840-1902), Austro-German physician and author of the authoritative *Psychopathia Sexualis*.
31 Albert Moll, (1862-1902), German psychiatrist. Author of Die *Konträre Sexualempfindung* (Contrary Sexual Feeling).
32 *Homogenic Love*, p. 20.

ineradicable".[33] So deeply is it fixed in a person's mental and emotional life, that such an individual has difficulty in imagining himself being otherwise than he is: "[T]o him at least the homogenic love appears healthy and natural, and indeed necessary to the concretation of his individuality".[34] Emphasising the instinctive, congenital characteristic of homosexuality is critical in distinguishing born lovers of their own sex from persons who, out of curiosity or excessive sexual arousal, or from a lack of opportunities for heterosexual intercourse, adopt homosexual practices.

There is a further significant distinction to be made. During Wilde's trials, with his appeal to classical Greek literature and life, same-sex love will become identified with paedophilia, with a sexual desire for boys, thereby casting the homosexual as a corrupter of the innocent. Whilst never denying the existence of the paedophile, Carpenter aims to sever this connection by presenting the ascendant homosexual drive as a desire for adult sexual partners. His defence of a homosexuality which is exclusively *androphilic*, not in the least concerned with boys, was timely because even before Wilde the link with paedophilia was invariably made.

He then repeats one of his most provocative claims: that the expression of the sexual instinct should be detached from the act of procreation. There is far more in the physical intimacy between two individuals than the reproduction of the species, and this arbitrary limitation greatly influences the popular mind against any physical expression of same-sex love. He is a realist, recognising that to represent same-sex attachments as purely spiritual in nature will be regarded as disingenuous, but forthright enough to acknowledge that, for the homosexual, some degree of physical intimacy is as much a necessity, and a condition of healthy life and activity, as it is for

---

33   *Homogenic Love and its Place in a Free Society*. p. 18.
34   Ibid.

the heterosexual. It is hardly surprising that here he hedges, stressing that there is a tendency for this love to express itself more through the emotions, going as far as to suggest that in a large number of cases it is "not distinctly sexual at all".[35]

Having condoned same-sex physical relations, he had to deal with the difficult question of what degree of intimacy was "fitting and natural".[36] He could not avoid tackling head-on the association of physical intimacy between males with one form of sensuality only, sodomy, the most rigidly proscribed and denounced of all sexual practices. The latinate term, *venus aversa, contra naturum*, was often used to avoid naming it. During the Wilde trials, sodomy will become fixed in the public mind as the defining act of the male homosexual, for no other sexual act will be named. It was therefore essential to insist that any physical intimacy between two persons of the same sex should not be "set down as a sexual act of the crudest and grossest kind".[37] He points to Krafft-Ebing's finding that, whilst physical intimacy is desired, "the special act with which they are vulgarly credited is in most cases repugnant to them".[38]

As the title of the pamphlet indicates, his defence of the homogenic temperament goes beyond a plea for its recognition and acceptance as part of human sexuality. He takes forward the cultural arguments so dear to Symonds, extolling the moral value and social worth of such individuals. Some thirty pages of *Sexual Inversion*, provided by Symonds, will be devoted to accounts of individuals of exceptional intellectual and artistic abilities, showing the falsity of the claim that such individuals could not function normally as non-sexual beings. Freed from the responsibilities and impedimenta of family life, Carpenter argues, such

---

35 *Homogenic Love and its Place in a Free Society* p. 15.
36 Ibid. p. 14.
37 Ibid.
38 Ibid. p. 20.

individuals can "supply the force and liberate the energies required for social and mental activities of the most necessary kind", doubting whether "the higher heroic and spiritual life" of a nation is possible without the institutional sanctioning of this attachment. Just as the ordinary sex-love has a special function in the propagation of the race, "so the other love should have its special function in social and heroic work, and in the generation – not of bodily children – but of those children of the mind, the philosophical conceptions and ideals which transform our lives and those of society".[39]

And the advance of women also required a fuller recognition of the place of the homogenic sentiment in their emotional and sexual lives:

> It is noticeable, too, in the deepest relation to politics that the movement among women towards their own liberation and emancipation which is taking place all over the civilised world has been accompanied by a marked development of the homogenic passion among the female sex... such comrade-alliances – and of a quite passionate kind – are becoming increasingly common, and especially perhaps among the more cultured classes of women, who are working out the great cause of their sex's liberation...[40]

In recognising the cultural importance of the homogenic attachment, he invokes Whitman in arguing that comradeship, at this juncture in history, had "the deepest relations to general politics"; a role in "the life-long building up of new forms of society, new orders of thought, and new institutions of human solidarity".[41]

The pamphlet concludes with a call for the ending of the prosecution under the 1885 Criminal Law Amendment Act

---

39 *Homogenic Love and its Place in a Free Society* pp. 42-44.
40 Ibid. p. 48.
41 Ibid. p. 44. Discussed more fully in chapter 10.

of male homosexual acts that take place in private. In the face of growing evidence that the homosexual orientation was an innate drive, not an acquired perversion, it was unjust to legislate against a natural inclination, which no amount of compulsion could change:

> If the dedication of love were a matter of mere choice or whim, it still would not be the business of the State to compel that choice but since no amount of compulsion can ever change the homogenic instinct in a person, where it is innate, the State in trying to effect such a change is only kicking vainly against the pricks of its own advantage, and trying, in view perhaps of the conduct of a licentious few, to cripple and damage a respectable and valuable class of its own citizens.[42]

Law could not control the expression of feeling, and in employing the clumsy bludgeon of the statute book to criminalise homosexual acts between consenting adults in private, the government was acting as a moral censor; adjudicating upon conduct that was properly a personal choice. This was not the law's province, and even were it its province, such a law could not possibly be enforced. In particular, because it did not require such private acts to be witnessed, it had opened wider than before the door to the blackmailer.

> That the homosexual passion may be improperly indulged in, that it may lead, like the heterosexual, to public abuses of liberty and decency we of course do not deny; but, as in the case of persons of opposite sex, the law limits itself on the whole to the maintenance of public order, the

---

42 *Homogenic Love and its Place in a Free Society*, p. 51.

protection of the weak from violence and insult, and of the young from their inexperience: so it should be here.[43]

The quality of the arguments in the pamphlet was recognised by Ellis, who sent a copy to Horatio Brown.[44] Writing from Venice, Brown was fulsome in his praise for the special talents of its author:

> I should like to tell you with what admiration, sympathy & enthusiasm I have read it. It is in this cool, quiet, convincing, scientific way that I think this difficult &, at present obscure problem should be brought to the notice of an ignorant and hostile society. At present I am rather afraid of the effect upon the world if the polemic is confined to the region of belles lettres. I ought to say it more simply; I mean that I think we want a cool, unimpassioned statement of the situation & that Doctors & Lawyers must be induced to take off their spectacles and look.[45]

Brown's assessment of the pamphlet was accurate. Carpenter had shown himself to be a shrewd tactician, craftily weighing and measuring his words. It is the work of a subtle persuader, a rhetorical questioner gently mocking the bigoted and the erroneous. His method is one of collusion with his readers, with their empathy and their reasonableness. Euphemisms are discarded and there is an absence of the special pleading that is occasionally found in Symonds's *Modern Problem*.

Brown asked for copies of the essay: "I want to send it to many unconvinced – also to some who need no convincing

---

43   *Homogenic Love and its Place in a Free Society,* p. 50.
44   Horatio Forbes Brown (1854-1926), historian, life-long friend of Symonds and his literary executor.
45   Brown to Carpenter, 14 February 1895, SA MS 386/52.

but who would be drawn towards the writer of this calm statement of an observed case".[46] Carpenter obliged by sending six copies to Venice, but not all his friends were as enthusiastic as Brown. The closeted Goldsworthy Lowes Dickinson[47] ruminated: "I suppose it is all in order, though I have a kind of feeling that these things are better left unsaid. Perhaps it is just because science has a way of treating these things as phenomena merely, that I think they should not be printed".[48] But he clearly admired Carpenter for his bravery in daring to write such a pamphlet: "How it is that public opinion hasn't managed to get him into prison and murder him, is a mystery to me. We must be thankful for small mercies!"[49]

It was reviewed in *Humanity*, the journal of the Humanitarian League, edited by Carpenter's friend Henry Salt. His first three pamphlets had dealt with "the most difficult and delicate questions" and deserved to be even more widely known. But it was right that the homogenic love pamphlet was privately circulated, "since anything which may be said on the subject is likely to be misunderstood at the present time", no doubt a reference to the Wilde trials. The reviewer regretted that, "through dread of public opinion", English scientific men were silent on the subject.[50] Ellis's *Sexual inversion* had yet to see the light of day.

---

46 Brown to Carpenter, 14 February 1894, SA MS 386/52.
47 Goldsworthy Lowes Dickinson (1862-1932), political scientist.
48 Dennis Proctor, ed. *The Autobiography of Goldsworthy Lowes Dickinson and Other Unpublished Writings*, (Duckworth 1973), p. 104.
49 Ibid. p. 157.
50 *Humanity*, vol. 1, April 1895.

A Literary Inquisition

Encouraged by the success of the pamphlets, Carpenter put them together, added new material, and got a book ready. The rigidity of public opinion towards sexual matters, "the absolute determination of people to *misunderstand* if they possibly could", meant that nearly every chapter was rewritten four or five times over before he was satisfied with it.[1] The book was to be called *The Sexes in a Free Society*.

He sounded out the publisher Fisher Unwin, whose titles now included the third edition of *Towards Democracy*. The quite progressive Unwin agreed to publish the book at his own expense, but only a few weeks later, as Carpenter was fond of saying, the bottom dropped out of his little bucket. On 26 April 1895, the libel action brought by Oscar Wilde against the Marquess of Queensberry collapsed, after Wilde's counsel learned of the witnesses Queensberry intended to call in his plea of justification: young men who had prostituted themselves with Wilde. But Queensberry was determined that Wilde should face a criminal trial and instructed his solicitor to send the youths' incriminating statements, and a copy of the court shorthand notes, to the Director of Public Prosecutions.

A warrant for Wilde's arrest, for 'committing acts of gross indecency with other male persons', was granted by Sir John

---

1   Edward Carpenter, *My Days and Dreams*, (Charles Scribner's Sons, 1916), p. 197.

Bridge at Bow Street Magistrates Court. According to some accounts, Bridge, possibly to avoid another sensational trial in which the sexual peccadilloes of persons in high places might well be revealed, dated the warrant for a quarter of an hour after the departure of the last continental boat-train from Dover. It gave Wilde time to flee, but he ignored his friends' entreaties and retired to the Cadogan Hotel, a stone's throw from his Knightsbridge home, where he remained, fortified by copious alcohol and cigarettes.

His arrest set alarm bells ringing in homosexual circles. For some, prudence was the order of the day. Frank Harris, Wilde's erstwhile friend and biographer, described, surely tongue-in-cheek, its effect on those who feared that the trial would lay bare London's homosexual *demi-monde* and draw others into the net closing around Wilde:

> Every train to Dover was crowded, every steamer to Calais thronged with members of the aristocratic and leisured classes, who seemed to prefer Paris or even Nice out of season, to a city like London, where the police might act with such unexpected vigour … They had imagined that in 'the home of liberty' such practices passed unnoticed.[2]

Wilde had incensed his detractors during the libel trial by detaching art from morality and the writers of newspaper editorials were quick to make a connection between 'aesthetes' and sexual deviancy: when the cross-examination moved to the dim-lit, perfumed rooms where the poet of the beautiful joined with valets and grooms "in the bond of the silver cigarette case".[3] Wilde was in the habit of bestowing such a gift on his lovers; its quality seemingly determined by the

---

2   Frank Harris, *Oscar Wilde, His Life and Confessions*, (Covici, Friede, 1930), p. 171.
3   *Evening News*, 5 April 1895.

social status of the receiver. The Westminster Gazette attacked him for fastening art to "the immoral the morbid and the maniacal", branding him a hypocrite whose elevated boasting hid a degraded personal life.[4]

The two criminal trials (the first ended in an inconclusive verdict), proved to be pure gold for august and lurid publications alike. The sexual scandals in the eighties and early nineties involving establishment figures had fed the public's voyeuristic appetite. As the tale of Wilde's cuckoldry with working-class youths unfolded, something akin to rejoicing gripped the self-appointed guardians of public decency. The guilty verdict, and the imposition of the maximum sentence of two years' imprisonment with hard labour, was widely applauded by the English press. *The Daily Telegraph* lauded the outcome as a stern rebuke to "the artistic tendencies" of the time:

> We have had enough, and more than enough of Mr Oscar Wilde, who has been the means of inflicting upon public patience during the recent episode as much moral damage of the most offensive and repulsive kind as any single individual could well cause.[5]

And the *National Observer* trumpeted:

> There is not a man or woman in the English-speaking world possessed of the treasure of a wholesome mind who is not under a deep debt of gratitude to the Marquess of Queensberry for destroying the High Priest of the Decadents.[6]

---

4   *Westminster Gazette*, 6 April 1895.
5   *Daily Telegraph*, 6 April 1895.
6   *National Observer*, 6 April 1895.

Given the stigma attached to Wilde's behaviour, to defend him would have been social suicide. Even an attempt to save his reputation by distinguishing the man from his work would be equally fraught with the danger of guilt by association. Those who were brave enough to speak out confined themselves to questioning whether, after the widely publicised libel case and inconclusive first criminal trial, Wilde could ever have received a fair hearing; or in drawing attention to the disparity between the punishment meted out to Wilde and men who corrupted girls. Ironically, one individual who drew such a distinction was William Stead, the man responsible for precipitating the furore that led to the passing of the 1885 Criminal Law Amendment Act. Stead attacked the double-standard that condemned Wilde but ignored the sexual exploitation of young girls and women by unscrupulous men:

If Wilde, instead of indulging in dirty tricks of indecent familiarity with boys and men, had ruined the lives of half a dozen innocent simpletons of girls, or had broken up the home of his friend by corrupting his friend's wife, no one could have laid a finger upon him. The male is sacrosanct: the female is fair game. To have burdened society with a dozen bastards, to have destroyed a happy home by his lawless lust – of these things the criminal law takes no account. But let him act indecently to a young rascal who is very well able to take care of himself... then judges can hardly contain themselves from indignation when inflicting the maximum sentence the law allows... If all persons guilty of Oscar Wilde's offences were to be clapped into goal, there would be a very surprising exodus from Eton and Harrow, Rugby and Winchester, to Pentonville and Holloway.[7]

_____

7   *Review of Reviews*, 15 June 1895.

Although Carpenter believed that Wilde was foolish to respond to Queensberry's goading, when notices for his *The Importance of Being Earnest* were removed from theatre billboards, in an anonymous letter to the *Star*, he insisted that, when passing judgement on sexual behaviour, a clear distinction had to be drawn between law and morality. He also penned a piece for the anarchist journal *Freedom*, criticising the 1885 Act for licencing blackmail, and defended the purity of homosexual relationships.[8] Emboldened, he also asked Stead if he would take the *Homogenic Love* pamphlet for the *Review of Reviews,* but Stead considered that its defence of male relationships was too overtly sexual. He made a further attempt to air the subject, telling Ellis: "I have sent a paper entitled 'An Unknown People' to the *Humanitarian*, which I think they may insert".[9] But the editor declined to print it, although the journal later carried a review of the other pamphlets, the writer declaring: "Believing as we do in the full and free discussion of questions which concern the moral, mental, physical and spiritual health of humanity, we are glad to extend a welcome to the efforts of this earnest and able seeker after truth".[10]

Wilde gave his counsel his word as a gentleman that there was no truth in the charges laid against him. He then proceeded to tell lie after lie. Once imprisoned, he sought a reduction of his sentence by cravenly describing his behaviour as a "form of sexual madness", and pleaded to have himself put under medical care in order that "the sexual insanity" from which he suffered might be cured. Other phrases which appeared in his petition were "monstrous sexual perversion" and "loathsome modes of erotomania".[11] But once released, he

8   Edward Carpenter, 'Some Recent Criminal Cases', *Freedom*, June 1895.
9   Carpenter to Havelock Ellis, 28 June 1895, HRC.
10   'Edward Carpenter's Tracts on Sex', *The Humanitarian*, 2 August 1895.
11   Rupert Hart-Davis, *The Letters of Oscar Wilde*, (Butler and Tanner, 1962), p. 414.

fled to the continent and returned to his old mania of chasing after boys.

His reckless stand against Queensberry, and the subsequent criminal trials, poisoned the public mind against homosexuality. However much he elevated same-sex love, his own behaviour fastened it to debauchery. His conviction was a labelling event: given the extensive coverage in the popular press, homosexuality became synonymous with decadence, although it is hardly the case that Wilde's personae, that of the "aesthete, dandy and campy witticist", became a model for generations of homosexual men.[12] For the majority, then and subsequently, a noisome odour always surrounded Wilde. His character was one to be escaped from, not emulated.

Wilde set, indelibly, in the public mind that homosexuality was male lust and nothing more. His appeal to the 'higher philosophy' never reached beyond the courtroom in which the 'Professor of Aesthetics' enunciated the creed. From the golden youths of his own class, he descended to consort with unrefined, uneducated, 'renters'. His unbridled sexual satiation destroyed any claim he might have had to be the defender of same-sex love. It also reinforced the deep-seated prejudice that homosexual behaviour was a socially destructive vice. For many, seeking sexual pleasure with those of inferior social status was an even greater offence; the mere association with such individuals being subversive of class hierarchy. And the aristocratic Douglas's predatory lusting after working-class boys was even stronger than Wilde's.

Carpenter, like Symonds, knew that it was important to separate love from lust; the 'homogenic impulse' from 'carnal curiosity'. They were committed to showing the normality of the homosexual orientation, but at every turn Wilde had kicked sand in their faces. Together with his fellow aesthetes

---

12   Donald E Hall, *Queer Theories*, (Palgrave Macmillan, 2002), p. 33.

and the Uranian poets (almost to an individual pederasts) he fixed in the public mind that homosexuality was about men corrupting boys. The insult 'oscarite' stuck.

Wilde's trial was the first of any prominent individual under the 1885 Act and was a pointer to the establishment's nervousness that he was not prosecuted for sodomy under the 1861 Offences against the Person Act, which carried a much harsher sentence of a maximum of ten years' imprisonment. The renters who were to bring Wilde down were unlikely to have agreed to testify had he been charged under the Act, which would have inevitably left them facing the same fate. Charlie Parker, one of Wilde's sexual partners, in his deposition to Queensberry's solicitor, made no mention of sodomy, but under questioning during the criminal trial he freely admitted that Wilde had sodomised him. Arraigning Wilde with what was a *misdemeanour* under the 1885 Act allowed his sexual partners to escape such a charge, in return for testifying for the prosecution. However, underlying this decision, the authorities must have feared that there might be a repeat of the Cleveland Street scandal of 1889, which had ensnared individuals at the very pinnacle of the social pyramid.

Then there was the decision not to prosecute Douglas. Letters in the National Archives indicate that this decision was made at the highest level: he was to be treated as a victim, corrupted by Wilde, against the clear evidence that he had willingly had sexual relations with several of the witnesses. Queensberry may have insisted that Douglas should not be prosecuted by threatening a bigger sensation involving senior members of the Liberal Government. Talk of a homosexual affair between his eldest son, Lord Drumlanrig, and Lord Roseberry, the Prime Minister, was widespread, leading Queensberry to conduct a scarcely concealed vendetta against him.[13] Drumlanrig was killed in a

---

13   Neil McKenna, *The Secret Life of Oscar Wilde*, (Arrow, 2004), p. 376.

shooting incident in October 1894, which looked suspiciously like suicide. With so much potential scandal swirling around Wilde, containing its spread would have been a government priority.

As Carpenter expressed it, from the moment of Wilde's arrest "sheer panic prevailed over all questions of sex, and especially of course questions of the Intermediate Sex".[14] Although he had not intended to include the *Homogenic Love* pamphlet in his book, copies had circulated quite widely and caused some "fluttering and agitation" in the dovecotes of Fleet Street. When the pamphlet came to the attention of Fisher Unwin he got cold feet and wanted to back out of publishing the book:

> He wrote asking me for the HL pamphlet (which he had heard of) and when I saw him a day or two after, he wanted to wash his hands of me and all my works. Well he didn't say anything about TD (*Towards Democracy*) but about the others. I told him the others contained nothing about the HL subject, and that as for that subject, there was a panic about it in London just now, which would all pass away. However, he wouldn't listen and wanted me to cancel the agreement about the sex volume then and there. I refused to do that – but told him to reflect calmly on the whole matter and then write to me. He has not written yet, but of course it will be no good forcing him to publish if he does not want to. So you see the boycott has set in already. Isn't it a caution?[15]

In the end, Fisher Unwin cancelled the agreement. Even though a good part of the book, still with the proposed title, *The Sexes in A Free Society*, had already been typeset, he was

---

14   Edward Carpenter, *My Days and Dreams*, p. 196.
15   Carpenter to George Hukin, 31 July 1895, SA MS. 361/25.

so anxious to be rid of it that he readily cut his losses.[16] He went even further. Believing that it was dangerous to be the publisher of anything remotely sexual, in a final act of cleansing he turned out of his shop all remaining copies of *Towards Democracy*, which he had been selling for three years, and told Carpenter that he could not continue as his publisher: "There seems to be a perfect panic on the subject in London and you have to take your life in your hands if you broach it… I think they are all going out of their senses". But he remained determined: "We have to push on, and shall win our way I scarcely doubt before long".[17]

He told Ellis:

I think there is no doubt that the H.L. pamphlet upset his apple cart, and I daresay he has heard talk going on at the clubs which alarmed him. I guess he will try to get other publishers to boycott me! I have removed stock of T.D. to the Labour Press Manchester, and am going to work through them in future; meanwhile we are trying to get a London house to work with us. Have you any suggestions in this line? I want to get a London publisher or agent to work with the L.P. [Labour Press] and then I would bring out T.D., the Sex-volume etc, through this channel. I hope you will get *your* arrangements fixed before long, (a reference to *Sexual Inversion*). How absurd it all is. It is very aggravating because it takes such a lot of time angling for these publishing fish and then playing them when hooked.[18]

He was determined to continue with the book, even though

---

16   This was the title of the work that Fisher Unwin was preparing for publication, not *Love's Coming of Age*, as incorrectly stated by Brady, in *Masculinity and Male Homosexuality in Britain,* p. 206. And, as it had not been published, it was not 'hastily withdrawn'.

17   Carpenter to Charles Oates, 26 August 1895, SA MS 351/4.

18   Carpenter to Havelock Ellis, 14 October 1895, HRC.

embarking on such a project whilst Wilde languished in jail was obviously hazardous. Publishers were now fearful of a literary inquisition, and to openly examine sex-relations struck at the heart of many Victorians' sense of decency; whilst to put into print anything remotely concerned with homosexuality might be the death of a respectable publisher. In January 1896, Carpenter was commiserating with Ellis over his, so far, unsuccessful attempts to find a publisher for *Sexual Inversion*:

> What a panic there still is on the subject! Sometimes one feels depressed about it all. It seems as if one had just got the coffin-lid up a little way, and then down it comes again with a bang! But I believe in continuous and sustained forward pressure. We shall appear above ground some day".[19]

Carpenter next offered the book to Swan Sonnenschein, which specialised in sociological and political subjects. It was turned down, although the company took it a decade later, by which time it was almost respectable. Five publishing houses declined *The Sexes in a Free Society,* before Bertram Dobell agreed to take the book, and to republish *Towards Democracy.* But in March Carpenter's plans were "further decomposed" by the bursting of yet another publisher's bomb:

> Bertram Dobell, after settling everything with me about the publication of my two books, has now suddenly had a panic about my Homogenic pamphlet – of which he has heard, evidently an exaggerated account; and wants to throw it all up. What an arch fiend I must be! I have written to pacify him, but I almost fear in vain – in which case I shall have fresh arrangements to make and fresh delays.[20]

19 Carpenter to Havelock Ellis, 15 January, 1896, HRC.
20 Carpenter to Charles Oates. 14 March 1896, SA MS 351/66.

Dobell refused to listen to the voice of the charmer. The "perfect panic" in London had finally reached all corners of the publishing world. There was no alternative but to shake the dust of London off his boots and fall back on the Manchester Labour Press Society. Unwin's 2000 or so unsold copies of *Towards Democracy* were shipped there, a new title page was inserted and it was reissued. He decided that anything with sex in the title would continue to scare off publishers and the title for the book was changed to the less provocative *Love's Coming of Age,* which was soon published by the Labour Press. At last, the first of his important sexual writings was out in book form, with the subtitle, 'A Series of Papers on the Relations of the Sexes'. [21]

It was ground-breaking: the first non-medical book published in England to explore the intricacies of gender, sexual, and marriage relationships. During his lifetime there would be twelve editions in England and seven in America, with French, German, Italian and Swedish translations. The Home Office's belated decision a decade later to consign this and other of Carpenter's sexual writings to the silence of the waste paper basket, rather than prosecuting him for obscene libel, seems to have been poor judgement. Such wide interest established him as a significant popular writer on sexuality, although initially the book made its way into the world, not through a host of welcoming reviews in established journals, but by word-of-mouth, largely within socialist and radical networks.

But the book was given a particularly warm reception in radical women's circles. Apart from its elegant and witty

---

21 The pamphlet *Sex Love* became two chapters, The *Sex-Passion* and *Man, The Ungrown*. The pamphlet *Woman* was also split into two parts, *Woman the Serf* and *Woman in Freedom*. The pamphlet, *Marriage* became *Marriage: A Retrospect* and *Marriage: A Forecast*. Two further chapters containing previously unpublished material, *The Free Society,* and *Some Remarks on the Early Star and Sex Worships* completed the book.

dissection of the bourgeois idea of masculinity and its marriage codes, together with its unqualified support for a new kind of womanhood, its frank presentation of sex as life-enhancing was a startlingly new outlook. The acerbic Henry Salt[22] unwisely claimed that he did not understand women, but reviewing the book for the *Labour Leader*, Lily Bell (Isobella Bream Pearce) praised him for having a deeper grasp than most men of the realities of women's lives, and for being one of the very few men who could "write acceptably on matters of sex", especially in relation to women:

> Most men write with such an air of superiority, such an assumption of masculine authority and right to lay down the law as to what women may or may not do, what may or may not be her 'proper' sphere in life, that I usually take up their articles merely to lay them down again with a feeling of impatience and irritation... I wish every man and woman in the country could give such books as this, a careful, thoughtful and earnest study.[23]

Olive Schreiner had earlier written from South Africa: "The marriage pamphlet has come. I think it splendid".[24] Ellis too, in his response to the pamphlet, had recognised Carpenter's special skill in dealing with sexual topics in a non-medical way: "I have read your Marriage paper with much satisfaction and, I think, like your argument, admiring the felicitous way in which you demolish the ordinary foolish quibbles, and also the calm and contemplative manner in which you view the whole proceedings".[25] Now he was equally impressed with the

---

22 Salt's wife Kate was lesbian, and a close friend of Carpenter's, which coloured his relationship with him.
23 Lily Bell, *The Labour Leader*, 27 June, 1896.
24 Olive Schreiner to Carpenter, 8 October 1894, SA MS 359/73.
25 Ellis to Carpenter, 22 January 1894, SA MS 357/6.

book: "I have been looking at *Love's Coming of Age,* though not yet had time to read it properly, I find it full of most beautiful things".[26] Ellis was about to attend a medical conference in Russia and Carpenter persuaded him to take a copy with him as a gift for Tolstoy, who admired Carpenter's views on science. It travelled across European borders sewn into the lining of Ellis's jacket, although he never had an opportunity to deliver it.

Edith Ellis was overjoyed by the dropping of his "sex bombs": "It has come and I've read it and I'm real proud of you. It is a downright fine piece of work and worthy of you. It is most stimulating and clear and makes a body glad you're alive".[27] Years later, she wrote that few people realised at the time that it was a "revolutionary" book. It held "such unconventional suggestions for experiment in new sexual ethical living that one may almost classify it with Karl Marx's *Capital*, which held similar suggestions in the economical field".[28] If Edith's comparison with Marx was somewhat overdone, there had certainly never before been such a forthright condemnation of Victorian sexual and marriage codes, combined with a frank and open celebration of physical love.

He was particularly pleased to receive Havelock's commendation: "It is selling pretty well – though no doubt it would be better if we had a London publisher. To give you an idea – the *Literary World* refuses to insert an advertisement for it on the ground that the title looks rather suggestive!"[29] He must have wondered what the response would have been had he retained the original intended title. Meanwhile, he was looking forward to seeing the final proofs of *Sexual Inversion*.

26   Ellis to Carpenter, 24 April 1896, SA MS 357/7.
27   Edith Ellis to Carpenter, 20 April 1896, SA MS 358/3.
28   Edith Ellis, *The New Horizon in Love and Life*, (A & C Black, 1921).
29   Carpenter to Havelock Ellis, 28 April 1896, HRC.

Although a chapter on homosexuality had not been included in *Love's Coming of Age*, Carpenter was still determined to find an opening for material that had not formed part of the *Homogenic Love* pamphlet. When the furore over the Wilde trials had quietened, he resurrected his *An Unknown People* paper and asked Ellis if he could suggest who might take it: "Any English magazine I suppose is hopeless; and in some ways I think I should prefer an American or International public".[30] He was surprised when it was accepted by an English magazine, the *Reformer*, a leading liberal periodical of the day. Its editorial stance was that all opinions were to be "freely admitted", as long as they were expressed "reasonably and in proper language". Carpenter was by now a consummate master of this art, well aware that he risked rejection if any provocative issues, such as the outright approval of same-sex physical intimacy or the call for the reform of the 1885 Criminal Law Amendment Act, were discussed in the piece.

When it appeared,[31] the publication of the first English edition of *Sexual Inversion,* although it was never intended to be a defence of homosexuality, was still some months away. The *Reformer* article, which was published in two parts, was the first such defence to appear in England in a prominent journal with a national circulation. It is this article, not the 1894 privately-circulated *Homogenic Love* pamphlet, that stands first in Carpenter's fully-public defence of the homosexual. Later that year, the publisher issued it as a pamphlet.[32]

Carpenter had two audiences in mind. Firstly, he wanted to gain the sympathetic understanding of the intelligent layman,

---

30   Carpenter to Havelock Ellis, 20 July 1896, HRC.
31   Edward Carpenter, *An Unknown People, The Reformer*, July/August 1897.
32   Edward Carpenter, *An Unknown People*, (A & H.B. Bonner, 1897).

pointing out that individuals with a homosexual orientation were not rare examples of a deviant sexuality but formed, if beneath the surface of society, a significant group. A frank and open discussion of their situation should not be avoided: society had a duty not only to understand them, "but to help them to understand themselves".[33]

> Anyone who realises what Love is, the dedication of the heart, so profound, so absorbing, so mysterious, so imperative, and always just in the noblest natures so strong, cannot fail to see how difficult, how tragic even, must often be the fate of those whose deepest feelings are destined from the earliest days to be a riddle and a stumbling-block, unexplained to themselves, passed over in silence by others. [34]

As this passage suggests, his second purpose was to give homosexuals a feeling of self-worth and well-being. It was bad enough that they suffered inwardly because of their sexuality, without also suffering from the refusal of society to recognise their existence or to give them help. It was especially hard for the young: the veil of complete silence drawn over the subject led to painful misunderstandings, and confusions of mind, with no recognition of "the solitary and really serious inner struggles they may have to face!"[35]

Some key ideas from the *Homogenic Love* pamphlet are repeated: in particular, the rejection of the morbidity thesis and support for the innateness of the homosexual orientation. Although, in *Homogenic Love,* sexual intimacies are freely admitted, the *Reformer* article avoids this issue, instead laying stress on the fact that such attachments are not necessarily

---

33 Edward Carpenter, *An Unknown People, The Reformer,* July/August 1897, p. 14.
34 Ibid. pp. 14-15.
35 Ibid. p. 17.

sexual, or connected with sexual acts. He knew that it was especially important to counteract the latter. To confuse homosexuals with libertines "having no law but curiosity in self-indulgence is to do them a great wrong".[36]

For the first time in the development of his ideas on the nature of the homosexual person, he advances the idea that homosexuals make up an *intermediate* sex. This takes it beyond the arguments found in the *Homogenic Love* pamphlet, and into a new area of controversy, dealt with in chapter ten.

In writing so prominently on human sexuality, Carpenter attracted hostility from many quarters, not least from some fellow-socialists. He was almost alone in his belief that changes in gender relationships and sexual attitudes and behaviour would form part of the transformative power of socialism. But the unfettered expression of the sexual instinct, presented as wholesome and life-enhancing, was greeted with misgivings. In particular, the idea that a woman's 'sex-relations' might not be purely a union for the birth of children was seen as dangerous to the cause. And, if the uncontrolled expression of female sexuality was a threat to social cohesion, for some, the condoning of homosexuality was beyond the pale.

When *Love's Coming of Age* appeared, George Bernard Shaw's wife despatched him to chastise Carpenter for associating socialism with "this sex nonsense." Although Shaw had not read the book, he dutifully undertook the mission. When he broached the subject by asking Carpenter why he had written it, he is said to have replied: "to liberate the emotions". Carpenter then asked Shaw why he wrote plays. According to Henry Salt, who was present, Shaw replied to the effect, "to think aloud. I don't mind being overheard. You're playing with fire Edward. You'll have to be undoing the harm you've done for the rest of your life. Now the socialists will be accused of

---

36   *An Unknown People*, p. 16.

believing in free love". But when Shaw read the book, he was "charmed" by it and wrote abjectly to Carpenter, apologising for his "disgraceful exhibition of bad manners".[37]

Robert Blatchford, editor of *The Clarion*, was typical in his response to sexual issues. He had taken offence when Carpenter sent him an essay on nudism: "Perhaps I'm a prejudiced old Tory but the whole subject is nasty to me". Blatchford was willing to accept that relations between the sexes were "all wrong now", but he felt that public prejudice was so strong on such matters, that if socialists were identified with radical sexual reform it would seriously impede their work: "[T]he sexual change will not concern us personally; but only concern the next generation…"[38] When the fourth, most homoerotic, most autobiographical part of *Towards Democracy* appeared in 1902, Blatchford, who had liked earlier parts, turned against it, complaining that Carpenter should not "effront us by echoes of Walt Whitman's lubberly frankness about sex".[39] Another of Carpenter's socialist friends, Bruce Glasier, also recorded that he found the "celebration of sexual sensation" difficult to stomach, strongly abhorring "orgiastic literature". [40]

37   Stephen Winsten, *Salt and His Circle*, (Hutchinson & Co, 1951), p. 111.
38   Robert Blatchford to Carpenter, 11 January 1894, SA MS 386/46.
39   Robert Blatchford, *The Clarion*, 19 December 1902.
40   Quoted by Tsuzuki Chushichi, in *Edward Carpenter, Prophet of Human Fellowship*, p. 143.

A Wicked, Scandalous
and Obscene Book

Carpenter took every opportunity to urge Ellis to continue with *Sexual Inversion*. After Symonds's death, Horatio Brown, now his literary executor, wrote to Carpenter promising to send him "letters of yours I find among Mr Symonds's papers. All his papers, letters, diaries etc., are in my possession... the mass is very great and the labour considerable".[1] He later sent Carpenter a number of these, which he passed on to Ellis. The book proposal had brought them closer than at any time during their friendship. He was now to become Ellis's principal point of reference on matters to do with homosexuality. From this time onwards, for over twenty years, they would regard each another as sounding boards; each able to ask the other's opinion and seek critical advice on work under preparation. They would loan each · other books, recommend books to each other, read drafts of each other's writing, advise each other on possible publishers, write reviews of each other's publications, and generally seek to advance each other's work. The Reading Room of the British Museum became their regular meeting place.

Early in 1894, Carpenter had begun advising him on the works on homosexuality that he should read, offering his own

---

1   Horatio Brown to Carpenter, 14 February 1895, SA MS 386/52.

careful analyses and evaluations of these books; providing him with more case histories, reading, at Ellis's invitation, his drafts, and suggesting changes. There is no indication in their papers or letters that Carpenter might have replaced Symonds as Ellis's collaborator. But the fact that he was now fully engaged in his own work on homosexuality, and at the time clearly more on top of the current literature than Ellis, gave him an important, not fully recognised, role in the book's gestation and progression. It is clear, from their written exchanges, that Ellis benefitted greatly from his guidance and advice, consolidated by their face-to-face meetings, which had begun at the very outset of the project with Symonds.

Typical of Carpenter's substantial input is the long letter he sent Ellis in January 1894. He singled out for his special attention the two books which were the most influential contemporary texts on homosexuality: the 1893 edition of Richard Krafft-Ebbing's *Psychopathia Sexualis*, and the 1894 edition of Albert Moll's *Di Conträre Sexualempfindung*. In his reviews, he is both complimentary and critical in his assessments. He commends Krafft-Ebing's development of the "psychiatric case-history" and his taxonomy of sexual-types based upon the detailed analysis of a large number of histories. Initially, most were of lower-class individuals found in the public asylums and clinics where Krafft–Ebing practised as a medical superintendent. But he also saw patients in sanatoriums and took private patients, which brought him into contact with a different class of homosexual. Many were educated individuals from the higher ranks of society, and after the publication of *Psychopathia Sexualis*, many men wrote to him with accounts of their sexual histories. These autobiographical narratives formed an indispensable component in the fashioning of sexual categories and the classification of sexual behaviour. For the first time, in any significant numbers, homosexuals spoke, and these self-analyses provided material for new psychiatric and physiological insights. If, as is often claimed, the 'homosexual' was a late nineteenth century social construction, then self-construction by such individuals was an essential element in the process.

A frequent assertion by many of these individuals was that they possessed perfect physical health and mental stability, and regarded themselves as being neither ill nor degenerate. But the basic premise of Krafft-Ebing's early work, which both Symonds and Carpenter strenuously contested, was the distinction drawn between pathological and healthy sexuality. 'Contrary sexual feeling', or 'inverted gender identity' (circumlocutory terms then used to describe a homosexual orientation) was placed in the first category. As his findings were, primarily, used by lawyers involved in the prosecution of sexual crimes, individuals whose non-procreative sexual acts were hitherto condemned as immoral and criminal were now to be stigmatised as pathological. The liberation from social condemnation and legal prosecution, which the scientific examination of human sexuality promised, was at the price of a new prejudice. In the final 1902 edition of the work, although greater emphasis was placed on its *congenital* form, Krafft-Ebing still insisted on the reality of *acquired* homosexuality, and of the role of masturbation in its aetiology.[2]

Knowing the authority that Krafft-Ebing's work carried, and its likely influence on Ellis, Carpenter urged him not to pursue this "too pathological a view", by regarding sexual inversion as a sign of "functional degeneration and (hereditary) nerve ailment". As he pointed out, by holding this position, Krafft-Ebing would have to allow that "whole races like the Dorian Greeks, of the healthiest type, must

---

2   When the World Health Organisation was established in 1948
    homosexuality was classified as a 'psychiatric disorder' and remained as
    such on British official lists until 1993.

have been, according to his theory, nervous weaklings!"[3] Like Symonds, he did not deny that being homosexual could lead to morbidity in individual cases, but this was a *consequence*, one linked to repressive social attitudes towards the homosexual. As for Moll, Carpenter considered that his findings were those of a man who lacked "authentic" experience outside "the resort of male prostitutes and pathics". Neither writer seemed able to envisage "a thoroughly healthy manifestation of inverted sexuality", even though this was very evident in many of the cases quoted by them. And, like Krafft-Ebing, Moll lacked a "wide and sane outlook over History and Ethnology".[4] The letter ends with a friendly caution to Ellis: "In the subject generally, as in so many others, the more facts one knows the more exceptions does one find to any rule given".[5]

Ellis was grateful to receive Carpenter's letter. He had been in "blissful ignorance" of the fact that there was a second edition of Moll's book: "Can you tell me if there is much new material in this second edition which I ought to read?... I should be glad to send you portions of my book... if you do not object, for criticism."[6]

In the same letter, Ellis gave a deftly compromising response to Carpenter's, and Symonds's, frequent insistence on the 'normality' of sexual inversion:

I shall make my cases the kernel of my book, insisting on the fact that they are none of them medical cases & shall simply argue, so far as I require, from the cases I present. I only recognise two classes – complete inversion and psychosexual hermaphroditism. I call these both 'abnormal' (in the sense in which genius and criminality

---

3   Carpenter to Havelock Ellis, 19 January 1894, HRC.
4   Ibid.
5   Ibid.
6   Ellis to Carpenter, 22 January 1894, SA MS 357/6.

are abnormal) which does not involve morbidity though it permits of more or less morbidity in any particular case. This is not quite your way of presenting the matter but I do not think it is a way to which you would seriously object.[7]

When Ellis tackled this issue in *Sexual Inversion*, he challenged the idea that what was abnormal was necessarily diseased, and was careful to use language that avoided any suggestion of pathology: "The study of the abnormal is perfectly distinct from the study of the morbid".[8] His natural inclination to avoid dogmatism was also evident when he dealt with the issue which most vexed Carpenter, and upon which his whole defence of the homosexual rested: whether homosexuality was innate or acquired. His own wife being, at least, bisexual, Ellis may have had difficulty in accepting fully that it was congenital and not a disordered orientation open to treatment. But, as always, science was the arbiter. He answered yes to both, by distinguishing between *real* sexual inversion and "situational homosexuality". Simply engaging in homosexual acts might be an acquired practice open to treatment (if an individual so desired) but, if sexual inversion did have a congenital origin, to try to cure it would be both futile and immoral. He was also at pains to eliminate the pejorative language of pathology from his writing, using words such as 'aberration' and 'deviation', but meaning simply a departure from the norm, and using the word 'abnormal' in a statistical sense to mean not the *average*. He would use 'perversion' to mean a preference for an abnormal form of sexual activity, whilst a 'deviant' was simply a person who deviated from the normal; in this case, sexual behaviour. And, if there was any sense in which the sexual invert could be said to be 'degenerate', it was only that he had "fallen away from the genus", as had, for example, a colour-

---

7   Ellis to Carpenter, 22 January 1894, SA MS 357/6..
8   Ellis, *Sexual Inversion*, p. 136.

blind person. It was, he said, a vague word, "little fitted for scientific use".[9] All such nouns, verbs and adjectives were to be employed in a non-pejorative, morally-neutral way. Writing by return, with further ideas and guidance on what had been added in Moll's second edition (he loaned Ellis his copy), Carpenter approved of his careful definitions: "I don't feel that any objection ought to be made to the use of the word 'abnormal' as you explain it".[10]

The mutual sympathy and admiration between them had grown steadily after the early days of the Fellowship of the New Life. Now their friendship was at its closest and most productive. Responding to Ellis's invitation, Carpenter offered to "look over any part of the book by way of criticism". He also asked for the Symonds's papers provided by Horatio Brown to be returned to him: "I will revise and perhaps amplify them. There are one or two points I know which want correction, and which I thought of writing to you about; and I may be able to get some further biographies".[11]

With London now galvanised by the Wilde trials, Carpenter saw danger ahead: "I'm afraid just now you will have difficulty in finding a publisher", he commiserated, but steeled Ellis against giving up the project: "It is a difficult campaign, but by going on slowly twill all come right perhaps". Some in Ellis's circle were advocating abandonment of the book but, in combative mood, Carpenter was "glad to hear there is strong opposition to it in some quarters as that is always satisfactory".[12] Ellis could even be of some help to the beleaguered Wilde: "As you are seeing friends of O. W's you are perhaps putting Sir Ed Clarke (Wilde's leading counsel) in the way of some of the scientific literature – I think he ought to be introduced in that

---

9   *Sexual Inversion.* pp. 136-7.
10   Carpenter to Ellis, 25 January 1894, HRC.
11   Ibid.
12   Carpenter to Ellis,19 April 1895, HRC.

direction".[13] But at the time, Carpenter would not have known of the scurrilous content of the Marquess of Queensberry's plea of justification.

In June Ellis sent him the completed manuscript, which elicited further encouragement: "It is too silly about the publishers: but I think things will improve before long. I find all this stir has roused up the Urning community here & pulled it together a good deal".[14]

Ellis first offered the book to Williams and Norgate, a publishing house with a history of promoting scientific works, but it was rejected by its reader, who happened to be his friend Dr Daniel Hack Tuke. Tuke advised the publisher that, although the book was a specialist work aimed at the scientific community, given its subject matter, it would be impossible to confine its circulation to such a readership, and there was a risk that it would come to the attention of the authorities. It was Tuke who made the memorable remark: "There are always the compositors".[15] As a physician, he shared the profession's aversion to the subject, but also, as a Quaker, he did not favour the ventilation of sexual matters in public, and "could not possibly view sympathetically any detailed approach to the problems of sex".[16] Moreover, his advice to the publisher was likely to have been influenced by more personal considerations, as his son, the painter Henry Scott Tuke, was well-known for his interest in boys. He had also been a close friend of Symonds's father and inclined to protect his memory. Later, as editor of the *Journal of Mental Science*, he will publish an anonymous critical review of the German edition, which may well have come from his own pen.[17]

---

13 Carpenter to Ellis, 19 April 1895, (HRC).
14 Carpenter to Ellis, 28 June 1895, (HRC). 'Urning' was a term for homosexual.
15 Havelock Ellis, *My Life*, p. 297.
16 Ibid. p. 296.
17 Journal of Medical Science, no. 43, 1897.

The atmosphere prevailing in the wake of the Wilde scandal had probably extinguished any hope that a leading English publishing house would be prepared to risk prosecution by issuing a work that questioned the criminalisation of male homosexual relations conducted in private. After Williams and Norgate declined to take the book, Carpenter offered to get up a fund, if Ellis decided to publish the book at his own expense. Frustrated, although he very much wanted the book to appear first in England, he did not take up Carpenter's offer. Instead, he asked his friend Dr Hans Kurella, a distinguished physician and anthropologist, if he would prepare a German translation. The decision to publish abroad was entirely strategic, and given the substantial work on sexual inversion that had already been published in Germany, Ellis told Carpenter "it isn't required", although he hoped it might pave the way for an English edition.[18] Because of the greater acceptability there of publications on sexual subjects, and Germany being the home of a number of pioneers on whom Ellis would have wanted to make an impression, it did make sense to have it issued initially there. Kurella had already made translations of Ellis's *Man and Woman* and *The Criminal*. The Leipzig publisher, Wigand, issued it with the title, not altogether pleasing to Ellis, of *Das Konträre Geschlechtsgefül* (Contrary Sexual Feeling), with both Ellis's and Symonds's names on the title page. Its appearance there caused little stir.

Carpenter was fulsome in his praise: "Well done! …it will make a sensation when that comes out in England – there will be silence in heaven for half an hour". But for the English edition, he advised Ellis that he should remove an appendix by Symonds on soldier love (*Soldatenliebe*) for being affected with "erotic sentimentality". "[All] that about the odour of soldiers & sailors, grooms and jockeys, & the attraction of uniforms,

---

18   Ellis to Carpenter, 24 April 1896, SA MS 357/7.

& is dwelt on too much in detail – and has a rather absurd effect…They would have a queer effect on Symonds's fame and name, and I think would raise a lot of prejudice against him and against the book – without having anything in them worth the sacrifice".[19] In addition to removing other material found in the German edition, Ellis also revised the order of content.

Still looking for an English publisher, Ellis heard through a friend that a certain J Astor Singer, "a man of some wealth… interested in scientific and philosophical subjects" was setting up a small publishing house "for the unostentatious issue of a few such works". His agent in London was his brother-in-law, Dr Roland de Villiers, and an agreement to publish Ellis's book was "speedily and easily arranged".[20] But, unbeknown to Ellis, de Villiers was a swindler who had fled from Germany, where he had been sentenced to twelve months' hard labour for forgery and other offences. 'J Astor Singer' was a figment of his imagination, as were the names of his publishing companies. As Ellis had wished, it was "issued quietly" under the fictitious trade name of 'Wilson and Macmillan'.[21] Its publication was only announced in prospectuses posted to doctors and lawyers, and it was sent for review to a few medical and scientific journals.

Before the book could, in Carpenter's words, "silence heaven", it was silenced from another quarter. From Venice, Symonds's literary editor, Horatio Brown, had all along offered encouragement to Ellis. In the spring of 1894, Ellis had stayed with him, when Brown helped with providing case histories, including his own. He later read parts of the manuscript, which he admired for "its calmness" and "judicial

---

19 Carpenter to Ellis, 2 December 1896, HRC.
20 Havelock Ellis, *My Life*, p. 297.
21 Havelock Ellis and John Addington Symonds, *Studies in the Psychology of Sex*, vol. 1, *Sexual Inversion*, (Wilson and Macmillan, 1897).

unbiased tone", adding, "And if anything can persuade people to look the question in the face this should".[22] But Brown came back in London very soon after the book was out, to find that a number of Symonds's influential close family friends had seen the German edition and advised suppression of his involvement with the work, believing that it would be injurious to his reputation and damage the family.

Brown was asked to halt distribution of the book, in order that Symonds's name could be removed from the title page and any material in the volume directly attributed to him taken out. A small number of copies had already been distributed but Brown bought up the remainder and had them destroyed. This first English edition was therefore never in general circulation.

Brown had been caught between two stalls. On learning of what had happened, Carpenter grumbled that there would be "no trace of him left. Isn't it too silly – and a sheer betrayal of J.A.S?".[23] He wrote a letter of protest to Brown, who, in response, pleaded that he had been torn between loyalty to Symonds and respect for his family's wishes. The family's request had caused him "great difficulty", and he resented the charge of acting unfairly to Symonds, pointing out that his place in "the history of the controversy", was recorded in the German edition, "which contains all he had to say, and more than Mr Ellis was prepared to publish in English".[24]

J.A.S. had all this matter by him for years, most of it, in print; the problem in Greek Ethics was finished & published (this was done privately) more than ten years before his death and yet he never published it; never even put his name to the few copies he printed – this proves to me that he had at least grave doubts about publishing...

---

22   Brown to Ellis, 8 August 1895, HRC.
23   Carpenter to Kate Salt, 31 August 1897, SA MS 354/49.
24   Brown to Carpenter, 21 November 1897, SA MS 386/76.

and I don't feel sure that he would have faced the inevitable anxiety and possible pain to his family.

You probably do not know that the very last words he wrote, when he was past speech, and within a few hours of death, were a strong injunction to me to regard his family in all matters of publication. An appeal from one of his family; the strongly expressed opinion of his oldest and most intimate friends when I got to London, the best legal & medical opinion I could obtain, all combined to take the step I did: and though I may not have done quite what he would have liked (but did not do) I think I have done what he would have done in the circumstances.[25]

As we have seen, Symonds had certainly agonised over whether to publish any of his sexual writings: first being bold in his determination to do so and then drawing back when he thought about the likely consequences for his and his family's reputation. Knowing at first-hand how Symonds had wavered, Brown's action was, on balance, justified. Carpenter, when he protested to Ellis "And what has he to do with the matter?",[26] was unaware of how close Brown was to Symonds, who had taught him over twenty years earlier when he was a sixth-former at Clifton College.

The German edition had included a fair amount of Symonds's material that was not used in the English edition, being, in Ellis's view, "of minor importance". The most substantial pieces attributed to him consisted of three appendices: the whole of his monograph *A Problem in Greek Ethics* (which they had agreed would merit a chapter); *Ulrichs' Views*, a chapter taken from the *Modern Problem*; *Notes on the Concubinus*, the practice of aristocratic young men permitted to consort sexually with slaves in ancient Rome, and *Letter*

---

25 Brown to Carpenter, 21 November 1897, SA MS 386/76.
26 Carpenter to Ellis, 2 July 1897, HRC.

from Professor X (one sent to Symonds by James Mills Pierce, a Harvard professor of mathematics, arguing that homosexuality was normal and not immoral). In the main text, there were four brief references to Symonds, together with ten footnotes. As we have already noted, without a close comparative analysis, it is not possible to identify what Ellis, if at all, took from the *Modern Problem* and wove seamlessly into the text.

He acknowledged that the finished result was not what his collaborator had wished for. It was "somewhat more shapeless than it was planned to be, and Mr. Symonds's part in it, which would otherwise have been fitted into the body of the book, mostly appears as fragmentary appendices".[27] Unsurprisingly, he added that he did not think the essay on Greek homosexuality threw "any great light on sexual inversion as a congenital psychic abnormality…"[28] Of course, strictly speaking, this was true, but it should be repeated that Symonds would never have agreed that ethnography had nothing to contribute to the understanding of homosexuality. It was not sufficient to show that congenital homosexuality was not a perversion. He had wanted, as Ellis clearly understood, a unified work which synthesised scientific, ethnographic and historical material. He saw this as a critical part of the case for legal reform; deeper than Ellis's purely utilitarian arguments. Without the contribution that he had anticipated making, it was not a comprehensive account of homosexuality. Such a treatment would have been innovative, and further, distinguished it from the work of continental writers. It could have educated the general public and better challenged the existing law governing male-on-male sexual relations.

With minimal editing, and no significant rewriting, Ellis was easily able to remove all traces of Symonds and produce

---

27   Ivan Crozier, *Sexual Inversion: A Critical Edition*, p. 93.
28   Ibid. p. 93.

a new English edition. Having recast the work, he told Carpenter: "In some ways the change will be an improvement, and it certainly renders it safe from attacks of all kinds"[29], an assumption that would soon be blown out of the water. As no other leading London publisher could be found to take the book, Ellis, seemingly still unaware that de Villers was a crook, again turned to him. He was assured that the book would be republished in Leipzig, but an expensive linotype printing plant had been built at Watford, and it was published there, using a second fictitious trade name, 'Watford University Press'.[30] When the new edition appeared, Carpenter congratulated Ellis:

> I think it so fine – one of the best things that you have done – clear and balanced – yet leading to definite conclusions… It is (I think) the best scientific treatment of the subject wh (sic) I have seen. And the character of your cases (their healthiness &c.) gives a special value to the book. I now feel that the subject has got a hearing and expression in England.[31]

But he did not challenge Ellis on what he had written about the physical expression of homosexual love.

The book had, again, been issued quietly, with notices posted to suitable recipients, mainly doctors and lawyers, and review copies sent to the medical and scientific journals. For six months it sold steadily, and one organisation that acquired copies was the Legitimation League, a radical society for the promotion of sexual reforms, including the legalising of illegitimate children. Promoting free love, it was also sympathetic to same-sex relationships, recognising

---

29 Ellis to Carpenter, 3 August 1897, SA MS 357/8.
30 Havelock Ellis, *Studies in the Psychology of Sex*, vol. 1, *Sexual Inversion*, (The University Press Limited, 1897).
31 Carpenter to Ellis, 27 November 1897, HRC.

"the absolute freedom of two individuals of full age, to enter into and conclude at will, any mutual relationships whatever, where no third person's interests are concerned".[32] The League had, for some time, been of interest to the police as an organisation with aims that threatened public morals, and as a haunt of subversives. John Sweeney,[33] an under-cover police officer posing as an anarchist, began attending meetings and won the confidence of its secretary, George Bedborough, who was also the editor of the League's journal *The Adult*, in which both Ellis and Carpenter had published. Bedborough was selling copies of the League's publications and various books, including *Sexual Inversion,* from the front room of his home. Sweeney purchased a copy, and later returned to reveal his true identity and arrest Bedborough on a charge of selling an obscene book.

A shocked Ellis was advised to obtain legal advice, but was not arrested, as the real objective of the police operation was not the prosecution of his book but the destruction of the Legitimation League. News of the impending prosecution quickly led to the setting up of a Free Press Defence Committee, to which leading literary figures of the day, George Bernard Shaw, Frank Harris, Walter Crane, Grant Allen, George Moore, Belfort Bax, and several others, including Carpenter, lent their names. But Ellis was angry that not a single member of the medical profession could be persuaded to join the committee. Shaw penned an indignant letter of support, complaining that the attempt to place an "authoritative scientific book" beyond the reach of those who could not read German, was "a masterpiece of police stupidity and magisterial ignorance".[34] Letters of support also

---

32   *The Adult,* vol. 1, May 1897.
33   Sweeney later wrote a book, *At Scotland Yard* (1905), in which he gave a colourful account of his infiltration of the League.
34   Dan H Laurence, ed. *Bernard Shaw – Collected Letters*, (Max Reinhardt, 1972), pp. 57-8.

came from distinguished American and European psychologists and physicians. The translator of the German edition, Hans Kurella, wrote: "the whole of scientific psychology and medicine on the Continent is on your side".[35]

For the authorities, anything published on the subject, whatever its scientific pretensions, would certainly be seen as an apologia for homosexuality. This was reinforced by the attitude of the medical profession: in England, not a single doctor of prominence supported it, and the leading medical journal, the *Lancet,* declined to review it. Ellis's mistake, it pontificated, was to allow a book containing such material to enter the everyday world, instead of going to a publishing house "able to take proper measures for introducing it as a scientific book to a scientific audience".[36] The public had to remain ignorant of this perversion, and any advance towards a wider understanding of it, quickly extinguished. For the clergy, it was anathema: William Inge, the Dean of St Paul's, allegedly threw his copy on the fire. More surprising was the reaction of women who were to be at the forefront of the fight for women to have control over their bodies. Marie Stopes likened reading it to "breathing a bag of soot", and Margaret Sanger, whose book on birth control was prosecuted in America, recoiled from the long accounts of homosexual indulgence found in the histories.[37]

The case was set down to be heard at the Central Criminal Court. Extracts from the long indictment vividly illustrate the horror of *unnatural* sex which informed the extraordinary drafting of the legislation:

George Bedborough being a person of wickedly depraved mind and disposition, and unlawfully and wickedly

---

35 Havelock Ellis, *A Note on the Bedborough Trial* (privately printed).
36 *Lancet*, 19 November 1897.
37 Recounted by Phyllis Grosskurth, in *Havelock Ellis*, a biography (Allen Lane, 1980), p. 187.

devising, contriving and intending to vitiate and corrupt the morals of the liege subjects of our said Lady the Queen, to debauch and poison the minds of divers of the liege subjects of our said Lady the Queen, and to raise and create in them lustful desires, and to bring the said liege subjects into a state of wickedness, lewdness and debauchery... unlawfully, wickedly, maliciously, scandalously, and wilfully, did publish, sell and utter, and cause and procure to be published, sold and uttered a certain lewd, wicked, bawdy, scandalous and obscene libel, in the form of a book entitled *Studies in the Psychology of Sex: Vol. 1. Sexual Inversion* by Havelock Ellis, in which said book are contained among other things, divers wicked, lewd, impure, scandalous and obscene libels, and matters, which said book is, pursuant to the provisions in that behalf, of the Law of Libel Amendment Act, 1888...

The Defence Committee briefed a brilliant young barrister, Horace Avory, to defend Bedborough on a plea of not guilty. He, unsuccessfully, sought to have the case heard in the High Court, on the ground that it was a scientific book that should be considered by a superior judge and jury. But he was unaware that the authorities were working behind the scenes to ensure that the book would never be ventilated in public.

In its defence, Ellis swore the following affidavit:

The said book was written by me as the result of many years' scientific study, investigation and observation and was written purely in the interests of science and scientific investigation and to the best of my ability in a scientific spirit. The said work is the first volume of a series of works which I am engaged in writing being studies in the psychology of sex. It deals with the subject of sexual abnormalities and in order to properly treat of these matters from a scientific point of view and to arrive at a conclusion with regard to the remedies for the practises dealt with (which frequently lead to crime disease and insanity) it has been necessary to instance cases which have actually occurred. The matter has been treated to the best of my ability in the least possible objectionable manner and with the sole object of elucidating the truth and arriving at a satisfactory conclusion as to remedial treatment. The general scope and objects of the book appears from the prefaces and also from the concluding chapter and I crave to refer to those portions of the book on those points.

He must have been advised by his counsel that he should stress the medical importance of the book, because he palpably contradicted two of its conclusions: that homosexuality was not a morbid condition but a congenital abnormality, and that, in such cases, no "remedial treatment" would be effective.

Before the case went to court, the police threatened to reveal embarrassing details about Bedborough's unorthodox family life, if he did not agree to plead guilty. If he co-operated, he was told, he would escape a prison sentence, which would be a satisfactory outcome for both sides; with no scandalising trial whilst Oscar Wilde remained incarcerated. It was sufficient that the book should be banned and the Legitimation League destroyed.

On the 31st of October 1897, Bedborough, who was also indicted on ten other counts connected with articles published in *The Adult,* duly pleaded guilty before the Recorder of London, Sir Charles Hall, who warned him:

So long as you do not touch this filthy work again with your hands and so long as you lead a respectable life, you will hear no more of this. But if you choose to go back to your evil ways, you will be brought up before me, and it will be my duty to send you to prison for a very long time.

He was fined £100 and bound over in his own recognizances.[38]

Except for the appearance of his name in the indictment, no mention was made of Ellis during the short hearing. As no charge of publishing an obscene libel had been brought against him, the book was never defended in open court. It may well be that, for Ellis, this was a price worth paying. He was disheartened to learn that none of his friends in the medical profession was prepared to go into the witness box to defend the book, but, with his extreme nervousness when faced with having to speak in public, he was also reluctant to do so. On the other side, the prosecution would have easily found individuals willing to speak against the book. It is difficult to see how Ellis's defence counsel could have defended the book without calling him as a principal witness, which might well have destroyed him. Under cross-examination, the veracity of his case-histories, on which the whole book was constructed, and where its 'obscenity' really lay, would have been pivotal. But, except for the cases of Carpenter, Symonds and Edith Ellis, he knew none of his respondents personally, and for their authenticity had to rely entirely on those who had provided them. How could he have spoken with authority? However, given the entrenched attitudes towards homosexuality at this time, it is doubtful whether *Sexual Inversion* could ever have been successfully defended as an important scientific book worthy of public dissemination. Until 1935, in England, only medical practitioners could legally possess the book. But, once labelled scandalous and obscene, a clandestine demand for the work was immediately created.

If relieved of the ordeal of appearing in the witness

---

38 Taken from the verbatim report of the trial, in Huston Peterson's
    Havelock Ellis: Philosopher of Love (Houghton Mifflin, 1928).

box, Ellis was severely shaken by the verdict. This totally unexpected setback to his progress had revealed a certain naivety on his part, as he recognised years later. He had supposed that a secluded student approaching his subject with precaution, making no direct appeal to the general public but only to the public's teachers; who wrapped up the results of his inquiries in a technically-written volume open to few, would be secure from attack. The treatment of the book had a lasting effect: he was only forty years old, but looked back on the event as a turning point in his life, "even the chief-turning point", the end of the upward climb and the beginning of what he felt to be a descent. "Until then, although I always looked older than my age, I had retained an instinctive feeling of youthfulness… But now, somehow, this instinctive feeling was suddenly and forever killed. I realised that I was no longer young".[39]

He wrote, and had printed privately in the United States, a small pamphlet about the book's prosecution. It was an uncompromising statement of his steely determination not to be diverted from his course. He was an impartial student whose path in life he had long marked out. He would leave to others the task of wrestling in the public arena for the freedom to publish work concerned with sex-life. It was not a task that he had ever contemplated for himself, and he did not intend to injure his work, or distort his vision of life, by entering upon such a struggle:

> The pursuit of the martyr's crown is not favourable to the critical and dispassionate investigation of complicated problems. A student of nature, of men, of books may dispense with wealth or position: he cannot dispense with quietness and serenity. I insist on doing my own work in

---

39   Ellis, *My Life*, p. 315

my own way, and cannot accept conditions which make this work virtually impossible.[40]

It had been a crushing blow to discover that his own country refused him the basic conditions of intellectual freedom. His book dealt with the facts of English life, and he wished to address English people. This opportunity having now been denied him, he vowed not to publish in England further volumes arising from his studies, and in 1901 transferred all future publication to the United States. He never forgot, or forgave, this attack on freedom of expression and the suppression of scientific knowledge. As Ellis put it, "the mighty engines of Social Order and Respectability" were set in motion to crush its publication.

Chastened by his experience, he would go forward, undemonstratively, to explore aspects of human sexuality that had hardly been touched in England until his meticulous mind was turned upon them. He had begun his study of human sexuality during the relatively short period between the high point of moralistic medical theorising and the emergence of ethically neutral models of human sexuality. With Freud, the congenital theory would be challenged by the idea of acquired homosexuality through the unsuccessful resolution in childhood of the oedipal complex. Ellis, on the other hand, by formulating new categories for the examination of erotic life, became a central figure in the development of an empirical sexology.

---

40   A Note on the Bedborough Trial.

A Stifled Anachronism

Ellis's principal conclusion in *Sexual Inversion*[1] was that homosexuality was a congenital abnormality, not a symptom of disease, associated with factors such as a criminal mind or insanity. He was not the first to question the so-called morbidity theory, but *was* the first to write an empirically informed book in English repudiating it. The occurrence of homosexuality in non-human species, and its prevalence among nations in all periods of history, convinced him of its falsity. He had partly justified his own study by arguing that it was necessary to examine homosexuality within the general population, so that only two of his cases were individuals who had come into contact with the law and only one, an American, had been an inmate of an asylum. Most were also men who had never consulted or been questioned by a physician about their homosexuality.

It was also a part of his claim to originality that his subjects were English or, as it turned out, British. Such cases were not easily obtained, and without those provided by Symonds, Carpenter and Brown, the investigation may well have foundered, for only twenty-seven male cases and four female cases finally made up the study. He had to resort to including three American cases to bolster the numbers. He

---

1   This chapter does not provide a comprehensive examination of the work. For this, see I Crozier's 2008 critical edition.

said that he was "unable to publish" a further five cases, but did not explain why. And on his own admission, he edited many of the cases, resulting in idiosyncratic presentations rather than systematic records using a common format. Only Symonds's, Carpenter's, and Edith Ellis's cases appear to have been published in full.

The most obvious weakness of his investigation was self-imposed: "I shall make my cases the kernel of my book ... & simply argue, so far as I require, from the cases I present".[2] He never claimed that any significant general conclusions could be drawn from such a small number of cases, but the scope of his study compared very unfavourably with, for example, Richard Krafft-Ebing's *Psychopathia Sexualis*[3] which, after going through numerous editions, contained over two hundred cases. Ellis had told Symonds that he believed, "a few carefully detailed (cases) are of much greater value than a large number of vague and fragmentary character",[4] but as has been observed, he "appeared unaware of the limitations of his restricted selection".[5]

There was also a distinct class bias in the study, as nearly all of his subjects were either middle- or upper-class individuals who, as Ellis observed, "may be said, on the whole, to represent the intellectual aristocracy of inversion".[6] This class bias probably explained why the study showed a much higher proportion of "self-approving inverts" than any previous study. The longest, and in some ways the most interesting case history, was that of Symonds,[7] who Ellis never had an opportunity to question. And although he used

2   Ellis to Carpenter, 22 January 1894, SA MS 357/6.
3   Richard von Krafft-Ebbing, (1840-1902), Austro-German physician. *Psychopathia Sexualis* (Stuttgart, 1887).
4   Ellis to Symonds, 9 February 1893, BUSC DM 109/31.
5   Phyllis Grosskurth, *Havelock Ellis*, p. 186.
6   Havelock Ellis, *Sexual Inversion*, p. 127.
7   Case *XVIII*.

Carpenter's much shorter history,[8] there is no indication in their correspondence that he had any intimate discussion with him about his homosexual life. He could have learned much from Carpenter's experience of same-sex attachments within the working-class, a topic which is dealt with second-hand and inadequately.

A second methodological weakness was that he did not identify clearly enough the sources of his material, leading to a number of ambiguous assertions: "Unfortunately I have not been able to investigate all my cases personally, so that many points in the following histories remain obscure..."[9] He did not say unable to investigate any of his cases personally; so, did he mean that he had investigated *some* of the cases? And, although he used the phrase "my cases", he nowhere made clear whether he had gathered any himself, and if he had, how they were distinct from those provided by others? Although only thirty-one cases were analysed, he listed his cases as "thirty-six in number". Were the numberless five, the "various other histories" which he was "unable to publish at all?"[10] He did not say where these came from, or why he could not publish them. It is also odd that he nowhere identified the cases that he said he had "personally observed", another ambiguous phrase. His most puzzling remark was that "all the cases not personally observed have been investigated with due care, through very reliable channels", and "may, I believe, be accepted".[11] But the majority of these cases were simply passed on to him, without any kind of mediation by the providers. To sum up: a critical reader might well have concluded that such puzzles surrounding, as Ellis expressed it to Carpenter, "my cases", cast doubt on the value, even validity, of the

---

8   *Sexual Inversion*, Case VI.
9   Ibid. p. 42.
10   Ibid. p. 104.
11   Ibid. p. 42.

conclusions drawn from them. When dealing with the issue of the possible role of heredity in homosexuality, there was further ambiguity over his cases. He admitted: "I have by no means escaped this difficulty, for *in most cases* (our emphasis) I have not even had an opportunity of cross-examining the subjects whose histories I have obtained".[12]

Whatever sense may be made of his confusing statements, there is no solid evidence that, apart from possibly his wife, the inordinately shy Ellis ever interrogated a single homosexual person. To ensure scientific objectivity, he should have explained very clearly, at the outset, the origins of all his cases and his precise involvement with his subjects.

Given the thinness of his own material, he had to rely particularly heavily on the work of Krafft-Ebing and Moll,[13] practicing physicians whose case histories included many that were based on face-to-face encounters, during which they *were* able to interrogate their subjects. Ellis used the 1893 edition of *Psychopathia Sexualis*, which he regarded as "the chief store-house of facts".[14] After reading the latest edition of Moll's *Conträre Sexualempfindung*[15] he adopted his position by rejecting the "fine-spun classification" of the sexually-inverted that Krafft-Ebing had constructed, recognising only *homosexuality* and *psychosexual hermaphroditism* (bisexuality).[16] Moll had also questioned the idea of *acquired* inversion, again a position that Ellis adopted. It is not unfair to say that he could hardly have reached either conclusion on the basis of his own limited histories. Perhaps the real value of the book was that, for the first time, English readers were introduced to the extensive work on homosexuality by continental writers.

---

12   *Sexual Inversion*, p. 105.
13   Albert Moll (1862-1939), German psychiatrist.
14   *Sexual Inversion*, p. 29.
15   Albert Moll, *Die Conträre Sexualempfindung*, (Berlin 1893).
16   Havelock Ellis, *Sexual Inversion*, p. 32.

In the division of labour agreed with Symonds, he had been allocated the task of writing the conclusion. His death meant that the form that this would take, whether it was to be a summary of the book's principal conclusions or something else, was never discussed. In the event, much of what Ellis wrote under the heading 'Conclusions' would never have been agreed by Symonds. It was not a summing up of the book's main findings but a chapter that opened with the topic, 'The Prevention of Homosexuality'.

Ellis recognised a human latent organic bisexuality, a shared hermaphroditic constitution, which made homosexuality more intelligible, and even more acceptable. Childhood and early adolescence were periods of *ambisexuality,* when the instinct was comparatively undifferentiated, so that "school-boy" passions arose spontaneously with the evolution of the sexual emotions, before turning into the "normal channel".[17] As this was a part of early sexual development, Ellis might have been expected to have regarded it as not unhealthy, but was shrewd enough to recognise that it would be unwise to condone such passions. He advocated "sound social hygiene" in order to, "render difficult the acquisition of homosexual perversity".[18] The best method was for boys to be educated with girls.

He then turned to the question with which Symonds had tormented Whitman: whether male comradeship permitted physical love-making. As noted in chapter two, in the 1860s Ulrichs had aroused indignation by claiming that the homosexual had a right to fulfil his physical desires. It was his nature, and what was natural could not be denied him: legal restraint and moral disapproval were equally misplaced. But he was rebuffed. Same-sex love, if acknowledged, was to be confined to 'spiritual' friendship, and if brimming with unfulfilled erotic desire, was only to be consummated

17 Applying equally to girls.
18 *Sexual Inversion*, p. 141.

in lonely auto-eroticism. This was the position adopted by Ellis.

His often-stated objective was to examine human sexuality in the round, dispassionately, without stigmatizing any particular form of its expression. His sympathy for the sexually-inverted, expressed in his letters to Symonds and Carpenter, and no doubt strengthened by his wife's lesbianism, seemed genuine enough. But his sympathy did not go beyond criticism of what he considered to be illogical and ineffective legal penalties against it. He urged the male homosexual to come to terms with his preference for abnormal sexual attraction and to refrain from physical intercourse:

[S]elf-restraint and self-culture, without self-repression, seems to be the most rational method of dealing with sexual inversion when that condition is really organic and deep-rooted.[19]

Such a statement exposed Ellis's lack of contact with homosexual men and an understanding of their psychological and physical needs. It also set aside the statements of many of the individuals who made up his cases. Given the rigid taboo against homosexuality, self-repression was almost inevitable. Symonds knew from bitter experience just how harmful his own self-repression had been, and how unnatural. He spoke from the grave: "I could not repress it internally any more than I could stop the recurrence of dreams in sleep or annihilate my native instinct for the beauty of the world".[20] Only those who understood such temperaments could grasp that the satisfaction of physical desire brought "peace and sanity and gladness". Individuals such as Ellis did not have "the evidence of their own experience to disprove and annihilate

19 Havelock Ellis, *Sexual Inversion*, p. 147.
20 Symonds, *Memoirs*, p. 128.

the misconceptions of prevalent opinion".[21] It was his early life of self-repression that led Symonds to declare that the sins of the body were less pernicious than the sins of the imagination. He included himself when he wrote: "Many a man who never stooped to any carnal deed has wallowed in the grossest sensuality of thought. Inside the sphere of their desires, such men are agent and patient, double-sexed, immersed in epicene voluptuousness, for ever longing, for ever picturing delights, for ever unassuaged".[22]

It is clearly wrong to claim that Ellis was "the first heterosexual investigator to grant them (homosexuals) dignity as complete human beings",[23] for his injunction condemned Symonds to a life in which it was his destiny "to make continual renunciation of my truest self", forcing him to live as "a stifled anachronism". [24] Ellis had written that Symonds "is quite certain that he suffers or benefits in health of mind and body according as he abstains from or indulges in moderate homosexual pleasure'.[25] When he began to express his inborn homosexual instincts he rapidly recovered his health. His neurotic disturbances subsided and his chronic lung disease was at least alleviated. Ellis observed: "Coitus with males... always seems to him healthy and natural; it leaves a deep sense of well-being, and has cemented durable friendships".[26] In other of Ellis's cases, where the individual had come to accept his condition without moral misgivings, physical expression was said to improve mental and physical health: "I am depressed at times, especially when I abstain from every form of erotic indulgence", one respondent wrote. Another wrote: "Physical continence is impossible... it is therefore better to

21 Havelock Ellis, *Sexual Inversion*, p. 203.
22 Ibid. p. 127.
23 Phyllis Grosskurth, *Havelock Ellis*, p. 187.
24 Symonds, *Memoirs*, p. 218.
25 *Sexual Inversion*, Case XV111, p. 61.
26 Ibid. p. 62.

spread abroad that spirit of open comradeship which is natural to many men and boys, and which results when the body is impassioned in mutual sex satisfaction". And Ellis reported of a third: "He finds that moderate intercourse with his own sex does him good, and he feels better and stronger for it".

These statements must have made it very clear to Ellis that the repression of all sexual desire was harmful to physical and psychological health, but there was to be no outlet for the release of the invert's sexual energy, except for nocturnal dreams and solitary masturbation. He commended André Raffalovich's *Uranisme et Unisexualité*,[27] a book that Carpenter had, inexplicably, drawn to his attention. Raffalovich is singled out by Ellis for his "just and sagacious reflections" and for urging the invert "to restrain the physical manifestation of his instinct..."[28] Raffalovich's essay was a moral diatribe of a catholic against the active expression of congenital homosexuality: the individual invert who restrained himself was superior to the heterosexual man who abandoned himself. Ellis followed his support for Raffalovich with a brief paragraph on Carpenter's *Homogenic Love* pamphlet; emphasising that Carpenter had urged "that its special value lies in its capacity of being exalted to a higher and more spiritual level of affectionate comradeship".[29] This overlooked Carpenter's insistence on the need for the physical expression of this love. For Ellis, it was "the ideal of chastity, rather than of normal sexuality which the congenital invert should hold before his eyes". It was necessary to "refine and spiritualise" the sexual impulse, in order that "the invert's natural perversion may not become a cause of acquired perversity in others".[30]

---

27 Mark André Raffalovich, *Uranism et Unisexualité*, (Paris, 1896).
28 Havelock Ellis, *Sexual Inversion*, p. 34.
29 Ibid.
30 Ibid. pp. 146-147.

He concluded his account of homosexuality by asking his reader what the "reasonable attitude" of society towards the congenital sexual invert should be. He answered that his behaviour (there is no mention of the female invert) must be subject to social control: "We are bound to protect the helpless members of society against the invert."[31] He did not qualify a statement that implied that all homosexuals were to be viewed as predatory. Did he, reaching his conclusions whilst Oscar Wilde was incarcerated, believe that the elevated homosexuality that Wilde had falsely professed in court, and which was shared by "finer spirits" like Carpenter, was confined to the few; whilst for the rest it was only a smokescreen for sexual licence? There seemed to be an assumption that lesser individuals constituted a danger to the "helpless" members of society.

Throughout the book, Ellis appeared determined to remain non-condemnatory; to avoid the attitude of "moral superiority", which he said he found to be so common in the literature on the subject. He wanted to remain focussed on the evil of ignorance, which could only be prolonged by suppressing public awareness of behaviour that could never be eliminated. But, in the end, he adopted the position that the male homosexual was a danger to society and his behaviour should be subject to some form of social control, although we should not seek to destroy him "before he has sinned against society". This would be to "exceed the warrant of reason". After all, he was not an entirely worthless individual and, in trying to eliminate him, "we may, perhaps, destroy also those children of the spirit who possess sometimes a greater worth than the children of the flesh".[32] It says a great deal about his lack of understanding of homosexuality, and his reluctance to discuss it, that when individuals who had managed to acquire a copy

---

31   *Sexual Inversion.* pp. 156-157.
32   Ibid., p. 157.

of *Sexual Inversion* wrote to him, he invariably recommended that they should consult Carpenter, having noted that the chief effect of attempts to suppress homosexuality had been to arouse "the finer minds among sexual inverts to undertake the enthusiastic defence of homosexuality".[33] As we argued in chapter three, it was only such an elevated homosexuality that had his approval.

A further blow was dealt Symonds, when Ellis turned to the issue of marriage and the fathering of children. He was well aware that many men with a homosexual drive, like Symonds, had married and fathered healthy children. However, if there was no 'cure' for sexual inversion, it was undesirable that the invert should possess the power of reproduction:

> Often, no doubt, the children (of inverts) turn out very well, but for the most part they bear witness that they belong to a neurotic and failing stock. Sometimes, indeed, the tendency to sexual inversion in eccentric and neurotic families seems merely to be Nature's merciful method of winding up a concern which, from her point of view, has ceased to be profitable.[34]

Ellis had promised that he would make his cases the kernel of his book, but in reaching a judgement on the role of heredity, as with the issue of physical love-making, he ignored what they revealed. Of the twenty-seven males, only one, a physician, believed that inversion was hereditary, but did not divulge his parents' or relatives' health. Fourteen reported that their parents or ancestors were healthy, whilst five made no mention of parentage or ancestry. A final group was made up of seven individuals who believed that a relative was, or

---

33 *Sexual Inversion.* p. 154.
34 Ibid., pp. 145-146.

may have been, inverted, but parents or ancestors were either recorded as healthy or not mentioned.

Ellis chose not to repudiate the still entrenched view that homosexuality was linked to heredity, together with a number of mental and physical disorders that could be traced in family histories. His stance would have pained Symonds, the father of four highly intelligent and perfectly normal girls. Several of the individuals who had provided Symonds with their histories were men of high intellectual and cultural achievement, who had married and fathered healthy children. In one of his written exchanges with Ellis, Symonds had asserted that "impaired health in ancestors" was a common condition "of all sexual development, normal and abnormal".[35] He accepted that it was not possible, when discussing homosexuality, to "evade the conditions of atavism and heredity", but saw its occurrence as a matter of probability. As sexual inversion was congenital, "[e]very family runs the risk of producing a boy or girl whose life will be embittered by inverted sexuality, but who in all other respects will be no worse or better than the normal members of the home".[36] He accepted that some conditions might be hereditary; in his own case the lung disease that had killed a sister and his eldest daughter, and would contribute to his own death: "I married when I was 23, ignorant of my own calamity, ignorant of my own pedigree. Had I realized the situation, as I realize it now, plain morality would have made me embrace celibacy".[37]

Since the publication of Francis Galton's influential *Hereditary Genius*,[38] the study of the factors amenable to social control which could influence the physical and mental qualities

35 Symonds to Ellis, *Letters*, vol. 111, p. 787.
36 Symonds, *A Problem in Modern Ethics*, p. 4.
37 Symonds to T.S. Perry, 15 July 1883, *Letters*, vol. 11, p. 832.
38 Francis Galton (1822-1911), *Hereditary Genius: an inquiry into its laws and consequences*, (London, 1869). Galton was a cousin of Charles Darwin.

of future generations had gained force. Galton was a close friend of Symonds's father and had often stayed with them. On one occasion, as he told a friend, "We had a most deeply interesting conversation on the laws of heredity & the theory of population. He told me lots of things".[39] Ellis accepted many of Galton's ideas, and would become a vice-president of the Eugenics Education Society. In *The Task of Social Hygiene*, he wrote:

> Eventually, it seems evident, a general system, whether private or public, whereby all personal facts, biological and mental, normal and morbid, are duly and systematically registered, must become inevitable if we are to have a real guide as to those persons who are most fit, or most unfit, to carry on the race.[40]

And in a 1922 collection of essays he wrote: "We can seldom be absolutely sure what stocks should not propagate… but we can attain reasonable probability, and it is on such probabilities in every department of life that we are always called upon to act".[41] He concluded:

> But it is not only our right, it is our duty, or rather, one may say, the natural impulse of every rational and humane person, to seek that only such children may be born as will be able to go through life with a reasonable prospect that they will not be heavily handicapped by inborn defect or special liability to some incapacitating disease.[42]

---

39 Symonds to Graham Dakyns, 16 October 1875, *Letters*, vol.11, p. 387.
40 Havelock Ellis, *The Task of Social Hygiene*, (Constable, 1912), p. 200.
41 Havelock Ellis, *The Individual and the Race,* in *Essays on Love and Virtue*, in *Morals, Manners and Men* (Watts & Co, 1939), pp. 6-7.
42 Ibid. pp. 6-7.

Ellis's position fits with this last assertion, confirming that he never entirely detached himself from a hereditarian position on homosexuality.

Finally, when he turned to the clause in the 1885 Criminal Law Amendment Act that, with the exception of buggery,[43] had made any act between males deemed to be sexual a *misdemeanour*, it was not to give support to the sexual liberation of the homosexual. Like many who did not approve of homosexuality, Ellis stated that the clause would have been in harmony with the most enlightened European legislation, had the law not made homosexual acts that took place in private an offence. The remit of the law should be confined to the protection of minors and the preservation of public order, and, as such private acts would rarely become known to the police, the law would increase the incidence of blackmail, whilst being unlikely to reduce the prevalence of homosexuality. As Ellis regarded its practice to be socially undesirable, which was the overwhelming view of the Victorians, it is only in the legal sphere, and on utilitarian not moral grounds, that he can be said to have challenged it. As he asserted, he was confident that in England, "social opinion, law or no law, will speak with no uncertain voice" on the acceptability of homosexuality. [44]

After the German edition, four English editions of *Sexual Inversion* were published. In the last, issued in 1915, substantial new material was introduced, much to take account of Magnus Hirschfeld's findings[45] and Iwan Bloch's encyclopaedic studies of sexuality.[46] But, as Grosskurth observed, "[t]he emphasis,

---

43 Buggery remained an offence under the 1861 Offences against the Person Act, carrying a sentence of at least 10 years' imprisonment.

44 Havelock Ellis, *Sexual Inversion*, p. 155.

45 Magnus Hirschfeld, *Die Homosexualität des Mannes und des Weibes*, (The Homosexuality of Man and Woman), (Berlin 1914).

46 Iwan Bloch, *Das Sexualleben unserer Zeit in seinen Beziehungen zur modermen Kultur, The Sexual Life of our Times in its Relation to Modern Civilisation*, (Berlin 1907).

the tone and the recommendations in all editions remained the same".[47] However, in the new era initiated by Freud, Ellis had to reconcile his work with claims that homosexuality, rather than being a congenital abnormality, was an acquired behaviour. But an empiricist to his core, he doubted whether the psychological mechanism posited by Freud could ever be demonstrated, and firmly rejected claims that the homosexual might be cured. It was not a disorder but a permanent condition, from which, as his cases had shown, most homosexuals had no desire to be released. He introduced new material examining so-called treatments by hypnotism, associational therapy and psychoanalysis, concluding that none offered a 'cure'. The ideal of chastity remained his recommendation for the homosexual intent on happiness. Such self-treatment was the path through which, he claimed, most of the more highly intelligent men and women whose histories he had recorded had "reached a condition of relative health and peace, both physical and moral".[48] He ignored the fact that, in most of his histories, the very opposite was claimed. He was content to repeat his statement from the first English edition: "I am inclined to say that if we can enable an invert to be healthy, self-restrained, and self-respecting, we have often done better than to convert him into the mere feeble simulacrum of a normal man".[49]

Ellis's clearly stated position does not support the view that he had set out to present a case for homosexuality,[50] or the claim that he wished to broaden the spectrum of acceptable sexual behaviour by presenting homosexuality as an innocuous departure from the sexual norm.[51] More recently, it

---

47 Grosskurth, *Havelock Ellis*, p. 184.
48 Havelock Ellis, *Sexual Inversion*, p. 146.
49 Ibid. p. 144.
50 See the discussion by Jeffrey Weeks, in Weeks and Rowbotham, *Socialism and the New Life: the personal and sexual politics of Edward Carpenter and Havelock Ellis*, (Pluto Press,1977), pp. 149-156.
51 Paul Robinson, *The Modernization of Sex*, (Eleck, 1976), p. 4.

has been claimed that Ellis had a political aim in writing about sex, which was to promulgate "... a sexual Elysium, where all types of sexual impulse could be expressed – including homosexuality".[52] This view is inconsistent with what Ellis wrote. Indeed, he went beyond disapproving of homosexual practices to actively discouraging them. On utilitarian grounds, he was not opposed to the repeal of legislation that penalised homosexual behaviour in private, but at the same time he denied the male homosexual the consummation of his love.

Having completed his examination of homosexuality, with an evident weariness and a veiled self-judgement on the wisdom of having undertaken such a study, he was keen to move on: "We have not wasted our time in this toilsome excursion. With the knowledge here gained we are the better equipped to enter upon the study of the wider questions of sex".[53]

Although we hold that Ellis abandoned scientific objectivity when he made moral judgements about the homosexual and the practice of homosexuality, his place as a sexual modernist is beyond dispute. His aim was to free the study of sexuality from the Victorian straight-jacket in which it had been confined. His subsequent studies helped to establish some of the basic descriptive categories of sexual phenomena that would inform much subsequent research. Above all, despite the glaring weaknesses of *Sexual Inversion*, he reinforced the strong scientific underpinning that the study of sexuality required: always concerned to employ ethically-neutral language free of pejorative overtones. And, if his congenital theory of homosexuality put him at odds with the supporters of psychoanalytical theories, the empirical foundations that he helped to lay for the study of sexuality

---

52 Crozier, *Sexual Inversion, Havelock Ellis and John Addington Symonds*, a critical edition, p. 29.
53 Havelock Ellis, *Sexual Inversion*, p. 158.

have never been significantly dislodged. As has been rightly observed, he became "an unavoidable point of reference in the study of human sexuality".[54] His role in advancing the case for homosexual rights was minimal but, in fairness, this was never a part of his project.

---

54 Nottingham, *The Pursuit of Serenity,* p. 7.

Eros, the Great Leveller

The idea that same-sex comradely love could dissolve class barriers had a powerful, but distorting, influence on both Carpenter and Symonds. Carpenter had written: "It is noticeable how often Uranians of good position and breeding are drawn to rougher types, as of manual workers, and frequently very permanent alliances grow up in this way..."[1] Many such lovers of their own sex were drawn to working-class individuals. Edward Fitzgerald, translator of the *Omar Khayam,* was famously enamoured of a young illiterate fisherman. After reading Carlyle's *Heroes,* Fitzgerald felt compelled to acquaint his friend with his own hero, "neither Prince, Poet, or Man of Letters, but Captain of a Lowestoft Lugger".[2] Carpenter's friend Charles Ashbee, pioneer of the Arts and Crafts movement, was happiest in the company of young London East End working-class men, who best met his idealised vision of comradeship. Another friend, Goldsworthy Lowes Dickinson, confessed that his secret desire was to be trampled upon by the shiny boots of a strapping young working-class man.[3] The pompous Oscar Browning resigned as an Eton master under the cloud of

---

1   Edward Carpenter, *Homogenic Love and its Place in a Free Society,* p. 155.
2   James Blyth, *Edward FitzGerald and 'Posh',* (John Long, 1908), p. 7.
3   Dennis Proctor, ed. *The Autobiography of G Lowes Dickinson,* (Duckworth, 1973), p. 72.

undue familiarity with his pupils, retreated to Kings College Cambridge and there indulged himself with soldiers, sailors and errand boys. A E Houseman, inspired to write A *Shropshire Lad* by his unrequited love for a fellow undergraduate, was believed to have had "a gondolier in Venice and rough trade in Paris".[4] Another of Carpenter's friends, Edward Morgan Forster, found transient contentment with an Egyptian tram conductor, and later an English policeman. Forster's young friend, Jo Ackerly, had his first glimpse of working-class masculinity in the form of a handsome boy delivering groceries to his parents' house. He afterwards found his ideal friend in the shape of a former seaman, whose "silken-skinned, muscular, perfect body was a delight to behold, like the Ephebe of Kritos. His brown-eyed, slightly simian face, with its flattened nose and full thick lips, attracted me at once". For Ackerly and others, such friendships "opened up interesting areas of life, hitherto unknown."[5]

But for many, such associations had little to do with an ideal of comradeship: they were born out of sexual desire. Bourgeois strictures against homosexuality made the pursuit of sexual pleasure with social equals dangerous, creating a demand for homosexual services, long met by working-class individuals through a subculture of clubs, brothels, male street-walkers and compliant guardsmen. The individuals satisfying the sexual needs of their social superiors were often heterosexual males willingly prostituting themselves for gain. Many a young working-class man was prepared to give his sexual favours in return for cash or gifts, without ever regarding himself as being either homosexual or a prostitute, maintaining his heterosexual identity by masculine role-playing during sexual encounters.

4   Noel Annan, *Our Age: Portrait of a Generation*, (Weidenfeld and Nicolson, 1990), p. 109.
5   J R Ackerly (Joe Randolph), *My Father and Myself*, (Bodley Head, 1968), p. 131.

The homosexual male crossed the class divide for sex, in much the same way as his heterosexual counterpart, but always with the threat of social ostracism. Trampling on class mores was subversive of social hierarchy, and for some a greater offence than homosexual indecencies.

For many of his social superiors, the working-class male was the ideal erotic object. It was imagined that he would be more spontaneous and natural in his love-making, have fewer moral scruples and be less impeded by social conventions. And his perceived superior masculinity, his muscularity and strength, were decisive. Here was a *real* man, and doubly so if, as was often the case with soldiers, he was heterosexual. The term 'rough trade' excited the imagination; conjuring up a picture of a powerful physical type bursting with primitive sexual energy.

When a nervous Symonds entered a male brothel for the first time to pass an afternoon with a brawny young soldier, the experience of sharing a bed with someone so different from himself had a powerful effect: the strapping young soldier with his frank eyes and pleasant smile, and Symonds, the "victim of sophisticated passion". The experience had a powerful but distorting. effect upon him:

> I learned from it – or I deluded myself into thinking I had learned – that the physical appetite of one male for another may be made the foundation of a solid friendship. Within the sphere of the male brothel, at least, permanent human relations, affections, reciprocal toleration, decencies of conduct, asking and yielding, concession and abstention, could find their natural sphere: perhaps more than in the sexual relations consecrated by middle-class matrimony.[6]

---

6   Phyllis Grosskurth, *The Memoirs of John Addington Symonds,* (Random House, 1984), p. 254.

So the comradely attitude of the young soldier prepared to sell his body to a stranger seemed to suggest, but Symonds was well aware that the coming together was a form of business for the soldier. At the end of the transaction, which had not involved sexual intercourse but simply enjoyment of being in the company of "a splendid piece of manhood", the conviction that "some at least of the deepest moral problems might be solved by fraternity" remained.[7] It was, indeed, a delusion, for in the German edition of *Sexual Inversion* he wrote a brutally frank piece on *soldatenliebe*, the love of soldiers, in which he explained why men of his class sought out sexual partners of a lower social standing:

> [F]irst the desire to explore hitherto uncharted waters and the vista of a simple life; secondly, the wish to enjoy the object of passion detached from all everyday considerations, feelings, conventions and traditional views; thirdly, the instinctive realisation that the sexual feeling which has to do with the primitive stirrings of human nature finds its suitable target and its proper sphere among men who are desirable only by dint of the physical and personal charms they possess, apart from any intellectual education and all refinement of culture.[8]

For Symonds, to be in the presence of a magnificent physical specimen gave him an immense sexual thrill. There was no need for talk, even if there had been any ground for the kind of discourse that a man of sophisticated culture might have wished for. Indeed, for many like himself, intellectual interests

---

7   Grosskurth, *Memoirs*. p. 254.
8   John Addington Symonds, *Soldantenliebe und Verwantes, (Soldier Love and Related Matter)*, translated and edited by Andrew Dakyns, (Eastbourne, 2007), p. 13.

were, as he had written, "completely incompatible with sexual desire; they simply disturb the rhythm of beauty of form and interrupt the stream of pure sensual feeling".[9]

Without a need to understand, or share, the inner lives of such individuals, demanding only unsophisticated masculinity, such men devalued them as persons; "all body and no soul" as Oscar Wilde was purported to have remarked. The truth is, that many used such youths and men crudely for their sexual satisfaction. Wilde, especially, took cynical advantage of the poverty of youths who prostituted themselves almost entirely for monetary and other rewards.

From the age of forty onwards, Symonds's poor health had forced him to live abroad, which distorted his thinking about the levelling possibilities of same-sex love. Within the Swiss canton of Graubünden, there was an absence of class distinctions and caste privileges, which made possible everyday associations that would not have been socially sanctioned in England. It opened up opportunities for friendships, and sexual encounters, with "peasants of every description, postilions, drivers, carters, conductors of the *diligence*, carpenters" and others.[10]

Whatever Symonds may have visualised, he inhabited social worlds that could never be reconciled. He conceitedly told his friend Charles Kains-Jackson: "My life is being spent too much among the great of this world. The Empress Frederick is here with her daughter Margaret and the nice young Prince of Hesse... They make considerable demands on my society... It is good for a man to live in both worlds". The other world was "a little old-fashioned wine-shop in a garden of vines, where the gondoliers congregate", and where he first set eyes on Angelo Fusato.[11] As

---

9   Soldantenliebe, p. 13.
10 Grosskurth, *Memoirs*, p.267.
11 Symonds to Charles Kains-Jackson, 30 October 1892, *Letters*, vol. 111, p. 767.

he sat among the gondoliers, it was only his capacity to speak Italian that gave him the slightest affinity with them. His sexual drive combined with his liberal thinking to produce a confused social philosophy. The delusion persisted, for only a few weeks before his death, he told Carpenter: "The blending of social strata in masculine love seems to me to be one of its most pronounced & socially hopeful features. Where it appears, it abolishes class distinctions & opens by a single operation the cataract-bound eye to their futilities..."[12]

Unlike Symonds, Carpenter had set out deliberately to escape the bondage of a class that he held responsible for his early maladjustment. His everyday involvement in the socialist movement gave him an affinity with working-class individuals, experienced by few from his own class. When he found fleeting emotional fulfilment with George Hukin, it was with an individual who was a model of self-improvement; an individual with whom, in spite of Hukin's initial feelings of inferiority, he came to establish an equality entirely absent from Symonds's liaisons. His belief in the possibilities for new forms of human solidarity encompassing homosexuals, examined in the following chapter, was at least grounded in reality. In stark contrast to bourgeois life, he found his working-class friends "saturated... with the thought of fraternity and fellowship".[13] His sexual bonding with Hukin was reinforced by their shared socialist convictions and it would have been difficult for him to separate these two elements in the relationship. As he had written:

It is hardly needful in these days when social questions loom large upon us to emphasise the importance of a bond which by the most passionate and lasting compulsion may draw members of the different classes together, and (as it

---

12 Symonds to Carpenter, 21 January 1893, *Letters*, vol. 111, p. 808.
13 Edward Carpenter, *My Days and Dreams*, p. 130.

often seems to do) none the less strongly because they are members of a different class.[14]

A year before penning this, he was on a train when he caught the eye of twenty-four-year-old George Merrill, exclusively homosexual and attracted to strong and mature men. He was already a skilful seducer, moving confidently within the homosexual underworld, uninhibited and incautious, as his boldness in promptly 'picking up' Carpenter showed. Carpenter could not have met an individual whose whole nature and personality so differed from his own. Apart from his brimming sexuality, Merrill was utterly untouched by the conventions and proprieties of Carpenter's world. He was the 'shameless lusty unpresentable pal' celebrated in *Towards Democracy*, inhabiting a world beyond the middle-class pale. A flattered Carpenter would have found it difficult to resist Merrill's determination to make a conquest.

From the outset, the age difference defined the relationship, Carpenter telling a close friend: "I feel a great tenderness towards him, as to a son".[15] He expressed this paternal feeling in one of the most simple and beautiful of his poems, *Hafiz to the Cup-Bearer*. It includes the lines:

Dear Son, that out of the crowded footways of Shiraz,
With hesitant step emerging,
Camest and laid thy life down at my feet...
I take thy gift, so gracious and sparkling-clear,
Thy naive offering, as of a simple Nature-child...
Come, son (since thou hast said it), out of all Shiraz
Hazif salutes thee comrade. Let us go
A spell of life along the road together.[16]

---

14   Edward Carpenter, *Homogenic Love and its Place in a Free Society*, p. 47.
15   Carpenter to Charles Oates, 14 July 1897, SA MS 351/75.
16   *Towards Democracy*, p. 416.

Five years later, Merrill went to live with him at Millthorpe, where he was registered as his servant. Their cohabitation, as we discuss in the following chapter, brought Carpenter closest to the public infamy that always threatened to engulf an open defender of same-sex love.

In their sexual loneliness, the ease with which middle and upper-class homosexual men found compliant sexual partners among the working classes distorted their sense of 'democratisation' through shared sexual desire. Such relationships did not remove, but often reinforced class distinctions. Transactions, essentially economic in nature, were also ones of "power and subordination".[17] Invariably, such men did not have long-term relationships with working-class individuals, although Noel Annan credited Carpenter with showing that "men of Our Age could live with a working-class lover". The majority who wanted sex with working-class individuals were looking for casual encounters:

> They might have two or three steadies, a sailor who could be depended on to come up from Portsmouth when his ship had returned from a cruise, or a regular frequenter of a well-known pub, but most of the time they would be on the search for fresh faces… encounter, courtship, consummation and parting all have to be achieved in a single evening.[18]

After many years of day-to-day living with George Merrill, Carpenter's enthusiasm for such "permanent alliances" had clearly waned. As he confessed:

> It sometimes happens that there are immense romances between people of quite different classes and habits of life,

---

17 H.J. Cocks, *Nameless Offences, Homosexual Desire in the 19th Century*, (I B Taurus, 2003), p. 157.
18 Noel Annan, *Our Age*, p. 11.

or of quite different race and colour; and they see, for the moment, flaming ideals and wonder-worlds in each other. But unions in such cases are doubtful and dangerous, because so often the common ground of sympathy and mutual understanding will be too limited; and hereditary instincts and influences, deep-lying and deep-working...[19]

Idealism had, if slowly, been replaced by realism. But if comradeship could never dissolve the influence of heredity and deep-seated cultural differences, it remained the case that homosexuals formed a fraternity of estranged individuals for whom Carpenter was prepared to fight.

---

19   Edward Carpenter, *The Drama of Love and Death*, pp. 63-4.

The Fraternity of the Estranged

In 1906, a decade on from the Wilde scandal, the fifth edition of Carpenter's *Love's Coming of Age,* for the first time included a chapter of twenty-one pages in length on the nature of the homosexual person, described as belonging to an 'intermediate sex'. It was based on his *An Unknown People* article of 1897, not the 1894 *Homogenic Love* pamphlet.[1] Material from this pamphlet was not used until 1908, when it formed a chapter in the first edition of Carpenter's new book, *The Intermediate Sex.*[2] This was the first widely-available, unambiguous defence of homosexuality to be published in England.[3]

It was now fourteen years since he had written his first pamphlet on homosexuality. If frequently attacked for his ideas, he had escaped prosecution. But not long after the publication of *The Intermediate Sex*, those who had warned of the danger of mixing up sexual reform with socialism seemed to have been justified. A rabid anti-socialist by the name of M D

---

1 As stated by Brady, in *Masculinity and Male Homosexuality in Britain*, p. 161. Brady is also incorrect in stating (p. 158) that *The Intermediate Sex* was first published in 1906.

2 Edward Carpenter, *The Intermediate Sex, A study of Some Transitional Types of Men and Women,* (Allen &Unwin, 1908).

3 The book soon sold out and was reissued the following year. Subsequently, it was reprinted a further five times, the last in 1930, a year after Carpenter's death.

O'Brien, a member of the England Patriotic and Anti-Socialist Association, began writing letters to Sheffield newspapers, unleashing a tirade against what he called an international conspiracy of moral corruption, of which Carpenter was a part. O'Brien, who lived close to Carpenter's Millthorpe home, then distributed a leaflet in neighbouring villages, *Socialism and Infamy*,[4] in which he attacked homosexuality as a vice that undermined marriage and the family. Carpenter was branded a moral poisoner, and George Merrill was accused of having propositioned local men.

Carpenter responded by urging the public to read what he had actually written. He had no intention of pursuing O'Brien in the courts, sharing the view of many that the self-important Oscar Wilde had precipitated his own downfall by taking the Marquess of Queensberry's bait. His accuser persisted and his next move was to attend a meeting at which Carpenter was speaking on the role of the state. Choosing his moment, O'Brien asked whether state intervention ran to introducing young men to the 'vice' extolled in his writings? Carpenter countered skilfully, but by now the hall was in uproar and O'Brien was forcibly removed.

O'Brien had no intention of surrendering his cause. Having failed to publicly damage Carpenter in Sheffield, he adopted a new strategy by writing to the Home Secretary, hinting at impropriety between Carpenter and George Merrill. Papers in the National Archives record what followed. The Home Office, the Chief Constables of the Sheffield and Derbyshire constabularies, all became involved and files were soon circulating between them. Although no action was taken against Carpenter, he had now been noticed by officialdom. His publications were drawn to the attention of Sir Charles

---

4   M.D. O'Brien, *Socialism and Infamy: The Homogenic or Comrade Love Exposed: An Open Letter in Plain Words for a Socialist Prophet*, privately printed, 1809.

Mathews, the Director of Public Prosecutions, who, five years later, would prosecute D H Lawrence's *The Rainbow*. However, Matthews judged that raising a prosecution would inevitably draw attention to Carpenter's books, posing a greater danger to public morals than leaving him alone. This, notwithstanding the fact that the chapter in *The Intermediate Sex* on 'the homogenic attachment' could easily have rendered the book an 'obscene libel'. Better, Matthews suggested, the silence of the waste-paper basket.

The decision not to prosecute Carpenter for his books disappointed the Home Secretary, who ordered that he should be watched. If he was to be trapped, or at least discredited, it would probably be through the wayward George Merrill. A concerted effort was made to find evidence of misconduct by him and eventually a local farmer was persuaded to report two incidents supposedly involving indecency by Merrill. But no action followed, and as for O'Brien, he later found himself in court to answer a charge of having published a pamphlet libelling his own family. It was he who ended up in prison. After surviving the assault, the pair went on sharing their lives until Carpenter's death twenty years later.

The Intermediate Sex[5] provided an opportunity to consolidate his achievement with *Love's Coming of Age*: a modernist approach to women's sexuality widely acknowledged as an important book, even by fellow socialists who saw it as a distraction from the cause. But a book on homosexuality was a much more difficult undertaking: one for which he needed all his considerable literary skills, as well as a degree of cunning. The chapter in the 1906 edition of *Love's Coming of Age* was anodyne, as it dealt only with the *nature* of the homosexual person. It was not an outright defence of homosexuality or,

---

5   Edward Carpenter, *The Intermediate Sex*, (Allen and Unwin, 1908).

importantly, an attack on the 1885 Criminal Law Amendment Act. *The Intermediate Sex* was both.

The case for the repeal of the Labouchère clause is clearly and succinctly stated. With its imprecise offence of *gross indecency*, it had made almost any familiarity between two men the possible basis of a criminal charge; throwing a shadow over even the simplest and most ordinary of endearments between males. But it was the attack on personal liberty, by extending the law's remit to the bedroom, that was most resented. It was an attempt, as Carpenter put it, "to regulate the private and voluntary relations of adult persons to each other".[6] This was moral censorship, and an intrusion into the lives of homosexuals that was not applied to two persons of opposite sex. And it was manifestly unworkable, as such a law could only ever be enforced with the aid of an informer, whilst opening the door wider than ever to the more serious crime of blackmail. In the interest of justice and fairness, homosexuality should be tolerated under exactly the same restrictions that were applied to heterosexuality,

A format, used by Carpenter for a number of his books, was to bring together material that had already been published, usually as pamphlets or journal articles. This was the case with *The Intermediate Sex*. There were four chapters: *The Intermediate Sex*, taken unchanged from *Love's Coming of Age*; *The Homogenic Attachment*, which used parts of the 1894 *Homogenic Love* pamphlet; *Affection in Education* (not dealt with here), which had begun life as a paper in the *International Journal of Ethics*, and *The Place of the Uranian in Society*, which expanded his ideas on the social functions of homosexuals first raised in the *Homogenic Love* pamphlet. All the key arguments in defence of the homosexual made in these publications, which were examined earlier, are brought together. These will only be referred to where

6   *The Intermediate Sex*, p. 79.

necessary, as the focus here is on the strengths and weaknesses of this bold, and brave declaration of the homosexual's right to social recognition and equality under the law.

He must have decided that beginning the book with a consideration of the homosexual's nature would be prudent: with the defence of homosexuality as a natural variant of the sexual instinct following on. He knew that this chapter would be the most liable to render the book obscene, and was best hedged around by less provocative material. Ten years on from Ellis's *Sexual Inversion*, a book focussed on the substantial supportive evidence on homosexuality, accumulated over thirty years, was still a very risky undertaking in England.

But there was a disadvantage in opening the book with his account of the cognitive, psychological and physiological characteristics of homosexuals, as it immediately introduced the controversial idea of *sexual intermediacy*, which effectively, 'feminised' male and 'masculinised' female homosexuals. It was Magnus Hirschfeld,[7] who had been the most recent to claim that homosexuals were *sexuelle zwischenstufen,* combining male and female qualities and characteristics,[8] which had attracted strong criticism from male-oriented groups in Germany. Members of the *Gemeinschaft der Eigenen* (Community of the Special) were the most insistent that a homosexual orientation was a cultural preference; not an inborn condition but a spiritual form of male-loving. It expressed virile masculine qualities, echoing Symonds's claim that, among the Dorians, a passion for males was considered proof of an extra-virile temperament.

The idea of homosexuals as a sex apart had been given some credence by the eighteenth-century subculture of 'mollies': of effeminate homosexual males assuming female roles and entering into mock marriages, although such behaviour did

---

7   Magnus Hirschfeld, German physician.
8   Sapho and Socrates, *Sapho und Socrates,* (Leipzig 1896).

not necessarily denote gender inversion.[9] In the 1850s, with the growth of forensic psychiatry, physicians were being called as expert witnesses in the prosecution of sexual crimes in large European cities, when notions such as the 'hermaphrosidy' of the pederast's mind and the effeminacy of so-called 'philopedes' became current. And a strict gender dimorphism *was* certainly being questioned as Carpenter wrote. Otto Weininger argued that all individuals combined male and female 'substance', and also described homosexuality as an 'intermediate' sexual form.[10] Charles Leland[11] emphasised the feminine and masculine characteristics of artistically-gifted homosexual men and women, and Edward Prime-Stevenson wrote of 'semisexualism'.[12]

Symonds had regarded the idea of homosexuals as a sex apart as extraordinary. He could not find in himself anything that justified the idea of a 'female soul' shut up in a male body, which he said savoured of "bygone scholastic speculation".[13] Similarly, Whitman's same-sex lovers were not biologically different from other men; half man, half woman. And Ellis dismissed the idea out of hand: "It merely crystallises into an epigram the superficial impression of the matter".[14] Sexual differentiation was elusive, but the clue to homosexuality probably lay in a latent organic bisexuality, a hermaphroditic constitution.

Aware of this literature, but seemingly relying on little more than his own observations, Carpenter asked the reader

9   See Rictor Norton's, *Mother Clapp's Molly House*, (Gay Men's Press, 1992).
10 Otto Weininger, Austrian philosopher. *Geschlect und Charakter*, (Berlin, 1903).
11 Hans Brietmann, pseud. Charles G Leland, *The Alternate Sex*, (Wellby, 1903).
12 Xavier Mayne, pseud. Edward Prime Stevenson, *The Intersexes*, (privately printed, 1908).
13 Symonds, *Memoirs*, p. 64.
14 Havelock Ellis, *Sexual inversion*, p.132.

to accept that many distinctions between the sexes had been stripped away, making the extremes of masculinity and femininity less apparent. The reconsideration of 'femaleness' detached from a woman's procreative role had revealed "the diversity of human temperament and character in matters relating to sex and love".[15] It was possible, he claimed, to identify males with a "double temperament": individuals in whom there was "a balance of the feminine and masculine qualities".[16]

Like Hirschfeld, Carpenter appealed to Karl Ulrichs to underpin his arguments, but misunderstood him in claiming that he had placed male homosexuals "on the dividing line between the sexes"; that whilst belonging physiologically to one sex they belonged "*mentally* and *emotionally* to the other".[17] This was wrong. For Ulrichs, what essentially distinguished the male homosexual was not the possession of a male-female double nature but an 'inverted' *love sentiment*, that of a female towards a male. The homosexual's nature was not, as Carpenter described it, "a balance of the feminine and masculine qualities". Ulrichs focussed exclusively on the nature of the *sex-drive*, whilst Carpenter's 'intermediate sex' is about the supposed possession of male and female characteristics, covering cognitive and psychological attributes, and the emotions. As discussed in chapter two, when identifying a female 'love sentiment' in the male homosexual, Ulrichs did, initially, look for female bodily and behavioural markers, and assigned feminine characteristics to all male homosexuals. But with greater knowledge of the diversity of homosexual types, and after men who had read his booklets wrote to him, Ulrichs accepted that the possession of feminine qualities did not *define* the male homosexual. Only his *inverted* love

15   *The Intermediate Sex*, p. 19
16   Ibid. p. 18.
17   Ibid. p. 19.

sentiment marked him out. In appearance and behaviour, there were male homosexuals who were decidedly feminine (Carpenter's George Merrill was unkindly referred to by some as 'Georgette') but there were masculine homosexual males who did not have so-called feminine mental and physical characteristics or behavioural traits, but whose 'love sentiment' was still, in Ulrichs's terms, feminine.

Carpenter, although holding that the typical homosexual male did not exhibit pronounced femininity, nonetheless insisted that he still possessed "the tenderer and more emotional soul-nature of a woman".[18] Interestingly, as a twenty-year-old, confused by his sexual emotions, he had asked himself: 'Was I really a woman born in some inner unknown region of my nature?"[19]

The assigning of female attributes to the male homosexual, as Hirschfeld had found, offended many men who did not care to be dubbed the 'intermediate sex' in a culture that projected a strong normative masculinity. Even after setting aside exaggerated types, the effeminate male and the butch female, Carpenter still insisted that there was "a general tendency towards femininity of type in the male... and towards masculinity in the female".[20] The male, he suggested, tended to be "of a rather gentle, emotional disposition", while the female was just the opposite, "fiery, active and bold". The mind of the male was "generally intuitive and instinctive in its perceptions", that of the woman "more logical, scientific and precise than usual with the normal woman".[21]

He seemed not to appreciate the consequences of linking a male homosexual orientation with femininity, which reinforced the prejudice that all male homosexuals were 'womanly' and

18   *The Intermediate Sex*, p. 32.
19   *My Days and Dreams*, early draft, SA MS 198.
20   *The Intermediate Sex*, p. 57.
21   Ibid. p. 27.

wished to be anally-penetrated. As has been argued, a feminine youth might easily be pushed into the homosexual world by such a depiction, but a masculine youth with homosexual feelings would be aware of the double stigma he might face, and would have reason to conceal his sexual orientation. Moreover, to present homosexuality as a form of gender inversion was marginalising: once stereotyped by society as feminine, the homosexual male did not pose a threat to the norm of masculine heterosexuality.[22]

Perhaps Carpenter thought that the idea of sexual 'intermediacy' would fit with the claim that homosexuality was a congenital abnormality. Instead, it helped to reinforce the association between homosexuality and femininity, which would not be broken until there was greater social recognition of the diversity of sexual tastes and practices. The visibility of 'butch' masculine men with same-sex desires, whether gay, bisexual or just sexually adventurous, has altered public perceptions of the homosexual persona. The very feminine homosexual, the camp 'queen', now endures as an object of parody but no longer signifies a gay identity.

It is understandable that Carpenter wanted to use every plausible argument that might help the case for the recognition and acceptance of homosexuals. These essentially biological claims, however questionable, were clearly intended to counter the widespread notion that homosexuality was a psychological disorder; a position endorsed by the English medical profession at this time. He lays down a challenge to those "inclined to deny to the homogenic or homosexual love that intense, that penetrating, and at times overmastering character which would entitle it to rank as a great human passion".[23] After reviewing the extensive literature on homosexuality and repeating the

---

22 Gert Hekma, *A Female Soul in a Male Body*, in *Third Sex, Third Gender*, ed. Gilbert Herdt, (New York 1994), p. 236.

23 *The Intermediate Sex*, p. 40.

many supportive arguments found in his previous publications, he repeats his foremost claim, that homosexuality is "quite instinctive and congenital",[24] not a morbid condition, urging the reader to accept that, step by step, on the basis of reliable evidence, this assumption was being abandoned.

If his views on the homosexual's nature may have appeared incongruous to some, and offensive to others, his claims for the recognition of the social worth of homosexuals are likely to have been more favourably received. Their repression in contemporary life was a loss, and posed a danger to social harmony. He was the first to call for homosexuals to be given "their fitting place and sphere of usefulness in the general scheme of society".[25] The homosexual form of love had "deep significance and social uses and functions..."[26] and should be placed on a level with heterosexual love. Marriage was of indispensable importance to societies, but this other form of union was "almost equally indispensable to supply the basis of social activities of other kinds".[27]

Audaciously, he suggested that a stable same-sex relationship should be given the "sanction and dignity" of public recognition, anticipating the civil partnerships and marriage for same-sex couples that would come over a century later. If the morality of marriage rested on public recognition, and an accepted standard of conduct within it, he asked, might not "something of the same kind" be true of 'the homogenic attachment?"[28]

Homosexuals should be valued by society for the contributions they made to the nation's cultural life. He doubted whether the spiritual life of the nation was ever

24   *The Intermediate Sex*, p. 55.
25   Ibid. p. 15.
26   Ibid. p. 39.
27   Ibid. p. 73.
28   Ibid. p. 82.

possible without the sanction of this attachment in its institutions.

> It certainly does not seem impossible to suppose that as the ordinary love has a special function in the propagation of the race, so the other has its special function in social and heroic work and in the generation – not of bodily children – but of those children of the mind, the philosophical conceptions and ideals which transform our lives and those of society.[29]

He likened a liberated homosexual fraternity to "a new and important" movement, which might accomplish "the noblest work" in some distant reformed social organisation.[30] He was aware that his call for new institutions of human solidarity might meet with opposition, certainly ridicule, but for forty years he had held true to the possibilities that Whitman had opened his eyes to. The recognition and acceptance of the homosexual was not just a personal imperative, it was a part of his socialist vision.

> If the day is coming... when Love is at last to take its rightful place as the binding and directing force of society (Instead of the Cash-nexus), and society is to be transmuted in consequence to a higher form, then undoubtedly the superior types of Uranians – prepared for this service by long experience and devotion, as well as by much suffering – will have an important part to play in the transformation.[31]

The Intermediate Sex was the highpoint of his defence of

---

29   *The Intermediate Sex*. p. 70.
30   Ibid. p. 12.
31   Ibid. pp. 122-3.

same-sex love, but issues surrounding sexuality continued to engage him. In 1902, he published *Iolaus,* an anthology of male friendships, and went on to publish a survey of ethnological research into homosexuality among native peoples, showing the social functions, and often high status, of sexually-divergent individuals, both male and female.[32] These latter studies, he felt, reinforced his argument for their full participation in society. Two further books both included reflections on human sexuality.[33]

*

Two decades after Carpenter had first ventured into the field of sexual politics, the time seemed right for a further advance in public understanding. In 1913, the Fourteenth International Medical Congress was held in London, at which Magnus Hirschfeld was one of the principal speakers. In Germany he had been a founding member of The Scientific Humanitarian Committee, set up in 1897 to campaign for the decriminalisation of male homosexual acts that took place in private between consenting adults. Carpenter and Ellis had forged links with the group, and there had been talk of establishing an English branch or an equivalent organisation. The Congress rekindled such expectations, and in July of the following year The British Society for the Study of Sex Psychology was set up, with Carpenter as its first president. As Jeffrey Weeks has written, Carpenter and Ellis "stood as giants of an earlier British generation who could provide the necessary prestige to get a reform society off the ground".[34]

The Society's main purpose was educational: to consider

---

32 Edward Carpenter, *Intermediate Types Among Primitive Folk,* (1914).
33 *The Drama of Love and Death,* (1912) and *Pagan and Christian Creeds* (1920).
34 Jeffrey Weeks, *Coming Out,* (Quartet Books, 1977), p. 128.

'problems and questions connected with sexual psychology, from their medical, juridical and sociological aspects'. Through public meetings and published papers, it hoped to contribute to a more humane, scientifically informed, understanding of sexual questions. Although it did not have the overtly political aim of seeking a change in the law governing homosexual relationships, early on a subcommittee was set up for its study, and the Society's second published pamphlet was *The Social Problem of Sexual Inversion.*

From the outset, it forged strong links with the women's movement, reinforcing the connection Carpenter had made twenty years earlier in his ground-breaking pamphlets. One of the early leading members was Stella Browne,[35] a campaigner for a woman's right to make her own sexual choices, again an issue earlier championed by Carpenter. To protect itself from prosecution, the Society was cautious in its dealings, often addressing its publications specifically to members of the educational, legal and medical professions. The law against obscene publications that had snared Ellis's book remained in place, as witnessed by the suppression in 1915 of D.H. Lawrence's *The Rainbow,* and the prosecution of *Lady Chatterley's Lover* in 1960. Support for the Society was strong among progressives and it helped to raised awareness and understanding of homosexuality, but as Jeffrey Weeks has judged, it is unlikely that it changed public opinion in any significant way or influenced government policy.[36] In 1920, the cumbersome name of the Society was changed to The British Sexological Society.

A further forty-seven years would have to pass before the Sexual Offences Act 1967, for England and Wales only,[37] made

---

35 Stella Browne (1880-1955), feminist, sex radical and birth control campaigner.
36 Jeffrey Weeks, *Coming Out*, p.136.
37 But for Scotland, not until 1980 and for Northern Ireland not until 1982.

consensual sex between two men in private legal. The age of consent remained at twenty-one and was not reduced to eighteen until 1994, or equalised with the heterosexual age of consent of sixteen, until 2000.

Finally, January 2017 saw the last act in this story of oppression, when individuals in England and Wales who had been cautioned or convicted under the 1885 Act, the dead and the still living, were pardoned. Legislation was initiated in Scotland in November 2017 for the same purpose. It has become known informally as the Alan Turing law, named after the renowned code breaker and computing pioneer who, following his conviction for gross indecency in 1952, took his own life.

Postscripts

Pirated copies of Symonds's two monographs, all with him named as the author, began to appear after his death. In 1896, an edition of *A Problem in Modern Ethics* surfaced. The text was likely to have been provided by one of the small number of original recipients: it was an expensive book, three-quarters bound in crushed Moroccan leather, gilt-edged and lettered with marbled endpapers. The publisher was Leonard Smithers, who had links with leading members of the *Decadent* movement, had published Sir Richard Burton's *Book of One Thousand and One Nights* and also a number of pornographic works. It is not clear how many copies were produced, but each was signed by Smithers. Also in 1896, a hundred less expensively bound copies in green cloth were issued 'for private circulation', without a named publisher. Not all of these copies were numbered, so more may well have been printed. These editions, because of their very restricted circulations, cannot be regarded as the first public defence of homosexuality to be published in England. This distinction must be reserved, partly for the 1906 edition *of* Carpenter's *Love's Coming of Age,* and fully for his 1908 *The Intermediate Sex.*

Also in 1896, an edition of A *Problem in Greek Ethics* was published by Murray, identifiable by its navy-blue cloth binding. Again, it is unclear how many copies of this edition were produced. The monograph was made more readily available the following year, when it was included as an appendix to the first English edition of *Sexual Inversion,* although Symonds edited the 1883 original for this purpose. It was followed in 1901 by an edition of one hundred numbered copies, again without a named publisher, bound in green cloth and intended 'for private circulation'. It carried the declaration that the type had been 'distributed'. Finally, in 1908 an edition was produced by the classicists' Areaopagitica Society. None of these various editions identified the source of the text used or claimed copyright. It is likely that, had the monographs been in general circulation, as was always Symonds's wish, they would have had parity with the best contemporary contributions to the understanding of the subject, and given Symonds his rightful place in the fight in England against homosexual discrimination.

*

Given his precarious health, Symonds was always conscious that he might be taken at any time. Feeling the shades of evening closing around him, early in 1889 he had put aside "all labours of remunerative literature" to prepare a record of a soul "still to settle its accounts with God".[1] He had just finished translating the autobiographies of Cellini and Gozzi and, motivated by these two masterpieces, he had begun setting down an account of his own life. This became known, and Ernest Rhys, writing about Symonds in the Pall Mall Gazette,[2] let it slip. Symonds was uneasy, telling him that he did not want to get a reputation for preserving anecdotal matter or gossip about people, when what he was writing was something

---

1 Phyllis Grosskurth, *The Memoirs of John Addington Symonds,* (Random House, 1984), p. 30.
2 Ernest Rhys, *Men and Women Who Write,* Pall Mall Gazette, 17 May 1890.

very different: "I feel that the intelligent & careful study of any person's development & psychical history, written from inside with sincerity, is what he may legitimately give to the world if he likes, & what is a valuable contribution to our documents of human experience".[3] He had also revealed its existence to the Whitmanite John Wallace, who "liked to see an old worker in the field of scholarship & criticism, come out in his own person & speak out of his heart".[4]

Early in its composition, he had decided that it would have to be left to others to deal with this "most considerable product" of his pen.[5] Having made Horatio Brown his literary executor, he emphasised the importance he placed on it, and made his wishes clear:

[It] was so passionately, unconventionally set on paper. Yet I think it a very singular book – perhaps unique, nay certainly unique, in the disclosure of a type of man who has not yet been classified. I am anxious therefore that this document should not perish. It is doubtful when or whether anyone who has shown so much to the world on ordinary ways as I have done, will be found to speak so frankly about his inner self. I want to save it from destruction after my death, and yet to reserve its publication for a period when it will not be injurious to my family. I do not just now know how to meet the difficulty. And when you come here, I should like to discuss it. You will inherit my mss. If you survive me. But you take them freely, to deal with them as you like, under my will. I have sketched my wish out that this autobiography should not be destroyed. Still I see the necessity for caution in its publication. Give the

3   Symonds to Rhys, 17 August 1890, *Letters*, vol. 111, p. 489.
4   Symonds to J.W. Wallace, 7 March 1891, *Letters,* vol. 111, p. 562.
5   Symonds to Graham Dakyns, 27 March 1889, *Letters*, vol. 111, p. 363.

matter a thought. If I could do so, I should like to accept it as a thing apart, together with other documents from my general literary bequest; so as to make no friend, or person, responsible for the matter, to which I attach a particular value apart from life's relations.[6]

Publication of the intimate life of a character "somewhat strangely constituted in its moral & aesthetic qualities"[7] would have destroyed his reputation and harmed his family. Although it did not seem imperative that anything should be published so soon after his death, those closest to him decided that Brown, his friend for over twenty years, should use the papers bequeathed to him, including the autobiographical manuscript, to prepare a biography. Even then, Catherine Symonds hesitated, recalling the note that he had written for her as he lay dying: "You see how the great question was supreme in his mind to the very last. Are we right in being cowardly & suppressing it?" To give credence to Brown's book, she wrote a short preface embodying a part of the note "to make his position clear to the outside world (not his friends, I mean) but critics & relations".[8] Brown went ahead and the biography was published in 1895. Although his aim was to make it as closely autobiographical as he could, to let Symonds tell his own story, it was a falsification: the drawing of a veil over life-changing events and intimate friendships. All the most salient and revealing aspects of his life were omitted or slurred over. Clearly, there could be no mention of the monographs, or *Sexual Inversion* and his association with Ellis.

Anticipating that some might be puzzled by its format, Brown wrote in the preface: "It may be asked why, as an

---

6   Symonds to Horatio Brown, 29 December 1891, *Letters*, vol. 111, p. 642.
7   Symonds to Graham Dakyns, 27 March 1889, *Letters*, vol. 111, p. 363.
8   A note from Catherine Symonds to Graham Dakyns, 2 November 1893, included in *Letters,* vol.111, p. 840.

autobiography exists, I have not confined myself to the publication of that?" His tortuous explanation hinted at obfuscation, ending with the assertion that what Symonds had left had to be supplemented by his diaries and notebooks, "in order that a true portrait may be painted".[9] When a second edition was published, parts of it had been rewritten, following objections from Symonds's friends that the portrait was uniformly gloomy: that his zest for life, his sociability, the sparkle of his conversation, had found no place in Brown's telling.

As literary executor, Brown had stipulated in his will that the autobiographical manuscript should pass to the British Museum, but when he died in 1926, for whatever reason, it was bequeathed, together with diaries, letters and other papers, to the London Library, with the stipulation that it was not to be open to scrutiny or published for fifty years. At the time, the chairman of the library committee was Symonds's old friend, by now Sir Edmund Gosse, an entrenched establishment figure.

A generation on, Symonds's daughter, Katherine Furse, was haunted by the presentiment that her father had been sacrificed to puritanical Victorian conventions. Even in 1940, when more was becoming known about homosexuality, "his story found in the Memoirs remained dead to the world". Brown's biography was "especially incomplete, omitting, except by inference, all reference to his study of homosexuality, producing an unbalanced effect and a misunderstanding of his attitude to a subject that occupied so much of his attention".[10]

Janet Vaughan, one of Symonds's grand-daughters, when a medical student occasionally took afternoon tea with the Gosses. One day Gosse said he particularly wanted to talk to her. "He said he knew how glad I should be to hear what he

---

9   Horatio Forbes Brown, *John Addington Symonds*, (Smith, Elder, 1895), p. x.
10   Katherine Furse, *Hearts and Pomegranates, The Story of Forty-five Years 1875-1920*, (Peter Davis, 1940) pp. 97-108.

had done to preserve the good name of my grandfather..."[11]
He told her that, with the librarian, Charles Hagberg, he had
lit a bonfire in the garden and burned everything bequeathed
by Brown, except for the autobiography:

> It was not safe to let myself speak as I thought of those
> two old men destroying, one could only guess, all the case
> histories and basic studies of sexual inversion that J.A.S. is
> known to have made, together no doubt with other letters
> and papers that would have thrown much light on J.A.S.'s
> work and friendships. Gosse's smug gloating delight as
> he told me, the sense that he had enjoyed to the full the
> honour fate had given him, was nauseating. There was
> nothing to be said. I walked out and never went back.[12]

In 1949, Katherine Furse asked to read the manuscript and
the box containing it was opened for the first time. Five years
later, it was decided that it would be obscurantist if access
to the autobiography was any longer denied to *bona fide*
scholars. Phyllis Grosskurth, when preparing her biography
of Symonds,[13] was able to make extensive factual use of it.
Then, in 1976, the embargo came to an end and she produced
an edited version of the manuscript, cutting the text by about
a fifth.[14] Grosskurth's biography, which revealed for the first
time the full truth about Symonds's homosexual life, and the
subsequent *Memoirs*, created a new interest in his work.

Did Symonds, with his intelligence, analytical abilities,

---

11 Extract from a letter to the editors of *The Letters of John Addington
    Symonds*, 23 September 1967.
12 Ibid.
13 Phyllis Grosskurth, *John Addington Symonds*, (Longmans, 1964).
14 Phyllis Grosskurth, *The Memoirs of John Addington Symonds*, (Random
    House, 1984). Symonds's handwriting is notoriously difficult to read, and
    Grosskurth, an outstanding biographer, produced a commendable text,
    which has guided scholars for many years.

powers of observation and enormous energy, misunderstand his calling? After his aborted study of law, ought he to have followed his father into medicine, or gone on to write on historical and scientific subjects, rather than labour to make his name as a *litterateur*; a path embarked upon, perhaps, to prove Benjamin Jowett wrong? His forensic examination of the then leading texts on homosexuality certainly equalled, if not exceeded, anything produced by Ellis, who, as we have recorded, readily acknowledged that much of the material provided by him for *Sexual Inversion* contained a large amount of "scientific inquisition".

Was most of what he wrote over a period of twenty years, a substitute for such work, which might have inspired him, whereas much of his writing clearly fatigued him? He often professed that he loved his art, that it was his solace; whilst complaining to friends that his literary offerings were sterile things, detached from a world in which he always longed to play a greater part. At the height of his reputation in England, he told Horatio Brown: "I am reconciled to literature and study as palliatives. I do not believe in them as substantial factors in life".[15] They were the creations of what he called "brain-labour". But the two monographs, and his memoirs, were carefully excepted from this judgement, for they alone connected his tortured life to a world, cruel to his kind, which he had the courage to confront. If the force of his literary criticism ebbed with the modernist tide, he was himself a modernist in the field of social and psychological science. It is captured in the title of his monograph, A *Problem in Modern Ethics.*

*

Within months of Symonds's revelation that he was writing

---

15   Symonds to Horatio Brown, 19 January 1890, *Letters,* vol. 111, p. 442.

an autobiography, Carpenter, in a very casual way, began to set down 'autobiographical notes', sitting in the old St Pancras Churchyard in London, the trysting place of Percy Shelley and Mary Godwin. He returned to the task in fits and starts over the next twenty-five years. Published in 1916 as *My Days and Dreams*,[16] with the exception of a small number of portraits of friends and acquaintances and an account of his books, it is almost wholly concerned with the outer events of his life. And even here, the narrative is slight for an individual who led such a long and unconventional life. There are brief passing references to his struggle with his sexuality but we seldom hear him interrogating himself. Much of it is what Ellis, reflecting on his own autobiography, dismissed as "harmless and agreeable".[17] The intensity of purpose in the task of self-delineation, so strong in both Symonds and Ellis, is entirely absent. Only *Towards Democracy* movingly captured his joyful escape from social and sexual bondage.

When he died in 1929, at the age of eighty-four, if still revered, he had slipped into obscurity as the force of his personality was no longer felt. On hearing of his passing, George Bernard Shaw, with whom in heady days he had played piano duets, told a mutual friend: "I found it difficult to realise that he was still here".[18] And E M Forster recorded in his Commonplace Book, "Astonishing how he drains away".[19]

Two years after his death, in a contribution to a *Festschrift*, Forster's judgement was that he would not "figure in history",[20] but in a radio talk in 1944, on the centenary of

---

16   Edward Carpenter, *My Days and Dreams*, (George Allen and Unwin, 1916).
17   Havelock Ellis, *My Life*, p. xiv.
18   Quoted in Stephen Winsten, *Salt and His Circle*, p. 161.
19   E. M. Forster, *Commonplace Book*, ed. Philip Gardner (Scolar Press, 1985), p. 52.
20   *Edward Carpenter, In Appreciation*, ed. Gilbert Beith (George Allen and Unwin, 1931), p. 80.

Carpenter's birth, he claimed that something from him had "passed into the common stock".[21] Concerned to draw the right picture, he had discussed what he should say with one of Carpenter's literary executors. It did not bode well for their friend: "Unless Labour is brought in, the centenary will be a small affair; you and I and a few others, value E. for his teaching and example about personal relations, but this won't cut enough ice; most people remember him as a social prophet and reformer and worker in the Labour movement".[22] Although it *was* Carpenter's teaching and example about personal relations that he knew had passed into the common stock, and influenced the ideas and ethical imperatives that had driven his own creative life, before the microphone, Forster did not say so. The closest he came to revealing why Carpenter had had a lasting influence was when he remarked that, for him, love was "the final earthly reality". And, possibly fearing complicity, he did not tell the truth about Carpenter's earthly love and his brave stand for homosexual rights.

After a lifetime of dissimulation about his own sexuality, Forster could not bring himself to talk about Carpenter's gay life. Twenty-seven years later he was to make amends for not giving him his due, with the publication of his novel, *Maurice*: which was also an act of posthumous truth-telling about his own homosexuality. It was Carpenter's belief in homosexual love that had attracted him in his loneliness. Imbibing the atmosphere of his household, presided over by the flirtatious George Merrill, released the spurt of creative energy that produced the homosexual-themed *Maurice*.

The novel was as much about the cruelty of class barriers as about intolerance of homosexuality: "The feeling that can impel a gentleman towards a man of lower class stands self-

---

21   E. M. Forster, The Life and Works of Edward Carpenter, BBC Book Talk, 25th September 1944, SA MS 387/5.

22   Forster to Gilbert Beith, 14 March 1944, SA MS 387/1.

condemned", Forster had Maurice say before he was seduced by the working-class Alec Scudder. He was determined that, in his fictional world, two men, of whatever class, should fall in love and remain in it "for the ever and ever", although Maurice and Alec would have to live outside family and class.

Carpenter was one of a small number of friends who read the manuscript, telling Forster that he was delighted that the story had ended "on a major chord". He was afraid that, at the last, Forster was going to let Alec go, "but you saved him & saved the story…" The end, if improbable, was not impossible, and was "the one bit of real romance wh. (sic) those who understand will love".[23]

After *Maurice,* Forster admitted to himself that he loved men and could no longer renounce physical gratification. In November 1915, a year after finishing *Maurice,* unable to enlist, he went to Alexandria as a Red Cross searcher, interviewing the wounded for information about missing soldiers. Sexually tormented, he unburdened himself to Carpenter:

Dear Edward, you continue the greatest comfort. I don't want to grouse, as so much is all right with me, but this physical loneliness has gone on for too many months, and with it springs and grows a wretched fastidiousness, so that even if the opportunity for which I yearn offered I fear I might refuse it. In such a refusal there is nothing spiritual – it is rather a sign that the spirit is being broken. I am sure that some of the decent people I see daily would be willing to save me if they knew, but they don't know, can't know… I sit leaning over them for a bit and there it ends, except for images that burn into my sleep; I know that though you have heard this and sadder cases 1000 times before, you will yet be sympathetic, and that is why

23   Carpenter to Forster, 23 August 1914, *Selected Letters of E M Forster* ed. M Largo and P N Furbank (Secker and Warburg, 1978), vol. 1, p. 223.

you are such a comfort to me. It's awful to live with an unsatisfied craving, now and then smothering it but never killing it or even wanting to. If I could get one solid night it would be something.[24]

Six months later he parted with respectability for the first time on the beach at Montazarh, possibly with a soldier but more likely with a local youth. He had finally connected his inner life with the life of the world.

Carpenter had blazed a trail that had liberated Forster and others: disentangled the sex instinct from artificial codes and provided the normative counterpart to D H Lawrence's resolve to make the sex relation precious instead of shameful. Forster understood, more than others, that the love that Carpenter most cared about had a defining figuration in many personal histories, and that his own life was one into which a part of Carpenter was permanently woven. The man presented by him as unlikely to have much earthly immortality, had taught him truths which he had absorbed and which had impelled his artistic life: supreme truths, above all, the primacy of personal relationships and the imperiousness of the body's commands. Close to death, Carpenter knew what form his earthly immortality would take: "I know we have done our work, even if not a soul remembers us. We live in their limbs, in their eyes and in their laughter."[25]

---

24   P N Furbank, *E M Forster: A Life*, vol. 2, (Secker and Warburg, 1978), p.25.
25   Quoted in Winsten, *Salt and His Circle*, p. 154.

Bibliography

Manuscript Collections

Sheffield City Council, Libraries Archives and Information
    Sheffield Archives: The Edward Carpenter Collection
    (SA)

The Harry Ransom Centre, University of Texas: The Havelock
    Ellis Collection. (HRC)

The University of Bristol Special Collections: The John
    Addington Symonds Collection. (UBSC)

The London Library: Manuscript of Symonds's memoirs.
    (LL)

I am grateful for permissions to consult and use material from these collections.

Letters

Letters from and to Carpenter: The Sheffield Archives.

Ellis's, Symonds's and Carpenter's Letters: The Harry Ransom
    Centre, University of Texas.

The Letters of John Addington Symonds, 3 vols., edited
    by Herbert M Schueller and Robert L Peters. Wayne State
    University Press, 1967-9.

The Letters of Olive Schreiner and Havelock Ellis, edited by Y
    C Drazin. London: Peter Lang, 1992.

The Letters of Olive Schreiner, edited by S C Cronwright
    Schreiner. London: Fisher Unwin, 1924.

Olive Schreiner Letters, edited by Richard Rive. Oxford:
    Clarendon Press, 1988.

Works by Carpenter

Towards Democracy (1883)
Civilisation: its Cause and Cure (1889)
Homogenic Love and its Place in a Free Society (1894)
Love's Coming of Age (1896)
An Unknown People (1897)
Iolaus: An Anthology of Friendship (1902)
Days with Walt Whitman (1906)
The Intermediate Sex (1908)
The Drama of Love and Death (1912)
My Days and Dreams (1916)
Intermediate Types Among Primitive Folks: A Study in Social
    Evolution (1914)

Works by Symonds

Studies of the Greek Poets (1973 and 1976)
A Problem in Greek Ethics (1883)
Essays Speculative and Suggestive (1890)
A Problem in Modern Ethics (1891)
Memoirs (1892, unpublished)
In the Key of Blue and Other Essays (1893)
Walt Whitman (1893)

Works by Ellis

The New Spirit (1890)
The Criminal (1890)
Man and Woman: A Study of Human Secondary Sexual
    Characteristics (1894)
Sexual Inversion (1896 and 1897)
The Evolution of Modesty; Phenomenon of Sexual Periodicity;
    Auto Eroticism (1900)
The Task of Social Hygiene (1912)
The Individual and the Race (1939)
My Life (1940)

Works Cited

Ackerly, J R (Jo Randolph). *My Father and Myself: A Memoir*. London: Bodley Head, 1968.

Aldrich, Robert. *The Seduction of the Mediterranean: Writing, Art and Homosexual Fantasy*. London: Routledge, 1993.

Annan, Noel. *Our Age: Portrait of a Generation*. London: Weidenfeld and Nicholson, 1990.

Beith, Gilbert. ed. *Edward Carpenter: In Appreciation*. London: G Allen and Unwin, 1931.

Bland, Lucy and Doan, Laura. eds. *Sexology in Culture: Labelling Bodies and Desires*. Cambridge: Polity Press, 1998.

Bowring, John. ed. *Deontology and the Science of Morality*, by Jeremy Bentham. London: Longman, 1834.

Blackwell, Elizabeth. *The Human Element in Sex*. London: J A Churchill, 1884.

Bloch, Iwan. *The Sexual Life of Our Times, in its Relation to Modern Civilization*. Berlin 1907.

Brady, Sean. *Masculinity and Male Homosexuality in Britain 1861 -1913*. London: Palgrave Macmillan, 2005.

Brady, Sean, *John Addington Symonds and Homosexuality: A Critical Edition of Sources*. London: Palgrave Macmillan, 2012.

Breitmann, Hans. pseud. Charles G Leland. *The Alternate Sex*. London: Welby, 1903.

Bristow, Joseph. *Effeminate England: Homoerotic Writing After 1885*. London: Buckingham 1995.

Bronski, Michael. *Culture Clash: The Making of Gay Sensibility*. Boston: South End Press, 1984.

Brown, Tony. ed. *Edward Carpenter and Late Victorian Radicalism*. London: Cass, 1990.

Brown, Horatio Forbes. *John Addington Symonds*. London: Smith, Elder, 1895.

Burton, Richard. *Arabian Nights: The Book of a Thousand Nights and a Night*. London: Burton Club, 1885-86.

Calder-Marshall, Arthur. *Havelock Ellis: A Biography*. London: Rupert Hart-Davis, 1959.

Chaddock, C G. trans. *Psychopathia Sexualis* by Richard Krafft-Ebing,

7th edition, London: F A Davis, 1892.

Cocks, H G. *Nameless Offences: Homosexual Desire in the 19th Century*. London: IB Taurus, 2003.

Cook, Matt. *London and the Culture of Homosexuality 1885-1914*. Cambridge: CUP, 2003.

Crozier, Ivan. ed. *Sexual Inversion: Havelock Ellis and John Addington Symonds*. London: Palgrave Macmillan, 2008.

Croft Cooke, Rupert. *Feasting with Panthers: A New Consideration of Some Late Victorian Writers*. London: W H Allen, 1967.

d'Arch Smith, Timothy. *Love in Earnest*. London: Routledge & Keegan Paul, 1970.

Dowling, Linda: *Hellenism and Homosexuality in Victorian Oxford*. Cornell: CUP, 1994.

Ellis, Edith. *The New Horizon in Love and Life*. London: A &C Black, 1921.

Furbank, P N. *E M Forster: A Life*. Vol. 2. London: Secker and Warburg, 1978.

Furze, Katherine. *Hearts and Pomegranates: The Story of Forty-Five Years, 1875-1920*. London: Peter Davis, 1940.

Gosse, Edmund. *Father and Son: A Study of Two Temperaments*. London: Heinemann, 1907.

Grosskurth, Phyllis. *Havelock Ellis: A Biography*. London: Allen Lane, 1980.

Grosskurth, Phyllis. *John Addington Symonds: A Biography*. London: Longman, 1964.

Grosskurth, Phyllis. ed., *The Memoirs of John Addington Symonds*, New York: Random House, 1984.

Hall, Donald. *Queer Theories*. London: Palgrave Macmillan, 2002.

Harris, Frank. *Oscar Wilde His Life and Confessions*. New York: Covici Friede, 1930.

Harrison, Fraser. *The Dark Angel: Aspects of Victorian Sexuality*. London: Fontana, 1979.

Hart-Davis, Rupert. *The Letters of Oscar Wilde*. London: Butler and Tanner, 1962.

Herdt, Gilbert. ed. *Third Sex, Third Gender: Beyond Sexual Dimorphism in Culture and History*. New York: Zone, 1994.

Hinton, James, *Life in Nature*: edited and introduced by Havelock Ellis. London: Allen & Unwin, 1932.

Hinton, James. *The Law Breaker and the Coming of the Law*: introduced by Havelock Ellis. London: Keegan Paul, 1884.

Hirschfeld, Magnus. *Sapho und Socrates*. Leipzig, 1897.

Hirschfeld, Magnus. Die Homosexualitat des Mannes und des Weibes. Berlin: 1914.

Hitchens, Richard. *The Green Carnation*. London: Heinemann, 1894.

Irons, Ralph. pseud. Olive Schreiner. *The Story of an African Farm*. London: Chapman & Hall, 1883.

Koestenbaum, Wayne. *Double Talk: The Erotics of Male Literary Collaboration*. London: Routledge, 1989.

Largo, M and Furbank, P N. eds. *Selected Letters of E M Forster*. London: Secker and Warburg, 1978.

Laurence, Dan. ed. *Bernard Shaw, Collected Letters 1826-1950*. New York: Viking, 1988.

Lombardi-Nash, Michael. trans. *The Riddle of 'Man-Manly' Love,* by Karl Heinrich Ulrichs. Buffalo NY: Prometheus Books, 1994.

Mayne, Xavier. pseud. Edward Prime Stevenson. *The Intersexes*: *A History of Similsexualism as a Problem in Social Life*. Privately printed, 1908.

McKenna, Neil. *The Secret Life of Oscar Wilde*. London: Arrow, 2004.

Mill, John Stuart. *On Liberty*. London: John W Parker, 1859.

Miller, Haviland. ed. *The Correspondence of Walt Whitman*. New York: NYUP, 1961-77.

Norton, Rictor. *Mother Clapp's Molly House*. London: Gay Men's Press, 1992.

Nottingham, Chris. *The Pursuit of Certainty: Havelock Ellis and the New Politics*. Amsterdam: AUP, 1999.

O'Brien, M D. *Socialism and Infamy: The Homogenic or Comrade Love Exposed*. Sheffield: privately printed, 1908.

Paul, M Eden. trans. *The Sexual life of Our times in its Relation to Modern Civilization*, by Iwan Bloch. London: Heinemann, 1920.

Proctor, Dennis. ed. *The Autobiography of Goldsworthy Lowes Dickinson and other Unpublished Writings*. London: Duckworth, 1973.

Robinson, Paul. *The Modernization of Sex: Havelock Ellis, Alfred*

Kinsey, William Masters and Virginia Johnson. London: Elek, 1976.

Rossetti, W M. ed. *Walt Whitman: Selected Poems*. London: Chatto & Windus, 1886.

Rowbotham, Sheila and Weeks, Jeffrey. *Socialism and the New Life: The Personal and Sexual Politics of Edward Carpenter and Havelock Ellis*. London: Pluto Press, 1977.

Rowbotham, Sheila. *Edward Carpenter: A Life of Liberty and Love*. London: Verso, 2008.

Salt, H S. *Seventy Years Among Savages*. London: Allen & Unwin, 1921.

Salt, H S. *Company I Have Kept*. London: Allen& Unwin, 1930.

Shively, Charley. *Calamus Lovers, Walt Whitman's Working Class Comarados*. New York: Gay Sunshine Press, 1987.

Showalter, Elaine. *Sexual Anarchy: Gender and Culture at the Fin de Siécle*. London: Viking, 1990.

Simpson, Colin. *The Cleveland Street Affair*. London; Weidenfeld & Nicholson, 1977.

Smith, Helen. *Masculinity, Class and Same-Sex Desire in Industrial England, 1895-1957*. London: Palgrave Macmillan, 2015.

Symonds, Margaret (Mrs W Vaughan). *Out of the Past: A Memoir of John Addington Symonds*. London: T Fisher Unwin, 1908.

Theile, Beverly. *Coming of Age: Edward Carpenter on Sex and Reproduction*, in *Edward Carpenter and Late Victorian Radicalism*, ed. T Brown. London: Frank Cass, 1990.

Traubel, Horace Logo. *With Walt Whitman in Camden*. London: Gay and Bird, 1906.

Tsuzuki, Chushichi. *Edward Carpenter: Prophet of Human Fellowship*. Cambridge: CUP, 1980.

Venturi, Silvio. *Le Degenerazioni Psico-Sessuali*. Torino: 1892.

Weeks, Jeffrey and Rowbotham, Sheila. *Socialism and the New Life: The Personal and Sexual Politics of Edward Carpenter and Havelock Ellis*. London: Pluto Press, 1977.

Weeks, Jeffrey. *Coming Out: Homosexual Politics in Britain from the Nineteenth Century to the Present*. London: Quartet Books, 1990.

Weininger, Otto. *Sex and Character*. London: Heinemann, 1910.

Whitman, Walt. *Song of the Open Road*. New York: Limited Edition Club, 1990.

Wilde, Oscar. *Phrases and Philosophies for the Use of the Young*. London: Gay and Bird, 1894.

Winsten, Stephen. *Salt and His Circle*. London: Hutchinson, 1951.

Suggestions for Further Reading

Bourne, Stephen. *Fighting Proud: The Untold Story of the Gay Men Who Served in Two World Wars*. London: IB Taurus, 2017.

Buckle, Sebastian. *The Way Out: A History of Homosexuality in Modern Britain*. London: IB Taurus, 2015.

Buckle, Sebastian. *Homosexuality on the Small Screen: Television and Lgbt Identity in Britain*. London: IB Taurus, 2017.

Davenport-Hines, Richard. *Death and Punishment: Attitudes to Sex and Sexuality in Britain Since the Renaissance*. London: Collins, 1990.

Davidson, Michael. *The World, the Flesh and Myself*. London: Gay Men's Press, 1985.

Dellamara, Richard. ed. *Victorian Sexual Dissidence*. Chicago: CUP, 1999.

Dover, KG. *Greek Homosexuality*. London: Duckworth, 1978.

Duberman, M. ed. with others. *Hidden from History: Reclaiming the Gay and Lesbian Past*. New York: NAL Books, 1989.

Greenberg, David F. *The Construction of Homosexuality*. Chicago: CUP, 1988.

Gibson, Ian. *The English Vice: Beating Sex and Shame in Victorian England and After*. London: Duckworth, 1979.

Houlbrook, Matt. *Queer London: Perils and Pleasures in the Sexual Metropolis 1918-1957*. Chicago: UCP, 2005.

Hyde, H Montgomery. *The Other Love: An Historical and Contemporary Survey of Homosexuality in Britain*. London: Mayflower, 1972.

Hyde, H Montgomery. *Sex Scandals in British Politics and Society*. London: Constable, 1986.

Kaplan, Maurice B. *Sodom on the Thames: Sex, Love, and Scandal in Wilde Times*. Ithaca: Cornell University Press, 2005.

Katz, Jonathan N. *Love Stories: Sex Between Men Before Homosexuality*. Chicago: CUP, 2001.

Ledger, Sally and Luckhurst, Roger. *The Fin de Siécle: A Reader in Cultural History c.1880-1900*. Oxford: OUP, 2000.

Mort, Frank. *Dangerous Sexualities: Medico-Moral Politics in England Since 1830*. London: Routledge, 1998.

Norton, Rictor. *The Myth of the Modern Homosexual: Queer History and the Search for Cultural Unity*. London: Cassell, 1997.

Plummer, K. *The Making of the Modern Homosexual*. London: Hutchinson,1981.

Reade, Brian. *Sexual Heretics: Male Homosexuality in English Literature 1850-1900*. London: RKP, 1970.

Rossario, Vernon. ed. *Science and Homosexualities*. London: Routledge, 1996.

Showalter, Elaine. *Sexual Anarchy: Gender and Culture at the Fin de Siécle*. London: Viking, 1990.

Sinfield, Alan. *The Wilde Century: Effeminacy, Oscar Wilde and the Queer Movement*. London: Cassell, 1994.

Sweet, Matthew. *Inventing the Victorians*. London: Faber and Faber, 2001.

Weeks, Jeffrey and Porter, Kevin. eds. *Between the Acts: Lives of Homosexual Men 1885-1967*. London: Routledge, 1991.

Weeks, Jeffrey. *Sex, Politics and Society: The Regulation of Sexuality Since 1800*. Harlow: Longman, 2012.

White, Chris. ed. *Nineteenth-Century Writing on Homosexuality: A Source Book*. London: Routledge, 1999.

Index